ARMAGEDDON FED UP WITH THIS

Armageddon

Fed Up With This

A Gunner's Tale

DEREK NUDD

Matador
9 Priory Business Park
Kibworth Beauchamp
Leicestershire LE8 0RX, UK
Tel: (+44) 116 279 2299
Fax: (+44) 116 279 2277
Email: books@troubador.co.uk
Web: www.troubador.co.uk/matador

ISBN 978 1784621 308

British Library Cataloguing in Publication Data.
A catalogue record for this book is available from the British Library.

Typeset in Aldine by Troubador Publishing Ltd
Printed and bound by CPI Group (UK) Ltd, Croydon, CR0 4YY

Matador is an imprint of Troubador Publishing Ltd

FSC
www.fsc.org

MIX
Paper from
responsible sources
FSC® C013604

To Dad

Author's Note

I have made strenuous efforts to track down the owners of material included or cited in this book. If you are a copyright holder and believe I have erred in any way, please contact me and I will rectify the situation as quickly as possible.

The cover illustration is 'A Soldier of World War Two' outside the D-Day Museum in Portsmouth. Some criticised the statue when it was unveiled in 1997 for not being 'heroic' enough.

I think it's perfect.

Contents

Illustrations

Maps

Drink and sing, and eat and laugh:
And so go forth to battle:
For the top of a skull and the end of a staff
Do make a ghostly rattle.

Thomas Love Peacock; *Maid Marian*

Preface

This book is based on my father's letters home during the Second World War, set in the context of local and global events. In 1940, like millions of others, he found himself unexpectedly in uniform: a raw conscript pitched into a heavy anti-aircraft regiment. He grew over the next five years into a seasoned professional with the Normandy and North-West European campaigns under his belt. A previously unsuspected talent for maths took him from heaving shells to the predictor[1] and then the radar crew, giving him a ringside view of the manic technological race at the time.

As an articulate journalist, prolific letter-writer and occasional poet he published improvised news-sheets from a succession of gun sites and dugouts.

The story is told mainly in his own words. His wry, sometimes scathing observation of the humour and idiocy of army life; the military, political and cultural events of the time are set against a backdrop of global cataclysm. I colour in the background for those of us lucky enough to have missed it, drawing on primary sources such as the Regimental War Diaries and newspaper reports as well as published works.

The period holds continuing fascination, as the best and the

---

[1] The predictor was a mechanical fire-control computer. It 'predicted' where to point the guns, the fuze setting, and the timing to place exploding shells near a target aircraft.

worst of times: many survivors remember it with grudging affection as the moment they achieved their full potential. Great, glamorous and disastrous careers are documented in detail. Oral histories are a valuable insight but lose the wider picture in the babble. It's worth listening at length to one of the reluctant 'civilians in uniform' who did the grotty bits with weary resignation. This civilian was an acute observer and literate recorder of what he saw.

The book provides a new perspective – from beneath – on a little-known aspect of the war. For a while after the fall of France anti-aircraft (AA) gunners were the only part of the army shooting back. Artillery is under-represented in literature considering it was a conspicuous Allied strength.

The 'Threads' chapter gives a running commentary on culture, politics and the remorseless grind of living with blackout, blitz, shortages, rationing and sudden loss. It tackles the impact of women gunners and the influx of black soldiers from the US. Many readers will find it particularly interesting and distinctive.

The title, by the way, was a contemporary joke.

Prelude

L et these snapshots flick past your mind's eye:

A bleary-eyed, half-concussed conscript heaving shells in the dark.

Trained radar operator now; calling range, bearing and elevation as the Blitz burns around him.

The hardened sergeant, drilling his crew to camouflage the trailer and get into action NOW!

Scrabbling from his Normandy dugout, Sten in hand, to find the 'attack' is the gunners' greeting for a beer shipment.

At the siege of Boulogne, back on the guns, working in shifts to feed them until they break.

Mud-caked clothes and kit; earth and water merging in the cold, wet, dark, gruelling Nijmegen stalemate.

Dashing home on his wife's death to care for his infant sons, then back to the assault on Germany.

A vast underground cavern, frenetic flurry fading as lights turn from red to green. Momentary stillness, a klaxon, and in unison the presses start to roll.

How did we come here?

Eric Nudd was born at Kingsdown near Deal, Kent in 1912; the sixth of a commercial artist's seven children. His elder brother succumbed to the 1918–20 'flu pandemic serving with the Royal Navy. His father died in 1923 leaving his mother and sisters to finish his upbringing. He described an *"unbalanced, unduly feminine atmosphere… in that unfortunate home"* where his sisters wouldn't even iron their underwear while he was there.

He left school without qualifications but with a burgeoning artistic talent, political awareness and a hunger for knowledge. Judging by the quality of his writing and the breadth of his reading he must have devoured the public library whole.

By 1933 the family had moved to West Drayton in Middlesex where Eric found work as an agency commercial artist. Around 1937 he joined the *Sunday Chronicle* as a graphic designer, falling immediately under the spell of the press. The enchantment lasted

Figure 1: Eric's brother and sisters at Kingsdown,
probably before his arrival

the rest of his life – along with growing disillusion at its cynicism, bickering and brutality.

> *"The middle thirties were an exciting introduction to those in their middle twenties – to those who could sense the short and inevitable trend to a new world reshaped by the conflict we most of us sensed was nearly upon us.*
>
> *'I wouldn't be living in a more exciting age'… That was thrown off at a party the night before Germany invaded France, Belgium and Holland.* [2]
>
> *In any case, the period preceding was as exciting – and precarious*

Figure 2: Eric as a designer

---

[2] The invasion was on 10th May 1940.

enough – to those of us who had our first-footing in the newspaper business... Those of us who were employed by Allied newspapers felt that this elephantile [sic] empire situated in Gray's Inn Road was a giant dying from slow paralysis of inspiration and dearth of talent. Thereupon, I suppose, the excitement and effort which seemed to be begotten of our own feelings of instability.

So many talents walked the corridors and frequented the pubs it gave you a nasty inferiority feeling just to have brief converse with them. But all, it seemed to me, were painfully aware of the plush carpet which divided their breath-taking ideas from the attention and approval of the man in the editorial chair.

Those who were occasionally blessed (or cursed) with that opportunity usually went forth with teeth chattering.

'I have a rendezvous with Death At some disputed barricade... '[3]

and were thereafter espied drinking off the effects in some undisputed corner of some not-so-local tavern.

All of that – and more – was my lot, because I had but faint hopes of breaking into this bewildering trade on account of humble beginnings in the publicity department... I was determined to emerge from the lower caste and mix on equal terms with those lads who at least had the opportunity of stuttering a potential idea to the man in the editorial chair.

After all, I HAD seen those who had emerged unscathed and

---

[3] The opening lines of a poem by Alan Seeger, an American who joined the Foreign Legion to fight for the Allies in the First World War. It was published after his death on the Somme in 1916.

successful, affecting long cigarette-holders and mixing with executives in the saloon…

One five-second introduction raised those hopes – not that I was over-impressionable (or was I?) – but the opportunity occurred one evening to meet a former executive of the old Sunday Chronicle… I had raised my status by defeating the acknowledged champion of Allied – and I had hardly thrown a dart before in my life. It was a sensation, and I was permitted distinguished company for the occasion. I was as innocent of beer-taking as I was of finishing on a double…

So, feeling pretty elevated by the beer, the victory and the company, I met Hugh Cudlipp, who had called in for a few minutes to recall his own excitements and victories as Features Editor of the Sunday Chron. The then editor and his former boss was Jimmy Drawbell (why has nobody attempted a book on HIM?) but I wasn't sufficiently acquainted with that great man to appreciate the prevailing jokes, anecdotes and hilarities. Anyway, it was over in a few minutes. Duty called.

But what was heartening was the instant feeling that the chap was genuinely pleased to meet you, and after the stories one had heard of him and of his progress on the Daily Mirror this was, well – this was an excuse to drink another light ale, forget darts and reflect that if there were such people in the business there were hopes…"

Cudlipp was a charismatic, punchy Welshman whose career in journalism started at the age of fourteen. Their paths crossed again in 1939 when Eric applied for a job at the *Sunday Pictorial*. He was successful and started work on 8th May.

"About two years had passed – pretty uneventful ones – when Jim Lee, head of the Sales Promotion department, mentioned there was a vacancy on the Sunday Pictorial, and he thought it would suit me. Hugh Cudlipp had been made editor of that paper about a year previously at the age of twenty-four, thus becoming the youngest editor

in Fleet Street. Despite warnings (of which more hereafter) I couldn't wait to have a go: presented myself, saw a quick nod pass to the Art Editor over my specimen book, and was told by the latter that I was in. In for a scare."

The change had a salutary effect on his self-belief.

"Then came a chance of a job on the 'Pic'. 8 guineas a week[4] and an extra one the first week! Maybe nothing to get excited over to a bloke with a more solid background and adequate education and training – perhaps mere chicken feed – but to me at that time it seemed a fortune. I can laugh heartily at myself now when I recollect how I sallied forth to hold that job down – but it was the first decent chance of my life, wasn't it?"

It was, in terms of the Chinese curse, an 'interesting' time.

"Was there anything comparable to the excitement of working on a newspaper (perhaps any newspaper – but particularly the Sunday Pic) during those months before the war… and the months after. We were especially favoured in possessing a young, enthusiastic staff: mostly in their twenties, led and inspired by probably the youngest – a demon for work, a taskmaster insofar as he expected an equal effort from all – that applied also to the ancients nearing forty… and, furthermore, endowed with a fantastic sense of humour which kept you perpetually laughing while you perspired.

No sign of a plush carpet, so far as I can remember. There must have been a carpet of sorts, but not of the thicker, intimidating variety. Instead, the whole office seemed to be a sort of free-for-all, with characters moving

---

[4] Approximately £480 per week (£25,000 per year) at 2013 prices.

at the double and with access to the editor only too easy, either through the ever-open door or via the hatch opening on to the features room.

That hatch had a language of its own, so exactly reflecting the mood of the occupant that explanatory words from him were hardly necessary.

Slow-slow. A quiet reminder, a sardonic compliment, or a reflective look-around.
Slow-slow-quick. 'Ah – he IS there. Can you now spend a flashing second…'
Slow-quick-reverse-shut. 'Not quite the moment… Five more minutes…'
Quick-quick-BANG. Conference. ACTION!"

The *Sunday Pictorial* had earlier looked into the gathering clouds. On New Year's Day 1939 it published a picture of a young girl sighting a machine gun. Bernard Gray's front page article claimed that Hitler had warned his generals to prepare for a move in March.[i] The headline was a depressingly accurate prophesy.

"Still, I admit it was a bit of a shock to me when I visited my family over the Christmas holidays and was asked: 'Have you seen this?' The effect was a startler as the front page of the SUNDAY PIC was held up for my inspection with its now-famous warning 'BE READY BY SPRING' spread across the front page as a New Year message.

Spreading of alarm and despondency? Many thought so at the time – but not so many when Hitler marched into Czechoslovakia almost at the moment predicted by the PIC. That brilliant and astute prediction, almost brutally flung at the country still praying for 'Peace in our time' was the real awakener, particularly so when proved correct."

Eric formed an enduring respect for Hugh Cudlipp at the 'Pic.' He – Cudlipp – later joined the army himself, but on his own terms:

"Hugh was curious about the shine on my boots and was horrified when he heard how much had to be done on them. His reaction was 'Oh hell, I'll give a guy a bob to do that for me!' "

Hugh formed an army newspaper unit in North Africa and launched the forces' paper: *Union Jack*. The *Pictorial* Assistant Editor, Stuart ('Sam') Campbell, stepped into the Editor's chair for the duration. He was less cherished; Eric wrote in April 1941:

"... I'm not too proud of the 'Pic' lately – Sam and co seem to be doing their worst to reduce it to gutter level. This time last year it was carrying the best of Lloyd George's articles and had a real status. What a waste! What a waste! Hugh shovelling coal[5] and his fatuous deputy bawling his silly head off! And even the 'Mirror' complaining of his gibberish. And at a time like this, too."

Cudlipp and Campbell were prominent movers in the post-war newspaper industry. Hugh returned to the *Sunday Pictorial* and *Daily Mirror* after the war. He steadily built his influence, and retired in 1973 as chairman of International Publishing Corporation (IPC). He was created Baron Cudlipp the following year.

Sam edited the *Sunday Pictorial* until Hugh's demobilisation in 1949 when he became Managing Editor of *The People*. He was appointed Editor in 1957 and held that post until his death in 1966. The *Sunday Pictorial* became the *Sunday Mirror* in 1963.

In 1937 Eric married Jennie Hanby, a teacher from Bristol. She was a few years older and, like him, fought her way from an unpromising background to an education and a responsible career. She passed her School Certificate with six credits at seventeen and

---

[5] Cudlipp at the time was delivering coal to officers' quarters at Catterick camp.

three years later qualified from Bristol University as a junior school teacher. Two years' supply teaching completed her probation after which she worked at Rye in Sussex. In 1931 a new job brought her to Cowley, Middlesex, where she met Eric and made her permanent home in the area. The couple bought a house in Ruislip for £850 (about £49,000 today) with a £600 mortgage.

War finally broke out in September 1939. The first tumultuous year saw Poland, the Netherlands, Denmark, Norway, Belgium and France fall in short order. In July 1940 the Royal Navy's attack on the French fleet at Mers-el-Kébir dispelled the widespread view (not least in Britain) that the government would have to seek whatever

Figure 3: Jennie

terms it could with Germany. The Battle of Britain came and went; Operation *Sealion* (the German invasion of Britain) was postponed indefinitely; and the *Luftwaffe* switched its attention to night attacks on British cities. The Blitz had begun.

It was clear from the start that the armed forces – already boosted to 875,000 men by voluntary enlistment – had to expand fast. The National Service (Armed Forces) Act 1939 introduced conscription by age group, youngest first. From that day it was only a matter of time until Eric was fitted (very approximately) for a suit in one shade of khaki. He wrote a thinly-veiled description of his departure:

> *"In 1940 a well-loved editor discovered that a comparative nonentity on his staff was due to be called up for National Service the following week. He immediately organised a small luncheon party. A foursome. He was an even finer newspaperman than xxx, and his fame is now worldwide. During the lunch he addressed himself exclusively to the parting guest, expounding his own theory of creating loyalty and dedication among his staff. It was, he said, the China Egg Theory. Inspire a man with a few words, to the effect that he is talented, reliable, indispensable. It could transform mediocrity into valuable material, produce a genius from potential talent. Put that china egg under a fowl, and it may produce (who knows?) golden eggs."*

Hugh Cudlipp repeated his 'China Egg' theory in his 1962 book *At Your Peril*.

Eric's journalistic skills didn't go to waste after conscription. He was an acute observer and later compiled *ad hoc* battery news-sheets *Blaze Away* and, in Normandy, the *Daily Shower*. While serving near London he could sneak into the office from time to time and swap stories with his old colleagues.

BLITZ

What Am I Doing Here?

As September 1940 drew to a close the Battle of Britain segued into the Blitz. Hitler postponed the invasion of Britain on 17th September, and again on 13th October. In the end his impatience to turn east ensured it would never happen.

None of this was obvious to the hard-pressed gunners of 58th (Kent) Heavy Anti-Aircraft (HAA) Regiment defending the southern Thames Estuary. They were in action every day, usually several times.

The 'Kent' was one of the six Territorial regiments (56th to 61st) formed between 1932 and 1935, as rearmament got underway. They shot down a raider in November 1939 in one of the first anti-aircraft successes of the war. By autumn 1940 they operated eight sites in north Kent, one of which was Northumberland Bottom just south of Gravesend (near the junction of the modern A2 and A227). A pre-war site for four 4.5-inch guns, it expanded rapidly to meet both operational and training roles. The site was destroyed in 1999 during construction of the Channel Tunnel Rail Link.

Recruit Squad 6 arrived there on 30th September, a busy day. Four raids crossed the coast at Dungeness and Lympne. One aiming for London was broken up short of its target, the other three concentrated on Biggin Hill and East Kent. In the confusion one of the London raiders strayed over 58th territory and was engaged by three sites, including Northumberland Bottom. Eric was duly impressed.

"We had a thrill on Monday – as soon as we arrived our guns brought down a Heinkel."

The regiment's war diary makes no claim for that day and there were no crashes in the area so he was a bit optimistic. Still, first impressions were good.

"Well, here we are, and it's not at all bad – good meals, good bed, issue of 3 blankets, pillow, and ground sheets, nice roomy sleeping huts and a hell of a nice Bombardier[6] in charge of our squad.

And the issue we are getting tomorrow! Full kit, underwear, 3 shirts, greatcoat, gloves, razor, towels etc, etc, and our 'smalls' are washed for us once a week!

It's hinted we may get leave shortly to take our 'civvies' home…"

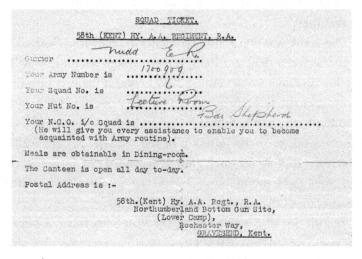

Figure 4: Eric's Squad Ticket

---

[6] Bombardier is a junior non-commissioned officer – artillery equivalent of corporal.

Leaving Squad 6 to their NCOs' tender mercies we should glance at the other end of the anti-aircraft (AA) organisation. Major-General Sir Frederick Pile, Bart, CB, DSO, MC was appointed to head 1st AA Division in 1937 then, in July 1939, took charge of AA Command. He held that post almost to the end of the war. He was an Irish aristocrat with a left-of-centre upbringing and little formal education. Graduating from the Royal Military Academy he joined the Artillery and distinguished himself in the First World War. In 1923 he transferred to the Royal Tank Corps where his enthusiasm for technology put him at odds with the cavalrymen who dominated armoured regiments at the time.

The journalist William Connor ('Cassandra') published *The English at War* in 1941. It eviscerates the complacency which lost Britain's lead in armoured warfare:

> "... *almost every British General or military authority who had proved his ability for the conduct of modern mechanized warfare was pushed, hedged, shoved or booted out of the position in which he might have rescued the British Army from its deadly coma of indifference, lethargy, snobbery and terrifying stupidity.*
> ... *General Pile, another authority on mobile mechanized war – edged out to command anti-aircraft guns.*"[ii]

'Edged out' maybe, but that put the right man into perhaps the army's most critical job between Dunkirk and the end of the Blitz. Pile was tireless and fearless in the never-ending struggle for the soldiers, equipment and training he needed. An innovative thinker, he set up wireless schools and recruited civilian engineers to turn gun-laying radar into a useful tool; introduced female and Home Guard crews – against stiff opposition – to gun and searchlight batteries; and later devised a quick way to move the 'fixed' 3.7-inch guns (which made up most of his strength) to where they were needed. He could hustle with the best of them but eschewed the parochialism too often typical of high command, even in wartime. For example, in 1941 he lent Fighter Command some of his precious radars to help develop night-fighter tactics.

In the first eighteen months of the war Pile's command almost tripled from 107,000 men to over 300,000. Most of the recruits were conscripts of variable quality who had to be turned into soldiers and trained in a highly technical occupation – or in many cases returned for redeployment.

For the trainees the desperate scramble to bring Britain's air defences up to scratch meant a dive into the deep end. Four days later:

> *"It seems a long time since I wrote to you, exactly the time it takes to turn a civilian into a pukka soldier! I used to hear a fable about a soldier's time being his own after 4.30. All rot. We never seem to finish!*
>
> *We have some consolations; our NCOs and officers are a very decent crowd, we have been informed we have been picked specially to make a highly efficient intake in the shortest possible time, we are getting plenty of theory as well as foot slogging on the parade ground, and the living is very good indeed. Canteens, washing, beds etc are beyond reproach.*
>
> *And, oh boy, the training! It seems just incredible we only came here Monday. We are marching, slow marching, saluting on the march, about turning, stamping and drilling generally like the Life Guards; anyway that's what we think! The sergeants compare us with Girl Guides, cripples and incurable lunatics on the parade ground, and what we say under our breath would put even their language in the shade!*
>
> *Still, on the whole, it's good fun, and the NCOs are very human when they're not shouting at you!*

We've started rifle drill today, which will give you some idea of our progress.

I will draw a net over the cleaning, polishing, sweeping and general 'chore' mania that infects the camp and will simply say that the best is not good enough!

As one unfortunate said 'If my old woman asked me to polish the step I'd have gone up in the air'. When this is over you'll see such a shine on the forks and spoons!

And another blessing – we are just too tired to bother about the air raids; Jerry simply doesn't hold a candle to the Company S.M. [Sergeant-Major]. *Not that we've seen much of Jerry, anyway."*

RAF Northolt was bombed on 3rd and 6th October. St Paul's was hit on 9th. Better weather on the 7th attracted daylight raids on Gravesend and East London, and strong attacks that night. London was hit daily and nightly at this time; the Thames Estuary was an unmissable landmark for *Luftwaffe* crews so the batteries were kept busy. For the recruits that meant learning on the job.

"We've had one visit to the gun pits in charge of a very jolly S.M."

"… The difficulties of wartime training are immense; you can't get near the guns during an alarm, of course – you can't stand about in the rain and must repair to the canteen for lectures, and you can't have the services of an instructor when he's been up all night – in which case you're taken for a route march until he manages to get on his pins (generally in rather a snappy mood!).

So you pick up your gunnery knowledge in bits and pieces as regards the practical side. And despite the difficulties we've done quite a bit and I've revelled in the theory."

Of course, it wouldn't be the army without a bit of drill.

"By the way, we've all had to have another hair cut: we are lucky to have a barber in our squad by name Poppolinski, of doubtful origin. His name is too much of a memory effort for most of the blokes who call him 'Rachmaninoff'.

The joke is that he was bawled out by our officer on parade regarding his long hair (which was tough considering he had helped the camp barber out quite a lot). The sergeant escort consulted his note books and shouted 'Poppolinski! You're a barber! Get your hair cut' – collapse of entire Battery!"

Another stock camp joke, or rather squad joke, is a bloke named Creamer. He just can't drill, no idea – always being called a bloody Girl Guide, the snag is that he keeps the whole squad on one exercise till we can all do it properly! After the 50th 'about turn' there is a frantic scuffle, and the sergeant shouts 'There's just one of you now...' and there follows a low growl of 'xxxxxxx Creamer' from the rank and file."

"... It comes a bit hard for most of us. We don't mind the work but the 'siring' and saluting gets us a bit!

But we are assured that discipline relaxes progressively as the time goes on so we work and hope!

Of course the lectures are interesting and very informative and by the way, the chance of getting on the predictors[7] is a very good one."

The technical side of the job was already catching his interest. It certainly beat spit-and-polish – and offered the chance to use his experience designing page layouts.

"And now I want you to help me about some books! I want to study maths, geometry and if possible trigonometry. I wonder if you

---

[7] Mechanical gunnery computers – see Appendix A.

could make some enquiries, say at the library, or draw on your own experience to get hold of something on these subjects?

There's no particular hurry about it, and meanwhile I would like 2 books from home, my book on perspective, which when I last saw it was in my tallboy! And the book on military map reading which I brought home in my case.

Would you also include my drawing pad, 2 or 3 fat pencils, a soft rubber if there's one in the box, and my pair of proportional dividers which is in the instrument box in the case? I am going to try my hand at one or two charts.

You will also find a couple of scribbling pads in the case which may be handy for drawing on."

The end of October brought a Brigadier inspection and – Oh Joy! – 48 hours' leave to mark the end of their basic training.

"Leave! Leave! The notice has been duly pinned up at the Battery office. To start 11 o'clock Sunday (a.m.) until 11 o'clock Tuesday morning, this Sunday, October 27th. At this moment there is a wild African war dance going on here, which I can hardly refrain from joining."

The only drawback was first having to impress the Brigadier.

"We are polishing up this week, also receiving instructions in Ceremonial Drill when for the first time 300 of us try a march past in troops, twelve abreast in 3 ranks, in honour of the Brigadier's visit on Saturday.

Such fun! Such swearing! The NCOs know as much about this as we do, and what a joy to hear them bawled out!

There's some very complex manoeuvrings. 3 ranks of 100 men each line up on one side of the square, and about turn, wheel into troops, about turn (with some trimmings) and proceed round the square in column of route.

'Dressing' is the difficulty – achieving that dead straight line in the long file and in wheeling. The Regt. SM is the expert and gallops snorting and bellowing up and down the line.

'Left dress, left dress! Hold it 'D!' Up No.1 C Troop! Up two! Back 3! Back the rest! Back seven! Back seven!! Bombardier Shepherd, what's that man's name?'

'Creamer!' groans the Bombardier amid suppressed snorts.

Then the incredible happens. At the next order 'To the halt, on the left, form squad' the Bomber completely loses his head. Instead of halting after the third pace and acting as pivot, he goes on marching gaily along, the rest of us following across the square with dubious looks and murmurs.

The pack, commissioned and non-commissioned, are after him in full cry.

'Bombardier! Bombardier! Where the BLOODY hell are you going Bombardier?'

Ah how one moment can atone for three weeks of insults! How Creamer's face simply radiated!"

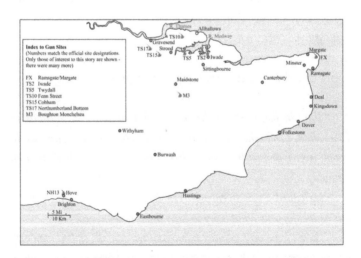

Map 1: South-East England showing gun sites and other locations mentioned in the text.

Now It Gets Real

At the end of October, the basics complete, the recruits were sent to their first operational posting – for most of them 206 Battery on a 4.5-inch site at Cobham near Gravesend in Kent. The unfortunate Creamer stayed behind.

> *"Well here we are at the gun station, and oh boy, is it good or is it good! It's the most free and easy place imaginable. The huts are situated in a wood, with a very jolly cook house (open air one of course) where you just line up and have as much as you like! The hut where eight of us sleep is a very comfortable one and is also our living quarters and contains a stove, bookshelves and books, large dining and writing table and some very picturesque hurricane lamps! Six of us are now intently scribbling to our loved ones – what a human picture! And what a difference in the officers! They come along for a chat as though they were NCOs. And we are starting on gun drill first thing in the morning. We get up an hour later (7.00). Breakfast is at 8.15, parade at 9.00 and no official 'Lights out'. We are, of course, expected to work hard and get through our training in record time, which you may bet we are all going to do."*

Anti-aircraft gun sites' design assumed they would be intermittently occupied by Territorials living or billeted close by, so most were built without accommodation. A post-Munich review exposed the fallacy and launched a programme of hutting. By then, however, rapid expansion of AA defences and competition for materials and skills ensured it would be years before supply caught up with demand.

The effect was that wartime conscripts often had better living conditions than the core of experienced volunteers – a cause of some scratchiness between the two groups.

They passed a peaceful night despite the battery's war diary entry: *"Much enemy activity at night & many bombs dropped."*[iii] Next day the promised gun drill materialised.

> *"At 9 o'clock we march down through the wood to the camp. There's a brief inspection – a mockery of the old – shades of the Sergeant Major! – and then we proceed to gun drill.*
>
> *We have spent today learning the names of the parts of the gun and how to take up action positions and to interchange. Tomorrow we have to learn how to operate the gun and read the instruments…*
>
> *It is far more interesting here and very free and easy, which atones for it being no longer a 'lark' if that's the right word. Meaning that during our initial training we were regimented and made to do everything by numbers in what we considered an overdone manner, consequently we reacted by treating lots of it as a joke! Well that's all over. We are facing a real job and do not feel disposed to find something screamingly funny about a 4.5. In fact one or two find the prospect anything but funny!*
>
> *I'm really enjoying myself and finding real Ack Ack work fully up to my expectations. I have been quite close to our guns when they have gone into action without experiencing any uncomfortable sensation. There is a hell of a lot to learn, and one could spend all one's time in studying it."*

> *"…We have practised loading drill today, and it's remarkable how easy the shells are to lift, once you get the knack. We practice with dummies, of course! By the way, I have an excellent chance of getting on to the predictors later, which is the most fascinating job in the AA."*

A writer described the noise of AA guns thus:

"These [3.7s], firing high-velocity shells, utter a short, sharp bark, when heard from about a mile away… The 3.7 gun… is mobile. For this reason it is sometimes heard outside your back door. When that happens the report is no longer like a bark, but becomes an ear-splitting roar and the barrel emits a 30-foot sheet of flame. The other standard AA gun is the 4.5, distinguishable from the 3.7 because the report is deeper. Heard from a distance the 3.7 gun's report may be compared to the yapping of a small dog, while the 4.5 may be likened to the bark of a sheep dog.[iv]"

Early November saw brisk activity with Cobham tackling daylight raids on 8th, 13th and 14th; and firing most nights. Eric – still heaving shells – found his muse in the exhaustion of a night action.

"DEBUT

You're asleep, but rudely shaken, you in some degree awaken
Whilst a bell's insistent shrilling sets you knocking at the knees
And you grab your respirator – you've been warned that sooner or later
You must reckon with some Phosgene in the estuary breeze!
– What an endless, breathless run, that first journey to the gun
As you batter into picket posts, and blindly poke your arm
At successive ghostly sights – why should this of all dark nights
Be a fellow's introduction to a ruddy big alarm?
You choke back all indecision, fearing censure or derision
Bring up, sling up ammunition – and oh, boy! do you work fast! –
Tho' each salvo's flash and thunder seems to rend the head asunder
And you wonder if you'll blunder at your ill-accustomed task
For tonight you fear the Huns slightly less than Q.F.[8] guns

---

[8] Quick-Firing

As they buffet, deafen, blind you, and incessantly crave more
Of those weighty, deadly rounds: high explosive, sixty pounds
That you carry, carry, carry till your every limb is sore.
But at last you get 'Stand Easy' then before you, bright and breezy
Looms a comrade who informs you that the guns have ceased to fire
And your brain and feet are leaden as you stumble into bed in
Something less than boots and helmet, something more than night attire
Wonder why you ever swore at the hardness of the floor
You're asleep in just a minute, soothing slumber dulls the pain;
Dreams of porridge, tea and bacon are dispelled, you re-awaken
Fighting mad and badly shaken –
IT'S THE RUDDY BELL AGAIN!"

At this stage unseen engagements usually involved barrage shooting at the predicted course of a raid, though there were some gun laying (GL) radar sets available. Success was rare but not unknown; Cobham was credited with shooting down a Junkers 88 bomber on 2nd November.[v]

A couple of weeks later the hoped-for predictor training materialised sooner than expected.

> *"There's not much news to give you, except for one important item – I've been picked for a course of training on the predictor! There are eight of us all told, and of course you can guess how delighted I am. I never dared hope for the chance as soon as this…*
>
> *I couldn't finish this last night as we gathered for an unofficial predictor lecture. We are definitely on it for good, and will relieve the other predictor numbers as soon as possible to release them for a special course. [9] I am hoping to qualify for No 4 who operates the time drum,*

---

9   Presumably radar

calls the fuze, and orders 'Fire'. I only hope Alf isn't on QE[10] jerking the damn thing up and down to give the gunner something to do! I'll murder him next time he interferes with one of my predictions."

Of course it wasn't all work and sleep.

"Our hut has lost its Little Ray of Sunshine, Les... He and Curly provided most of the entertainment. Their latest stunt was 'Lets Bomb Berlin'. Seated on a form Curly would drop his bombs and Les operate the machine guns (knives stuck into the crevices so that they rattle). Climax to a hellish din was 'On Fire, on Fire' the fools baling out all over our beds! Last night they naturally fell on the Bombardier's bed when he was asleep, capsizing the whole outfit."

The 58th's war diary mentions difficulty in housing recruits at four sites including Cobham. Open-air washing and cooking were uncomfortable with winter drawing in but at least they didn't lodge in hop-pickers' huts as at one of the Thames sites. Occasional parcels from home relieved army diet.

"The marmalade was lovely, making even our current type of bread eatable. I think we had our worst session of food ever this week. They are buying an awful type of brown bread like chaff and you can manage to get about one slice of white every other day. The cooking is just unbelievable. One day the meat had not been cut up properly or cooked sufficiently and the rice that followed hard as iron, just for want of a bit of soaking."

---

[10] Quadrant Elevation: signalling the required vertical angle to the guns.

The gunners were liable for guard or cook-house chores during their 48-hour 'off duty' stretches so only eight hours was actually their own. For the Londoners it was, infuriatingly, almost but not quite possible to get home and back.

> *"... apparently you're only entitled to see your wife if she is dying or your home if it's a heap of rubble."*

Beds – unknown at first – gradually caught up with them. Very gradually.

> *"I have solved the bed problem by borrowing a duty man's bedstead at night after he has removed his blankets to the dug out. As you say, it's a scandal that we have none of our own. I see that every German prisoner is provided with one, however!"*

So did a few luxuries.

> *"I am pleased to report a great improvement in living conditions! We have moved to the camp proper and are now installed in a nice roomy hut, beds expected any minute, and darling a Radiogram!*
> *Thank God. That place 'up top' was gradually getting us down. Thank God for electric light and a canteen near us, and some real work to do. We are on the predictor now (quick work eh?). My turn comes tomorrow."*

The same night – 14th November – brought the *Luftwaffe's* destructive raid on Coventry. 449 bombers reached the city led by pathfinders using electronic aids. The first wave dropped high-explosive bombs to disrupt services and communications, making it difficult to fight fires started by the incendiaries that followed. Over 4,300 homes and about a third of the city's factories were destroyed, and most of the rest damaged. Casualties were mercifully light compared to what might have been – an estimated 554 people killed, 863 badly injured and 393 less so.

There is a persistent story that Churchill allowed the attack so as to protect the secret of Bletchley Park's ability to read German 'Enigma' codes. This is unlikely. It was clear there would be a major raid but not – until too late – where it would fall. Rather, the failure of British electronic countermeasures that night combined with ideal weather conditions added up to the worst of luck. Telephone lines were destroyed early, preventing central control of anti-aircraft fire. Each gun position had to cope as best it could – mostly by guesswork. Only one German aircraft was shot down.

"The raid on Coventry was pretty lousy, wasn't it? The defences didn't seem very adequate to my mind. The swine got in too easily."

Coventry was a justifiable military target though the densely-packed city made civilian suffering inevitable. It was also, at least partly, a reprisal for the RAF's Munich raid on the night of 8th November. That night was an annual commemoration for sixteen of Hitler's followers killed in the 1923 putsch. He had survived an assassination attempt the previous year in Munich, and gave a speech there earlier that evening. The RAF attack was interpreted – probably correctly – as another attempt to kill the *Führer*.

Coventry set the tactical template for city-scale raids by both sides. The *Luftwaffe* sowed the wind; German cities reaped the whirlwind over the following years.

On 11th–12th November 21 Fleet Air Arm aircraft attacked Italian warships in port at Taranto, seriously damaging three battleships. The attack, flown from a single carrier, was a model for the vastly scaled-up raid on Pearl Harbour thirteen months later. The

Japanese assistant naval attaché in Berlin flew to Taranto to inspect the damage and a captured torpedo modified for shallow water.

Taranto, along with the bombardment of the French fleet at Mers-el-Kébir on 3rd July and the fleet action off Cape Matapan the following March, assured Royal Navy dominance of the Mediterranean's surface.

In Britain Captain Archibald Ramsay, a right-wing MP with strong anti-Semitic views, was interned for the duration. He was alleged to be Hitler's Gauleiter-designate for Scotland after the invasion.

The pace back on the estuary was unrelenting.

> *"Some of the blokes have turned out for an alarm at this minute, leaving their supper untasted, to the accompaniment of Bing Crosby singing 'I haven't time to be a millionaire'. He's telling us!"*
>
> *"… Did I tell you about our cinema? It's a mobile one that comes every Tuesday with the nearly latest films, and it's very good. Yesterday we had 'My Son, My Son'.* [11] *Unfortunately, the alarm rang in the first quarter of an hour, and I had to scram."*
>
> *"… I was terribly worried about that land mine in Broadwood Avenue*[12]*… Now I want to tell you something straight away which may be some little compensation for that night! I was in action all last night on the predictor for the first time, and we bagged a Jerry! I was layer for bearing. It was one of the most exciting nights of my life, I think. We were busy all night, and put up some lovely barrages. The one that got him was a beauty, all guns fired simultaneously, and we*

---

[11] A 1940 melodrama of dysfunctional relationships.

[12] These 500kg or one-tonne barrels of explosive, also known as parachute mines, were not the same as the buried monstrosities we call land mines. This one landed about 300 metres from their house.

heard him losing height immediately the shells burst. It was a great satisfaction to think 'that's one bugger who won't get near Ruislip!' ...

Well, last night did me the world of good. I'm conscious today of a job well done for the first time since leaving the Pic."

The casualty (Heinkel 111 of 1/KG26, based at Moerbecke and Courtrai) was first damaged by anti-aircraft fire then hit a balloon cable. It crashed at Beckton Marshes Essex at 12:19 AM on 20th November. All five crew, one a medical officer along for the ride, were killed.[vi]

Another success came on the night of Sunday 8th December. Eric stepped off the train from meeting Jennie in London – straight into an alarm.

"I was pretty lucky. I reached Sole Street at 8.30 and was at the camp at 9.00. Soon afterwards a bomb hit the line between Sole St and a station on the Victoria side. If I was travelling later I should have been stumped."

"... I felt very worried about leaving you to go home all by yourself on Sunday. It was just our luck to click for a raid and I hope the journey home wasn't too scaring or dangerous. We had a very busy night here. A plane dive bombed Northfleet and didn't come out of the dive. We heard the dive and crash quite plainly. Our guns were firing right over the hut and the blast frequently blew the doors open. Very awkward as the light was on most of the time, and it meant jumping out of bed to turn it off and closing the door."

A Junkers Ju 88 crashed at North Stifford, Essex (on the same bearing from Cobham as Northfleet) at 2.15 AM. The crew of four were all killed. This and another Ju 88 in Epping Forest were the first two night raiders brought down in December.[vii]

Weather limited *Luftwaffe* operations in early December 1940.

The easier pace released time for study and domestic concerns.

> *"I have made up my mind to work as hard as possible on theory and any practical gunnery knowledge I can obtain while things are quiet because when you feel like getting down to it it's fascinating stuff. The camp has also resumed P.T., which is very enjoyable, and I also have the regular job of cleaning and adjusting the predictor every morning. So there's no excuse for getting dull or depressed."*
>
> *"... Captain Porter is very worried about a high sickness average in the camp and he is making arrangements among other things, for a weekly bath for everyone at Rochester. About time too."*

Charlie Chaplin's film *The Great Dictator* was released on 14th December. Two hours' sustained parody of Hitler, very thinly disguised as 'Adenoid Hinkel,' concludes with an impassioned call for liberty, kindness and gentleness. It is one of Chaplin's hardest-hitting films as well as his most successful.

Eric and Jennie had a brief rendezvous at the Laughing Waters restaurant (now The Inn on the Lake Hotel, Gravesend).[13] This was a big help with the hut competition for best Christmas decoration.

> *"Tell you what I should like you to bring. A pot of red poster paint, if there's one at home, and a big paint brush. I'm doing a 'Merry Christmas' for the hut."*
>
> *"... I don't know if you have the chance of getting hold of any coloured paper now. If you can it would be very welcome for wall decorations. Green for silhouettes of trees etc. We want that bottle of port and cigarettes!"*

---

[13] Laughing Waters also housed ground-crew from the nearby RAF Gravesend. Live ammunition was found there in 1966.

"… This must begin with big apology for not writing to you yesterday. I went on guard which I half expected and developed a cold in the process. Then I was roped in to do a lot of decorating which included cutting out big replicas of holly and berries in crepe and pasting them all over the wall. The hut is looking really swell, and the officers are favourably impressed which is a good sign."

Christmas brought an unofficial three-day bombing truce on both sides. Eric, on guard duty, couldn't make it home and the battery didn't cater for visitors so Jennie visited her family in Bristol. The sky over the Thames Estuary was eerily peaceful.

"Everything is very quiet and unexciting here, we turn out for alarms, nearly always at night, fire a round or two, without getting much kick out of it."

Normal service resumed with a heavy raid on the night of 27th December, and a savage attack on the City – sometimes called the 'Second Great Fire of London' – on 29th. The latter prompted Home Secretary Herbert Morrison to call for volunteer 'fire watcher' guards on empty buildings at night and weekends. The practice of dealing with incendiary bombs before they took hold proved very successful and was systematically applied across the country. It was too late for the 160 civilians and sixteen firemen killed or the hundreds of people with serious injuries. In spite of an intense barrage no German aircraft were shot down.

Despite the destruction Eric managed a quick trip home on 30th; some recompense for seeing in the New Year on sentry duty.

An air defence innovation in December was to release untethered balloons trailing cables with explosive charges in the path of a raid. This technique ('Albino') posed significant danger to people on the ground, and almost none to enemy aircrew. 'Mutton,' an attempt to destroy bombers by towing a mine behind aircraft mingling with a raid, was equally futile. The use of gun laying (GL) radar – with its still too-scarce height finding attachment – to direct night fighters was more promising. 'Fighter co-operation' became a valuable tactic.

Meanwhile AA guns were forbidden to fire on moonlit 'fighter nights,' when RAF single-seat fighters attempted visual interception. The silence of the guns had an unfortunate effect on civilian morale.

At this stage the guns still accounted for around three quarters of the few enemy combat casualties at night. Accident, breakdown and weather were far more serious hazards for German airmen.

Poor weather in January cramped the *Luftwaffe's* style, but only relatively. Cardiff suffered its worst attack of the war on the night of 2nd. Bristol was hit on 3rd and 4th, London and Manchester on 9th, Portsmouth on 10th, London on 11th and 12th – counting major raids only.

206 Battery had a rare opportunity on 7th when low cloud prevented fighters operating, so they were allowed to fire at unseen targets.

> "We had a very busy day of it indeed on Tuesday. We were on the guns all day and most of the evening, and actually got a chance to do some day shooting. It was mostly 'hitting from memory' as the visibility was dreadful."

The big raid of 12th had them working hard:

> "We had a terrific session here last night. Jerry came in force over the estuary and it was one continuous roar of guns and bombs. We shot at least one down in the barrage. We were reinforced by a mobile battery just outside Cobham and boy, what a row when we all opened up!"

The booking hall at Bank Station took a direct hit in the raid, killing over 50 people. The defences claimed one German aircraft shot down and two 'probables.'

Eric snatched a day in London with Jennie on 4th, and a quick visit to his old colleagues on 8th. Unofficial trips were getting trickier though.

> *"Owing to the state of the roads I did not reach the office until 4 pm. But I made good use of the time, got Jack on to the details of that 'leave' game and presented Freddy with some material for his poems. Didn't see Sam [Campbell] aloof in his editor's room! I should have bowled in quick enough if H.C. [Hugh Cudlipp] had been there.*
>
> *It's a bit risky now to travel in London without a pass, which for some reason the C.O. is loath to issue. The town seemed lousy with 'red caps' and I got back through Victoria by the skin of my teeth."*

There was no need for subterfuge the next week: the army decided to get the recruits' leave entitlement out of the way so they were all given seven days from 17th.

> *"We have been having some hectic times here and owing to shortage of predictor men (they are rushing us through our leave as fast as possible) I have been on duty almost continuously. My guard duty has been postponed twice for this reason, so I click for it today.*
>
> *Lord, I shall be glad to be home for a few days. I'm simply living for it."*

Meanwhile the headlong expansion of anti-aircraft forces continued.

> *"We have a new intake here (December) and a lot have been bunged into our hut. Makes us feel like old soldiers!"*

"… The new boys are a nice crowd and are mucking in well. It's very amusing to see new recruits arrive, bearing the indelible stamp of the training battery and jumping three feet in the air if spoken to, and to remember we were exactly the same. And doesn't it make us feel old sweats!

Sergeant Wynell (you remember the red-faced bloke?) came in last night and started a rough-house which ended in a pitched battle with rubber boots between predictor men and height finders. The new blokes, quite unused to the spectacle of sergeants getting mixed up in this, huddled together in the centre of the hut and stopped most of the missiles."

Amy Johnson, the pioneering long-distance pilot, was lost during a ferry flight on 5th January. Lord Baden-Powell, founder of the Scout movement, died on 8th.

"What an amazing life he had. It seems superfluous to mourn a man like that who lived every minute of his long life and left such a heritage. It was his tragedy to see his world brotherhood dissipated and in some countries corrupted into young soldiers."

The law of unintended consequences kicked in at the gun site when the authorities tried to formalise meal breaks.

"'Falling in' for dinner – or any meal for that matter – is now an official parade and a late arrival is punishable as a defaulter. This led to a very amusing scene yesterday.

The boys decided that as they were not allowed to come late, they would come early and get first place in the queue – so that just before dinner was called the vicinity of the cookhouse was alive with furtive gunners prepared for the big rush. It was for all the world like the start of the great mutiny scene in 'The Big House'[14]*. And the orderly Bombardier had barely uttered the first syllable of 'Fall in' before plates were being smashed and knives and forks trampled in a great scrum. The orderly officer arrived in the middle of it and ordered everyone back to the huts!"*

Predictor drills never relented.

"I must leave now for a practice run on the old 'Predic'... Of course we are still training for day 'shoots' which is more complicated and I want that 'Time Drum' operator's job. During the day alarms I am No.2, who helps traverse and keeps 'lateral steady'."

"... We didn't get much time to ponder on the joys of 7 days of civilisation. We were roped in immediately on gas drill and within half an hour were marching and running in gas masks and 45 minutes of it. Then came predictor drill and lining up, and a spell of fatigues."

"...We had a grand practice run today. I was calling the fuze predictions and 'got off' a record number. Capt Porter is always pleased when this occurs and told me afterwards that, although I had probably half killed the gun crews, it was all to the good! Unfortunately I found the gun sergeants awaiting me with a different story! I rather fancy I will have this job for good."

Luftwaffe attacks continued from 13th–20th January. Plymouth, Derby, Bristol, Swansea, Southampton and London saw significant action with sporadic raids elsewhere, including a night venture by Stuka dive bombers which were too vulnerable for daylight use over Britain.

---

[14] A 1930 film featuring a violent prison revolt.

"There was some firing by our battery during the night but I was so fast asleep I didn't hear a thing. Considering that the guns shake the whole place and shake anything loose off the shelves you can guess how deep that sleep was."

Poor weather prevented anything more than nuisance raids from 20th to 29th when London was attacked again. London airfields and Thames shipping came in for a strong daylight raid on 31st.

"Rather funny this morning – the officers are desirous of bringing the changing of the guard up to date and generally brightening it up, so we all paraded at 11 a.m. for a practical demonstration. We were just complaining bitterly about blasted red tape when the alarm bell went in the middle of it. Of course the lecture dissolved like magic!"

120 German bombers transferred to the Mediterranean, and others were assigned to mine laying and anti-shipping duties. Hitler's directive of 6th February switched the *Luftwaffe's* priorities first to destruction of British shipping in conjunction with the U-Boat blockade, second the suppression of Britain's aircraft industry (including anti-aircraft armaments). The effort available for the Blitz began to tail off and refocus from the industrial centres to the ports. Near-impossible flying weather deterred further raiding in February but didn't stop the exercises.

"Returned to duty today on the predictor and had a good time laying on the planes that were flying out over the Channel. It was a very realistic exercise – gas masks and all, and we had two and a half hours of it."

St Valentine's Day marked a turning point in Eric's army career: radar.

"I'm feeling rather excited at the prospect, my old choice of a change rather than a rest."

*Figure 5: Southover Hall from the northeast. Photo taken in 1893
(English Heritage NMR BL12204)*

Wireless School

The anti-aircraft gunners' poor success rate – measured by shells per aircraft downed – against unseen targets prompted a thorough review in Autumn 1940. One conclusion was that the early radar sets were too complex and too temperamental for the people expected to operate them. The problem was compounded by technical manuals too secret to be issued to the gun sites.[viii]

The solution was to form AA Command Wireless schools, the first at Richmond Park, to bring fire control operators up to the theoretical and practical skill level needed to make the kit work. One such was Wireless Wing AACSI (Anti-Aircraft Command Signals

Instruction [?]) at Southover Hall near the pretty village of Burwash in the Sussex Downs, once the home of Rudyard Kipling.

The Hall was built around 1870. At the 1881 census it was occupied by Mariano de Murrieta, a 48-year-old widowed 'Foreign Banker & Merchant.' By 1909 it had passed to a Colonel E W Cradock. During the Second World War it was used both as an army training establishment and for an evacuated school – probably not at the same time. A Mr C J Thorn bought the hall in 1946 intending to turn it into a film studio; he was refused planning permission so it was carefully demolished between 1948 and 1951.

First impressions were positive.

"We are situated in lovely surroundings and in a very sumptuous mansion and living like lords. There are quite a lot of sailors here too, on the same course.

Leave is good – every other weekend…

The course seems to be a very interesting one tho' difficult and we will be at study from 9 a.m. until 7 p.m. Six weeks is an acknowledged 'cram' for the subject but they say they cannot afford more time, so that's that.

I have encountered one or two blokes from the original training battery at North Bot [Northumberland Bottom].

The grounds here are really lovely; lawns, tennis courts and gardens sloping down to a lake surrounded by trees – one of the most perfect settings possible. Most of the gardens are in bounds, so it is possible to do one's compulsory swotting out of doors on a fine day. The food is also very good and there's as much as you want, a distinct improvement on Cobham. Sleeping arrangements are on Cobham lines – sans beds – but I am getting quite used to that now…"

Then the scale of the task sank in.

"I'm afraid I'm a bit behind with this letter, but we are having one of the busiest sessions of our lives, and there's hardly time to do a thing outside the official programme.

… This business is so like being back at school again (hell and all) that I feel quite embarrassed when I remember I've married a teacher! The work is very interesting, though pretty stiff, and God knows what we shall be trying to assimilate in a few weeks time – that is if we pass our Bar exam, to be held Saturday week…

Life outside the classroom is very boring, very little chance of recreation and a God forsaken village 3 miles away! I think the idea is to make us concentrate! There's not even a wireless set to listen to – not bad for a wireless school!"

"… Our heads are aching pretty badly by this time as we are taking electricity right from the start and have to master formulas and work out resistances and potentials and watt-nots till we are nearly gibbering and scratching for imaginary electrons. It's some business if you've never done this sort of thing before, believe me. We have to master all fields of electrical work before we touch elementary wireless.

… If you possibly can, darling, could you get me two refills for that Woolworth's loose leaf book? I'm simply burning the pages up, even writing as small as I can.

Classes here are rather jolly, you can smoke and the instructors are a nice lot. We have a 'Lab' for the practical tests and experiments."

At least the work pushed army protocol into the background.

"Our staff sergeant is hoping to present a musical concert in the near future with the available talent. He himself was formerly an orchestra leader in quite a posh way. He's certainly no drill sergeant, makes no end of mistakes himself but is very fussy where we are concerned – 'He's no-one to ruddy well shout his-self!' is the general verdict. This morning the officer wanted us turned about and the

sergeant gave the order while we stood at ease! Of course the parade performed the evolution with the maximum of aggrieved shuffling – was his face red!

The atmosphere is (in the abstract sense) decidedly warmer as we get to know each other better and cease to be politely mistrustful. The sailors are universally liked; they are a nice crowd."

Jennie in the meantime started her fire watcher's training.

"Was interested to hear that you attended one of the fire watching lectures. I suppose it dealt with the explosive incendiary. As you say it's certainly no joke putting one of those out.

I don't think there is much doubt that you will be exempt – I should jolly well hope so anyway."

No such luck. A few weeks later:

"I think it's rather a cheek for Tuck to expect you to do fire watching – I suppose Kay [a neighbour] will do damn all? You have quite enough to do now – more than enough to please me. Anyway, I should choose your own time and convenience."

Meanwhile the total immersion approach was working. Some got the hang of it, others didn't.

"The course is now getting very interesting, we have had practical lessons on Diesel power engines today and are tackling wireless proper. There is the further prospect of seeing the 'real thing' tomorrow. You will be pleased to hear that I came 'top of the class' in the Bar exam with 90%. Of course, the real obstacle will be the trade test in which you have to score pretty heavily to qualify for that extra farthing a day or whatever it is. You might be offered that or alternatively a bed to *sleep in. However, I'll stick out for the dough and hope for plenty of weekends.*

Tom Morse has failed very disgracefully and returns to Cobham tomorrow. It was just damn carelessness on his part. He showed me his paper and one bit sent me into fits – he was asked to explain the workings and polarity of a magnet and contented himself with three scribbled drawings. The 'marker' had deciphered the first and awarded a tick pretty confidently (✔). The next was a lot more doubtful and you could see he was in two minds about it (✔). The third looked like something made with a planchette and the marker registered complete bewilderment (?). Tom says he doesn't mind anyway.

The pleasure side of Southover has bucked up today to the tune of a mobile canteen and a film show to be held later this evening. Seems almost like debauchery to our starved souls. Maybe even our sergeant (studious) major will smile sometime after this."

"… The course is at last getting a little illuminating, so the final exam should not be too impossible. Both Ken [a colleague from the same battery] *and I have increased the swotting tempo this week.*

Ken amused me very much on Sunday night. He visited the battery at Denton over the weekend and encountered the CO who has a particular aversion to him – in fact he put him on the course to try and get rid of him. Well, this officer was none too pleased to see him and asked him what he thought of GL and (sarcastically) how much he knew about it. Ken retorted 'Oh, quite a bit sir, but of course it isn't the sort of thing we talk about to anybody!'"

206 Battery's commanding officer attended a Burwash course himself in May.

The *Luftwaffe* used improving weather in March to step up the pace. Birmingham, Bristol, Cardiff, Glasgow, Hull, Liverpool, London, Plymouth, Portsmouth and Southampton took severe punishment. Back on the Thames Estuary the regiment was busy firing most nights. 206 Battery did a TEWT (Tactical Exercise Without Troops – war game) and then mobile training. Their rivals from 208 Battery won the Brigade Cup Final.

Jennie's home town (Bristol) suffered a heavy raid on the night of Sunday 16th March. The raiders, bombing blind through cloud, missed the docks but seriously damaged communications, residential and shopping areas despite the partial success of decoy fires (code named 'Starfish'). Some 200 people were killed; one bomber came down in Wiltshire and another three over Europe when returning. On Wednesday 19th nearly 500 aircraft struck at the East End in the heaviest raid since October. Eric wrote next day:

> *"Was rather perturbed to hear about the raid on Bristol and trust they are all OK. The planes were humming over here in the direction of London last night and I couldn't help wondering where they were heading and feeling a bit worried. It will be nice to be back on the guns again and feeling that one's justifying a somewhat curtailed existence."*

Nonetheless gradual deployment of AI (Air Intercept), GCI (Ground Controlled Interception) and GL radar, combined with the fighter and gun crews' developing skills, began to make a difference. German losses were rising, though still pitiful in relation to the number of attackers. Anti-aircraft guns claimed 37½ night bombers shot down from January to March 1941, fighters 29. To put this in context there were 4,707 Luftwaffe night sorties against British cities in the same period, giving a casualty rate of about 1.4%.[ix] By contrast RAF Bomber Command suffered overall losses of about 3.5% between July and December 1941.[x]

At sea, the *Kriegsmarine* had broken British naval and merchant ciphers. Losses escalated dramatically from 303,000 tons in January to 475,000 tons in March and 616,000 tons in April.

"Everyone seems to consider the food situation as pretty critical, as the U boat menace seems to be increasing without appreciable check. Let's hope we find the solution soon."

On 6th March Churchill ordered Bomber Command to focus on targets directly or indirectly associated with the sinkings. He later said the U-boat peril was the only thing that frightened him during the war.

Fighter Command took an increased role in shipping protection and, with convoys diverted to the North-West Approaches, western anti-aircraft defences had to be strengthened. In January 1941 the Clyde, for example, had 67 guns out of an approved 120; by April its ration had increased to 144 guns and was to be met in full. The reinforcement would affect Eric before long.

The course was followed by a few days' leave; just in time to save his sanity.

"We had a filthy night on fire picket (says he, proceeding in same cheerful vein). We were so damned tired that we all overslept too and the first thing we knew the sergeant was kicking our bottoms and asking us if we knew that the fires were out and we weren't supposed to go to bed anyway. Followed a snappy encounter with the sergeant cook, whose Welsh rhetoric flowed nobly on the subject of late breakfast. Then the bloody Diesel wouldn't start up. By that time we could have started on the equipment (and the permanent staff) with a large sized monkey wrench. Instead we had to sit down all out of breath and write about it. God knows what the result will be! I could have cheerfully written an essay on the Army in general and Southover in particular.

Oh well, darling, some day when this is over and we are enjoying a livable and lovable existence I will ask you if I have grumbled at anything since the war ended, and on recollection of any such happening you can dot me with the hardest thing to hand.

> *But we must be thankful for what we have got I suppose. I felt*
> *a bit ashamed of my little troubles when I heard that one of the boys*
> *has lost best part of his family in the blitz in the East End, and he*
> *didn't know till he went home this week end. And as long as you are*
> *well and happy when this is over I don't care if I have to start again*
> *with damn all."*

Back to the Bottom

On return from leave Eric found himself with 264 Battery – back at
Northumberland Bottom but this time operational. In a sign of
war's ability to cut through normal structures his immediate
superior was a civilian: GL radar, and the height-finding attachment
in particular, was still new enough to need babying by an expert.

> *"The man in charge of the GL is a civilian (seems funny having*
> *a 'Civvy' boss) quite a nice bloke. He was enquiring about our*
> *occupations and when I told him where I worked he startled me by*
> *saying 'And how is the great Hugh Cudlipp?' Afterwards saying 'I*
> *met his brother Percy frequently, my brother works on the Herald'.*
> *Subsequently I discovered his name was Ewer – so you can guess*
> *whose brother he is![15]... Mr Ewer is starting lectures again tomorrow."*

Poor weather at the start of April gave a brief respite in the raiding.
The gunners seized the chance for some recreation and maintenance.

---

[15] William Norman Ewer (1885–1976) worked at the *Herald* from 1912 to 1964. At
this time he was diplomatic correspondent and eventually became chief foreign
correspondent. He was an enthusiastic Communist (and Soviet spy) in the 1920s
but later adopted anti-communist Labour politics.

"The fellows here are a very good crowd indeed and I have at last found a sufficiency of chess players, six, to be exact! One is so hot that on my first game with him I was completely overwhelmed, which I may say does not happen very often."

"… Yesterday was my duty day and I was so busy that I didn't think once of it being Good Friday! We were calibrating and checking instruments with the aid of a plane flying at a known height and speed and it was most interesting work."

Most gun sites now had some form of radar support and the crews were gaining familiarity with the equipment.

"We are getting pretty conversant with the intricacies of the GL in action, it wants a bit of doing though, especially the high standard of operating required for Fighter Command information."

Bristol was hit repeatedly on the nights of 3rd, 4th, 7th, 9th and 11th April, the last and most destructive being Good Friday. Jennie was visiting her family at the time, causing Eric no little anxiety. They escaped unscathed; not everyone did.

"You will I know be sorry to hear that Mrs Hull died last Friday; and also that Sid Heaven died in hospital on Monday. He was a warden at Knowle on duty and caught the blast of a bomb (which wrecked his house) causing internal injuries from which he succumbed."

Eric didn't have much time to worry as the *Luftwaffe* switched tactics to raid over a wide area instead of single, concentrated attacks. The Medway batteries were kept busy most nights.

London suffered its heaviest raid yet on the night of 16th April. 685 bombers dropped 890 tonnes of high explosive and over 150,000 incendiary bombs causing 1,179 deaths and 2,233 serious injuries.

Five enemy aircraft were shot down. Even this assault was surpassed on 19th when 712 aircraft delivered over 1,000 tonnes of high explosive for the first and only time in a single raid on the UK. Over 1,200 people were killed and 1,000 seriously injured. Poor weather and the sheer scale of the attack combined to overwhelm the defences: just four raiders failed to return.

> *"We had the most hectic session ever down here. I reached Gravesend just as the sirens were sounding and was at the camp just as the raid was approaching its maximum – I went straight over to the transmitter and stayed there for the next six hours until a kind soul relieved me. The planes came in so thick and fast that Gun Operations Room just couldn't cope with them by plotting barrages and told us to go over to individual control, which was very helpful as we weren't transmitting to the predictor. So we just fed them information by phone and they banged away on that system. Something will have to be done soon about countering a mass attack. At present we can do damn all and we are all fed to the teeth about it."*

Seventeen high explosive bombs, two parachute mines and about 1,000 incendiaries landed around the regimental HQ, damaging the roof of the drill hall but without casualties. None of which dissipated tension between the 'intellectuals' of the fire-control team and the horny-handed gunners.

> *"An NCO showing another round put his head into our hut yesterday, viewed the recumbent 'personnel' and said 'THIS is the bloody infirmary!' They hold a very poor view of GL, chiefly because we are outside their jurisdiction. Sort of fox and the grapes."*

German attention then switched away from London. Plymouth suffered three nights in a row, from 21st to 23rd April, then again on

28th and 29th. Sunderland and the Mersey also experienced major raids, with many other places hit either by lesser attacks or opportunistically by aircraft unable to reach or find their main targets.

April had seen the heaviest bombing yet but the defences were finding their feet. 5,724 German sorties resulted in 48 aircraft destroyed by night fighters and 39 by artillery – the first time Fighter Command's claims had exceeded the guns' at night. Apart from physical destruction the defences were often effective in disrupting the bombers' aim or making them abandon their attacks. In this they were helped by decoy fires, smoke screens and constant fencing between the RAF's 80 (electronic warfare) Wing and German navigation and targeting systems.

In war news the Greek success against Italian attack lit a brief flash of hope.

> *"What do you think of the new war fronts? Glad to know there is a new BEF* [British Expeditionary Force] *in Greece – let's pray there will be no more 'Dunkirks'. They have a pretty big job on, but the elimination of Italy in Abyssinia should release big reinforcements. Good luck to them."*

But then on 6th April the Germans invaded Greece and Yugoslavia with eighteen divisions backed by a strong air assault. The defenders, a scratch force improvised from whatever General Wavell could spare in North Africa, stood little chance. The RAF was outnumbered by ten to one and the few anti-aircraft gunners had little early warning and no blind fire capability. Piraeus, the port of Athens, was unusable by 11th April.

George Orwell's diary for 13th April read: *"No real news at all about either Greece or Libya… Of the two papers I was able to procure today, the Sunday Pictorial was blackly defeatist and the Sunday Express not much less so. Yesterday's Evening Standard has an article by 'Our Military*

Correspondent'… which was even more so. All this suggests that the newspapers may be receiving bad news which they are not allowed to pass on… God knows it is all a ghastly mess. The one thing that is perhaps encouraging is that all the military experts are convinced that our intervention in Greece is disastrous, and the military experts are always wrong."[xi]

The unfortunate British conducted a disciplined, fighting withdrawal to the south taking in resonant names like Thermopylae, Olympus and Argos. The RAF's last fighters were destroyed on 22nd and all anti-aircraft defence overwhelmed by 26th. On 30th the Royal Navy finished evacuating nearly 51,000 of the 62,000 men landed in Greece; without their equipment. Another Dunkirk.

"News from the Balkans isn't so hot, is it? Hope it's not building up to another glorious withdrawal by the 'cream of the Imperial Forces'. It's a pity public opinion has been so buoyed up by our victories over the Wops. People seem a little hurt when the Germans refuse to behave in the same fashion. Still, our troops have yet to meet them. Good luck to them."

He didn't know that over 1,000 German bombers had been withdrawn to support the Balkan campaign; aircraft that would otherwise have been attacking Britain. Not that that was any consolation to the poor people facing them.

"The bad news from the East seems to be having a depressing effect on people here. It is hard to see our slender gains snatched from us so soon, but I do think that it is no worse than we expected last year. Nobody would have prophesied that the Greeks would have beaten the Italians and so delay the invasion of their country. In the meantime we have eliminated the Italian threat in East Africa and disposed of a large Italian Army in Libya, which by now would be augmenting the German divisions.

It is my bet that Hitler will now start at once on Turkey as the one remaining country between him and the oil fields of Irak [sic]. After all, what's one country more or less? And what reasonable resistance can the Turks be expected to put up now that they stand alone? If they had helped the Greeks Mussolini would have been flung out of Albania weeks ago.

It's a pity our generals spent the winter of 1939 congratulating themselves that there were no senior German officers with experience of the Great War! Of course that's pretty evident now."

This echoes Cassandra's observation in *The English at War*:

"Then comes a most significant and illuminating observation spoken by this sixty-year-old soldier [General Ironside]*: 'The German Army has one weakness that is largely overlooked. She has no commanders who were more than captains during the last war...' Events have proved that it was precisely because of this fact that the German Army was so brilliantly efficient in action."*[xii]

Invasion fears were still at the top of the gunners' minds. With small detachments scattered around the country, the nearest trained and equipped soldiers to any parachute landing would most likely be AA Command. General Pile was a strong advocate of engaging paratroops before they had time to organise, but his forces were controlled for ground fighting by regional commanders who favoured static defence. Accordingly each regiment maintained a Defence Schedule: a worked-out plan of action in the event of invasion alarm. Typically this involved the immediate issue of small arms and evacuation of the Regimental HQ to the nearest defensible gun site. The guns would fend off airborne assault as long as possible then adopt field artillery or anti-tank roles as needed. In the last resort the gunners were to destroy their equipment and revert to infantry.

> *"We were awakened at night here a short time ago by an awful hullaballoo and sprang out of bed expecting to cope with parachutists. It happened to be Ken having a nightmare in the grand manner."*

The focus on maritime trade even affected the battery. With RAF resources switched to the west the Navy had to find other ways of defending coastal traffic against air attack.

> *"'Sandy', our posh accordionist, has been posted to an anti aircraft vessel and has left amid general regret. He had just received a warrant for 36 hours leave when a note arrived summoning him straight away. Was he sick about it! It was a shame. Sandy received the news when he got in late last night, a little 'under the influence' and he just stood in the centre of the room and cussed for about ten minutes."*

Sandy went to *HMS Golden Eagle*: a paddle steamer built in 1909 as a ferry. She was requisitioned in the First World War, returned to her owners, requisitioned again in 1940, went to Dunkirk, then became an Auxiliary Anti-Aircraft Vessel. In that role she was fitted with a GL radar to counter mine-laying seaplanes off the coasts of Kent and East Anglia.[xiii] Later she helped cover the D-Day landings. She survived the war and her owners got her back again – no doubt slightly worn – in 1946. Sandy, a radar operator, found himself on a gun as well as fire control.

The three AA ships of the Nore Flotilla were a popular billet: Navy food was better and leave more generous than for their colleagues ashore. The ships were kept busy fending off *Luftwaffe* minelayers, destroying floating mines and rescuing survivors of mined ships.

Life on the battery continued as normal. This disturbance on a night when Belfast, Liverpool and Barrow-in-Furness were heavily attacked was too trivial to mention in the regimental War Diary.

"We had a five minute Blitz in the middle of the night when a plane came across and every gun in the district opened up at it. I only half heard it being extremely tired after my short night's rest previously."

10th May brought yet another heavy raid on London by over 500 bombers. It caused extensive fires and, as in December, fire fighters were hampered by very low water in the Thames. Many buildings had been left without fire watchers over the weekend, exacerbating the damage. Over 1,000 people were killed but the raiders didn't have it all their own way. Clear weather and moonlight helped the gunners and allowed the RAF to put up 325 fighters. Eleven bombers were lost.

Rudolf Hess, Deputy Führer, used the confused skies to cover his unauthorised and delusional dash to Scotland. He baled out of a specially adapted Messerschmitt 110 when almost out of fuel. He hoped to negotiate peace with Britain and free Germany to concentrate on the approaching fight with Russia. In fact he spent the rest of his life in prison, dying at Spandau in 1987.

"... what do you think of the Hess business? What a story! I'm looking forward to seeing what the press boys make of it tomorrow. Of course there will be the usual stories of the impending Nazi crack up! I suppose the poor bloke's off his nut! All the same the effect on Germany will be pretty electric.

Somebody said today that it may be a new invasion stunt with Germans coming over here, presumably running away, until there are about 30,000 of them! They can't fool us!"

On 3rd May a lance bombardier at 206 Battery's Denton site accidentally shot a gunner who died the following day. The poor lad was buried at Leytonstone on 9th and the offender court-martialled on 16th. Amid the chaos and destruction of the Blitz this was the battery's first fatal casualty.

The radar crew had a more pressing concern on their minds.

> *'A very severe but not altogether unexpected blow has befallen the GL. We have been ordered to supply men for guard duty, fire picket and fatigues! Four of us, including myself, are due for guard duty tomorrow. Isn't it a swine? The very thing I wanted to dodge!*
>
> *The trouble is we have far too many men here, about 22 in fact, and until we are split up a bit we shall probably click for a lot of camp duties. We are all very worried about the prospect of leave being cut down. What a life!... It makes you sick when you hear about how well wireless men are treated in the Navy and the RAF. Why didn't I try for the RAF?"*

Of course the rest of the battery didn't share their dismay. Glee would be closer – until the hacked-off radar men found ways of expressing their resentment.

> *"The whole affair created quite a sensation and practically the whole battery turned out to see the GL mount guard. We were so damned wild about it that we did it perfectly and got congratulated! And I was picked as attending man.*
>
> *Actually I quite enjoyed my spell – 10pm to midnight. I clicked for a crowd of NCOs creeping up late, challenged them with as much noise as possible, bawled them out for 'crowding up' and made them all come up separately and be recognised – in fact made a damn nuisance of myself. I don't think they considered this aspect when they agitated for the GL to mount guard. We shook 'em!"*

On 20th May the Anglo-Greek garrison of Crete (including many survivors of the Greek campaign) came under attack. Ten days' heavy fighting led to yet another humiliating, costly defeat and evacuation. The Allies lost about 1,750 soldiers and 1,800 sailors killed, 1,750 wounded and 17,500 prisoners. The Germans suffered 6,000 – 7,000 casualties and lost 284 aircraft.

Both sides took lessons from this first and only successful invasion entirely by air. The Allies noted the paratroops' effectiveness and immediately began to plan their own elite airborne formations, while German experience of their vulnerability deterred them from trying the same trick again.

The British public couldn't know that. Returning from an evening out Eric wrote:

> *"The evening's entertainment offset the depressing news from Crete. Bad show! There's not a man who isn't disgusted about it, and I'm glad to see the papers aren't accepting the usual excuses. The whole business was a complete bungle."*

The Royal Navy provided some consolation when it sank the *Bismarck* on 27th May.

By the end of May the pace of *Luftwaffe* activity was beginning to fall off as units transferred to the Eastern Front. Birmingham suffered a major raid on the night of 16th May, Manchester on 1st June and Chatham on 13th – but there were now weeks, not days, between efforts on this scale.

At about this time Eric was temporarily attached to 163rd Battery of 55th HAA Regiment at Fenn Street near Rochester.

> *"Well it's quite a nice little site here, quite reminds me of Cobham. Conspicuous absence of red tape and animosity. But as I said, the duty is a lot stricter, as we have to stay on the instruments and be prepared to go into action at a moment's notice. And we work in 6 hour spells, which rather interferes with the chance of a day out. Still, as you say, may be we shall learn to wangle something.*
>
> *We had a very lively first night here. A few planes came over the*

district, and as we opened up at one of them another aimed a 'stick' at our flashes. They burst about 100 yards away. I, being off duty, slept through the preliminaries as usual, and woke to hear everybody jumping for their tin hats and the bombs descending.

The GL is here chiefly for the benefit of the guns which makes an action much more interesting – and it's quite a good experience. The whole of this district is chock full of guns, especially Bofors."

It was however a bit isolated: *"… it's a swine of a walk to anywhere, and the last bus to the vicinity is about 6.15pm…"* He got around that by bringing a bicycle back from his next leave.

"We had a nice cycling expedition on Saturday when we toured the Isle of Grain district. You get a lovely view of the destroyers and other naval craft anchored off Sheerness including the A.A. boats. Otherwise the district is very dull, and the villages the most desolate you ever saw. It reminds me of your descriptions of the Rye country. A fellow who accompanied me had the misfortune to be at Grain during the first few months of the war and he said it nearly drove them mad."

In the news there were ominous rumblings from the east. The *Sunday Times* on 20th April reported a build-up of forces, construction of road and rail links toward the Soviet border, and orders for Russian-gauge railway wagons.

"Something does appear to be happening on the Russian border, doesn't it. Very exciting and speculative. Wonder if Stalin regrets 'starting something' when he invented parachutists?" [16]

---

[16] Marshall Tukhachevsky created the world's first dedicated paratroop unit in the 1930s. He was executed in the 'Great Terror' of 1937.

As German forces migrated to Poland the remaining *Luftwaffe* squadrons did their best to disguise their reduced strength with redoubled work rate.

> *"When in addition to this we have to do constant manning, it becomes very arduous, as this means 'searching' and reporting on friendlies and hostiles.*
>
> *We haven't had a night as bad as the first one, but scarcely one without some sort of action, including the first day shoot I have witnessed for a long time.*
>
> *The worst of 6 hour manning periods is that you never get a complete day off, and although the battery is easy going about some things, it is very strict about punctuality – worse luck!"*

A gas scare at a nearby site on 5th June was a false alarm, but it was never explained just why the detectors activated. Then, on the night of 14th:

> *"Sounds as though there's a raid in the offing – the sirens have blown off in the distance – probably Chatham, and we are standing by with the juice on. Will probably amount to nothing."*

Wrong. After a couple of weeks' lull about 100 German aircraft were in action over the South and Medway. The guns had a busy night and the *Luftwaffe* took unexpectedly heavy losses. One aircraft exploded in mid-air, presumably when a lucky hit set off its bomb load. Eric wrote:

> *"Last busy night was Friday. Objective, Thames Estuary and a convoy anchored there. Things were pretty hot from one till four in the morning."*

Still the air battle was tilting in Britain's favour. More guns and fighters, better technology and tactics all had their effect. Had the

Luftwaffe continued its attacks at their earlier intensity the cost would have escalated far beyond their derisory losses so far.

> *"Oh, and we had a spot of bother on the good old Estuary yesterday – last night rather. A few bombs, but nothing close enough to worry about. The bursting power of our shells seemed to be terrific; we all commented on that. Some quite distant bursts simply rattled the hut. I suppose they are using the new explosive. I should have hated to be up there among the 'flak'."*

On 22nd June, the storm broke. In a catastrophic miscalculation Germany launched Operation *Barbarossa*, the invasion of Russia, with over four million soldiers on a front 1,800 miles long. German strategy envisaged a rapid military collapse followed by capitulation on the pattern they had set across Europe; it didn't happen. Failing to achieve a quick victory against either Britain or Russia left the Third Reich in the situation its planners most feared – a long war on two fronts. In the east the four-year slugging match that followed saw some of the most brutal behaviour in history, where each side treated the other as sub-human.

Many Britons saw socialism as the last, best hope for a fairer society. The Soviet-German non-aggression pact of 1939 left them uneasy and confused. Now *Barbarossa* resolved the tension and brought clarity in its stead. We had a common enemy.

> *"Remarkable that when we debated yesterday morning about putting the wireless on we should have missed what is probably the greatest news of the war. Isn't it just incredible? I never believed it would happen, despite the rumours and troop concentrations. If there's one thing more fantastic than Comrade S[talin] lining up with Winnie [Churchill], it will be the sound of the International being played among the anthems of the Allies! Workers and plutocracies of*

the world unite! God, won't Jerome's head be spinning! And I can see my skates being of some use yet!

But with all due respect for Germany's well conceived campaigns – you must give the swines that much credit – I can't imagine why on earth she has taken on a proposition of this kind. It's either genius or desperation, in view of the vital stage of this war, with America hovering on the brink, and the RAF at its best. It's going to be very interesting to watch the course of events."

As Churchill put it: *"No one has been a more consistent opponent of Communism than I have for the last 25 years. I will unsay not a word that I have spoken about it. But all this fades away before the spectacle that is now unfolding."*[xiv]

The ever-growing need for fire control operators forced the army to advertise publicly, and admit the existence of gun-laying radar.

"The GL cat seems to be well out of the bag, doesn't it… If I get away early I may pop into the Pic office for an hour. I should like to hear their reactions on the subject of radio location. On my last visit there they were politely incredulous when I mentioned it."

The same pressure led to the recruitment of Auxiliary Territorial Service (ATS) women from April 1941 to supposedly non-combatant roles (everything except actually loading and firing the guns) in mixed batteries. They proved highly effective and released some 28,000 soldiers for other work.[xv] 1941 also saw the first Home Guard trained for anti-aircraft duties, initially on 'Z' (rocket) batteries though later they were used much more widely.

With the night Blitz fading to a grumble some of the defences dispersed to other tasks. 308 Battery mobilised for overseas service on 16th June; it ended up in Sierra Leone.

> *"We have lost a couple of the 'personnel' here. They are going abroad with their battery. Very short notice, too."*

Back with 264 Battery at Northumberland Bottom, Eric found rumours flying.

> *"Yes, the prospect of foreign service is a bit of a blow, but we must face up to that possibility, at least. Latest reports indicate that the whole regiment is being issued with embarkation kit – from sources at North Bot. Still it's no use thinking too much about it until the actual orders are issued and the GL personnel find themselves included."*

On 7th June the regiment was advised that 206 Battery was to come under War Office control, a prelude to service abroad. The instruction was cancelled the next day but, on 9th, the battery was ordered to transfer to 60th HAA (currently in the Birmingham area) on 10th July. Eric, suddenly switched to 207 Battery at Iwade, had no idea whether or how the change would affect him.

> *"I was… warned to expect a move and only notified about destination today. We were moved over to this site about half an hour after receiving your letters. We stay here for a week only, and God knows where we go to after this. The 206 is not going abroad, but is turning mobile and, by all accounts, is moving to Birmingham. Whether we go with them is not yet clear."*

Not that he was sorry at the prospect.

> *"This is a lousy dump compared with Fenn St and I'm not sorry we're not staying longer… Anywhere but here! It's nothing but marshes. As it's a danger area there is no local leave either."*

At the end of June General Pile congratulated 28th Brigade on its 200th claimed German aircraft, 58th Regiment having accounted for $52^3/_5$ths of them. 60th HAA were moving from Birmingham to the Crewe area and 206 Battery – including Eric – was to meet them there. They left on 8th July.

Hindsight

Eight months' night bombing of British cities left 40,000 people dead, at least as many seriously injured, and over a million properties destroyed in London alone. The capital was attacked 71 times, including 57 consecutive nights.[xvi] Despite the destruction the campaign failed seriously to affect British war production or civilian morale. It did tie down very large forces, which could profitably have been used elsewhere, in defence of the United Kingdom. If your enemy can attack anywhere, you have to defend everywhere.

On the other hand the *Luftwaffe* experienced far lighter casualties during the Blitz than their opposite numbers in RAF Bomber Command. This was changing: in the second half of 1941 it lost 114 bombers in UK raids and 33 more in shipping attacks;[xvii] despite a much slower tempo. Only 33 of the 252 air raids causing more than ten deaths in 1941 were after the German invasion of Russia, and by mid-August only 203 bombers (of which 84 were serviceable) remained on the Western Front. The equivalent numbers for September 1940 were 1,498 and 958.[xviii] From the gunners' point of view the number of rounds needed to bring down an unseen aircraft fell from 18,500 in September 1940 to just over four thousand in January 1941 – mostly owing to GL radar.

Apart from gradually escalating mutual reprisals the *Luftwaffe* tried hard to attack military targets. Their electronic navigation and aiming aids (*Knickebein*, *X-Gerät* and *Y-Gerät*) were better than anything the RAF had at the time and, when they worked, allowed them to bomb through cloud with reasonable accuracy. The location of factories in tightly-packed cities made collateral, in today's unpleasant language, inevitable.

The electronics also triggered the 'Battle of the Beams,' a technology arms race in which each side tried, often successfully, to block the other's countermeasures. It wasn't the first use of electronic warfare (EW). That honour goes to an unknown Russian radio operator at Port Arthur in 1904, who held down his spark-gap transmitter key to disrupt the attacking Japanese fleet's communications. EW now came to the forefront of tactics for the first time however. Fast learning, soon to be combined with American industrial muscle, made the Allies' later domination of the air war possible.

As for Eric, if he thought Iwade was bad…

MOVES, MOANS
AND MUD

Railway Children

60th (City of London) HAA Regiment was another territorial unit raised as the shadows lengthened in the late 'thirties. Unlike 58th it was mobile, a veteran of the British Expeditionary Force (BEF) and Dunkirk. It spent the Blitz months in Birmingham and had its share of adventure, forced to evacuate a gun site while three bombs were defused. 206 replaced 194 Battery, who joined 80th HAA Regiment and fought their way through North Africa, Sicily and Italy. The regiment's other two batteries (168 and 169) stayed.

The regime was a jolt for gunners from static sites. The first six months of the year had seen over fifty battery or troop moves, including live-fire practice at the Towyn range in North Wales and regular detachments to the Combined Operations Training Centre (COTC) at Inveraray – *not* a holiday camp.

After Dunkirk the war could only be won after an opposed, amphibious landing on the European mainland. No 1 COTC (abbreviated to CTC) was set up in October 1940 to develop and train the required skills. Inveraray, on Loch Fyne, was a village of about 500 souls but hosted up to 15,000 soldiers, sailors and airmen in the camps around it. Some 250,000 trainees passed through before it closed in July 1944. The regime was brutal, including landings under live fire. AA batteries were rotated through the centre both for training and to defend the loch.

On the plus side there was less paperwork.

The move coincided with 60th's transfer from Birmingham to Crewe, a lightly defended railway hub. To complete the disruption, 206's radar crew switched to 169 Battery.

> *"… we are at Crewe, Cheshire, 15 miles from Wales, 20 from Liverpool, on quite a nice site – our second since arriving here! We were quickly separated from our battery, who are just the other side of the town. Their site had Mark 2 GL[17] and very few of us had any experience of it, so we were rushed off to another site with the usual Mark 1. But we aren't so very far from our own battery.*
>
> *We get 48 hours every month, which isn't so bad. The journey can be made in four to five hours. One can also hitch hike on the Great North Rd which, considering the fare (26/-)[18] is just as well.*
>
> *I can't tell you much more about the district until I've been out and around, but it seems alright. We are on a farm and the cows have the run of the gun site and huts – in fact they are continually putting their heads into the huts to everybody's disgust.*
>
> *We had a very good journey up. We started late and the train finally left Gravesend about 11.30 pm. We came right through London without changing (via Addison Road and Willesden Junction) and arrived at Crewe about four in the morning."*

---

[17] I use Eric's radar naming (Mark 1, 2 etc) instead of the official designation (Radar AA No I, II etc) for consistency. This is confusing when we get to No III which went through several completely different Marks. For the purposes of the story, don't worry about it.

[18] About £61 at 2013 prices.

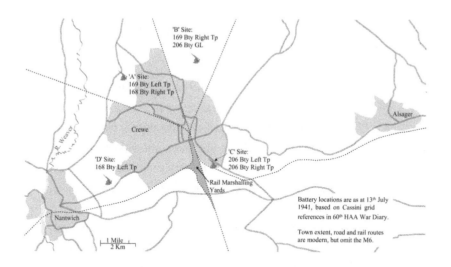

Map 2: Crewe HAA Gun Sites

Moving onto an unprepared site was an education for the Estuary gunners. They had to install basic services, set up the equipment and prepare ground defences.

> *"We have been doing plenty of ground exercising work, including telephone line laying and barbed wiring. We are also having our kit overhauled and refitted. I'm glad to say I've acquired a better tin hat – not new, but only slightly soiled.*
>
> *The Battery we are serving with have seen service in France and they are pretty hot. The NCOs and officers of 206 come down here every day for gun drill, so altogether we are being nicely 'hotted up'. It's rather a good job we are kept busy, for this district would be well in the running for a prize as the most God-forsaken spot on earth. The one surprise since we've been here was the presentation of a round of free drinks at a pub in Crewe – oh and there was the Marx Bros. film 'Go West', quite good."*

Return from a short leave didn't improve his view of the scene, by now a sea of mud.

> *"This really is the dullest Battery and the dullest place imaginable. The mere prospect of spending a winter here will drive us mad.*
>
> *Plenty might be done if the officers were the slightest bit interested. There's still no signs of a recreation room and not so much as a sing song organised, let alone a concert. And they've just damn all to do here. It's funny how the attitude of the officers reflects on the men. The whole crowd seem thoroughly dull and dispirited.*
>
> *However our own little party keeps pretty cheerful and we are quite busy on our own account camouflaging the instruments and building several strong posts in the vicinity. We are doing some tree felling for this purpose."*

Having set up and settled down, they set about making some entertainment.

> *"We are just back from field sports today. We have also formed a canteen committee with a view to acquiring indoor sports tackle."*

Eric joined Crewe library and managed a trip to Nantwich: *"… a most delightful little place, very picturesque and old fashioned and a great improvement on Crewe. It is famous for its brine baths and, by the way, this is a great salt producing place."*

One compensation for being with 169 Battery, just back from the delights of Inveraray, was that the radar section was spared when '206' was packed off there in late July. They didn't appreciate their good fortune.

> *"Hopes rose high last night when Liverpool district was raided but the planes kept well out of our area.*

206 go to Scotland soon for more training but we stay here, worse luck. We scarcely get a 'friendly' here to practice on, let alone a Jerry."

It was such a quiet life that when a shout came it caught them unawares.

"We had an alarm last night and were so surprised that we lay in bed listening to the whistles, quite unable to connect it with an alarm until the sirens joined in. Nothing transpired, of course, and we were all back in bed again after ten minutes.

They have a damn funny system here. We have orders not to fire until the planes have actually dropped bombs, the idea being not to expose the position of the marshalling yard and works. Probably a very sensible idea, but confoundedly annoying when we track a plane in and get it beautifully in firing range, as happened the night I returned. The boys got quite rude about it."

Drawing on the lessons of the Blitz, Parliament rushed through legislation to create a National Fire Service replacing some 1,600 local organisations of varying efficiency. Launched on 18th August it never had to face a challenge like the great fire raids of 1940–41, but was a vast improvement on what had gone before.

Eric formally qualified as Operator Fire Control Class 3. His rather daunted first impression of 60th was beginning to wear off.

"I was so bored the other day that I volunteered for prediction drill and quite enjoyed the practice run. The team here is not nearly so hot as the Cobham crowd."

The tedium drove them to extreme measures:

"Biggest news from our particular front is the capture and taming

*of a field mouse (!!) by the wireless section. As it makes a noise just
like Tullett, we've christened it 'Emma II.'*

*Rather horrible to think that we're descending to what the blokes
in the Bastille do to relieve monotony."*

'206' had all the fun. After the terrors of Inveraray they left for
Burrow Head (a peninsular due north of the Isle of Man) for firing
practice on 22nd August and stayed there until early September.

*"206 are off again to Scotland and are mostly downcast at the
prospect, having had enough of the first period. Les Bromage is
particularly so as he has lost his 'protection' stripe, but he rallied
sufficiently to send kind regards to you."*

In the meantime 168 Battery (Right Troop) went to Shropshire.
Eric's radar section followed a few days later.

"... I'm due for a long spell of fire piquet after ten.

*By which you will gather that the GL is having all the dirty
work slung at us as at North Bott. Only until tomorrow, however.
We all move out to a place called Donnington, near Brum; isn't there
a racing track there?*

*Seems to be a pretty good place from what we hear. Wireless
search station cum training centre – so we are preparing a biggest
ever 'soldiers farewell' to this dump, and have appointed cheer
leaders.*

*... Must break off now and parade for 'fire piquet' which is
another way of saying 'fatigues' (potato peeling a speciality). Will let
you know about the new address as soon as poss."*

Shropshire Lads

It was a big step up despite the primitive living. 168 Battery was much more congenial than 169, and they finally got their hands on a GL Mk 2 radar. No more boredom for a few days while they got it working.

> *"We are now on a site in Shropshire about 4 miles from Donnington near a village called Oakengates. The site has been built on the highest point in the county and we have a really marvellous view of the surrounding country, can see the balloon barrages of Crewe and Wolverhampton and the Welsh hills about 14 miles away.*
>
> *When we arrived here we found that we had to erect tents as there was no hut accommodation. We therefore prayed for fine weather and have been very lucky so far…*
>
> *We found a brand new Mark 2 outfit here for us to assemble and have been very busy ever since in getting it 'ready for action'… At present there are two guns and not more than forty men here. The 168 are a great improvement on 169."*

At least, it worked apart from the trivial matter of fuel for the generator.

> *"It seems damn silly our HQ operating from Crewe still. They actually send a ration lorry all the way from there nearly every day. We have been out of action now ever since we've been here because we could not get oil fuel transferred from our old site! It's just arrived."*

The new toy was as good as a holiday.

> *"We are all still very excited about our 'Mk 2'. They are really wonderful instruments and do everything but talk. The O.F.C. make*

up for that. They have just started up and rushed over to 'man'. Isn't it wonderful what something new will do?"

The easy-going atmosphere sparked a livelier social schedule.

"We had a very jolly darts match in the canteen the other night between GL and the rest of the section – and we won! The section team included the two officers."

Sometimes it was a bit *too* easy-going.

"Instead of parading one morning we assembled in the canteen for a lecture on discipline. The officer pushed off with a complaint about smoking in 'on duty' periods and was warming up nicely when suddenly he broke off, goggling, and we became aware of a column of blue smoke ascending from our midst – from one of the GL men who had become blissfully unaware of it! You should have seen it put out in record time!"

The next task was learning to use the new radar. An air co-operation exercise had the team reverting to traditional methods.

"We had quite a snappy session of 'co-opping' today. I'm still laughing over a typical 206 session during the last period. We had some difficulty in locating the bearings of planes as they approached close and appointed a roof spotter! He proceeded to open up a considerable portion of the roof in order to shout down orders and finally some bright spark climbed to the top of the aerial and perched precariously there with a pair of binoculars. All this had the effect of drawing large crowds in the road outside, and presently the GPO [Gun Position Officer] arrived fuming and said he had no objection to anything in reason but there was no need to behave like a troupe of ruddy acrobats!"

The change, the challenges and the company rekindled Eric's enthusiasm for the job – and progression.

"I wonder if you could order me a booklet of math tables, dear?... We are having some good theory sessions just now and one is rather hampered without some calculating tables."

"... I have been doing a lot of swotting in maths and wireless theory lately as there is a probability of vacancies for a technical instructor's course. I should very much like a stab at it. I am glad to say that my 'trig' is now on a sound basis."

He leaped at any chance of extra-curricular activity – especially if it paid.

"Things being still pretty dull around here, a couple of us volunteered for harvesting. Accordingly we spent all day yesterday on a neighbouring farm. We both enjoyed it though as work goes it must rank second only to stone breaking. Anyway, our skill with the pitchfork was much appreciated and we received 7/6 each for a day's work and an invitation to come as often as possible. So, fortified by the prospects of such worldly wealth we turned up again this morning but the fields were too wet to start on. Then we paid a visit to a coal mine in the vicinity, saw the boss and said how about a look? He was very decent about it and has arranged for us to 'have a look' tomorrow night. We are wondering if it is possible to harvest by day and then make a bit extra at the mine on the night shift! What a war!"

And a few days later...

"Well, the harvest continues to be safely gathered in by yours truly, so spare a thought for me when the winter storms begin and you munch your bread (Shropshire brand). It really is good fun plus £1.2.6 for three days work, and the session seems less like Dartmoor

after the first day. I can now make up a stack, toss up two sheaves into the cart at one go with unerring aim, manage three walloping great brutes of farm horses all at once (including harnessing) and talk Shropshire lingo, besides other technical accomplishments. Speaking of horses, the biggest one of the lot takes a lot of starting (i.e. woona pull, the booger!) One of the tips I received about starting him was to light a fire under him. Well, homeward bound with a full load he breasted a slope and then stopped dead, and all other persuasions having failed, I crossed my fingers and had a go. I'm afraid it was somewhat larger than intended for it flared up alarmingly, and he started off like a Derby winner, nearly upsetting the 'jag' of hay (sorry, corn). I don't think it was worth while, both for his heart and mine.

As a relief from farm life we turned up at the colliery last night, having obtained permission to go down with the deputies – the men who have to examine the workings before the night shift arrives. We had the special gas indicator lamps, helmets (like jockey's caps, only you wear the peak at the back to protect the neck), and we carried short sticks to help us along the workings. There were three of us and one (an ex-salesman) couldn't resist the inevitable 'Going down, ladies underwear' etc as the cage started. It went down at a hell of a lick, and although it's not deep for a coal mine (900 ft) it seemed ages before we espied the lights below through the floor of the cage. Well, we climbed out and looked around with great interest. We saw the tiny office and then went to the stables and inspected the pit ponies (Phew!) before departing for a tour of the workings. It was then that we were glad of the helmets, as the supports are only four feet high in places.

Then the deputy fired a shot in the coal face. The previous shift prepare the face by boring about 4 feet into the seam, and the deputy's job is to fire these alone. The cordite and detonator are pushed into the drill and well tamped with clay, and then you retire at once with 20 yards of wire, make contact with a battery and up she goes! We all rushed forward to have a look, and the deputy said he would fetch a pick, and retired. Our

*ex salesman picked up a sledge and commenced at once, with the result
that about half a ton of the top came down! You should have seen us move.*

*Well, nothing much more exciting occurred except that small
traces of 'Blackdamp' were discovered and traced to faulty ventilation;
then we came up. A very enjoyable experience."*

At Crewe 169 Battery had been put on a two weeks' concentrated
programme, presumably to improve their morale. The training
covered air co-operation, field gun practice, lectures on camouflage
and security, marking out and digging new gun sites, mobile drills
and switching troops between sites. In between all this
entertainment they polished the equipment for a staff officer visit.
206 Battery returned from Practice Camp in time to help with the
digging. Shortly afterward the RAF 'attacked' the Crewe gun sites
in a joint air exercise described as 'of great value.' In early September
a fourth battery, 359, was attached to the regiment.

Having done the heavy work on the new sites, the regiment was
ordered to Glasgow. 168 Battery, with one troop at Donnington and
the other at Inveraray, was not consulted.

*"We have been waiting here more than a week for definite news
of our transfer and we are still completely in the dark about it.
Meanwhile, leave is held up indefinitely in view of a small move to
Crewe, a matter that an intelligent NCO could put right in five
minutes. Unfortunately, these arrangements are left to the higher ranks."*

Eric dreaded the return to (as he thought) Crewe and made the most
of his remaining time.

*"I had a nice afternoon at Shrewsbury yesterday. It's a lovely
town almost enclosed by the Severn with the old Norman castle still
intact, a relic of the Welsh border wars. There is a fine museum and*

library, also an art school. I spent some time in the cattle market – a huge affair – and watched the auction, also got mixed up plenty with droves of cattle. Finally went to the pictures and saw Jean Arthur in 'The Devil and Miss Jones'[19] *(very good) and caught the next train back to Oakengates. As I hitch hiked over it was a very cheap outing. I want to see as much of this country as possible during our stay here."*

168 Battery finally pulled back to Crewe, straight into the mayhem of the Scottish move.

"We were suddenly told to pack up on Thursday, so assuming that we were going that night I thought I would postpone my letter until then. However, we moved out Friday morning and rumour had it that the whole Regt was leaving for the Northern Command and we would re-entrain for somewhere in Scotland. But the train arrangements had been bungled (as usual) so we have had to spend the night here. There are two complete Batteries on this site as well as transport and wireless men of a third so you can guess how chaotic it is."

They entrained for the Clyde Sunday evening 21st September.

Song of the Clyde

After a sleepless night Eric found himself back with 206 Battery at Flaterton Camp, Gourock, guarding the southern entrance to the Clyde about 25 miles downstream from Glasgow.

---

[19] A 1941 comedy about a flinty store boss who goes undercover to weed out union agitators. Needless to say he finds love and enlightenment instead.

> *"We arrived at Clydeside about 4.30 a.m. and were taken by lorry to the camp. We haven't seen much of our surroundings except that it is mountainous and very picturesque, with a lovely view of the Clyde from the surrounding hills.*
>
> *The prospect of a prolonged stay in these surroundings is pretty grim, but there is a speck of consolation in the fact that we are not for foreign service and are back with the Battery… Ye Gods! It has to be Scotland!*
>
> *I'm nearly falling asleep over this, as we had practically no sleep last night, so I will end now and get some shut eye, as we are due to man the instrument at midnight until six a.m."*

Things didn't improve when they got to work. Having mastered the GL Mk 2 (a radar actually engineered rather than bodged) they discovered their new site still had the old equipment.

> *"We are back on the old, old mark 1 set and all hopping mad about it. We have had one or two unpleasant surprises: the Battery isn't what it was and the sense of distance still hangs heavily over us."*

After a couple of days he began to see the positive side, perhaps encouraged by his Donnington mates' departure for Inveraray.

> *"We got round a bit yesterday. First we went to Gourock which is quite a nice little place on the Clyde with a great variety of craft at anchor, including flying boats. Then we visited Greenock. I should imagine that it is to Glasgow what Avonmouth is to Bristol, a real dock town… I am hoping to visit Glasgow and Edinburgh soon as those towns are quite accessible and Edinburgh sounds particularly inviting… We are very fortunately placed here compared with the rest of the gunners. Our G.L. section gets leave every other afternoon and as we do night manning we are excused all parades and fatigues. It's a great pity we are not operating the newest instruments as ours is an important master site."*

"… Scotland is slowly improving on inspection. The people are grand, very friendly and sociable, and the Corporation buses make no charge for service men, a very thoughtful innovation which the railways might copy when it comes to leave. By the way, there is ice-skating in Glasgow!

It's been raining cats and dogs here, and boy, does it rain!! Still it's my day in and the rain held off yesterday, so who am I to grumble? We went to the pictures Saturday and saw 'Cheers for Miss Bishop'[20] a sort of 'Mr Chips' style of story. Quite good."

As September's mud slithered into October's Eric recalled that he'd now been in the army a whole year: *"All the same I don't fancy spending another anniversary here, much as I fear we shall."*

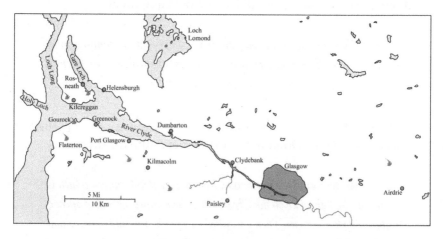

Map 3: The Clyde. Showing only gun sites mentioned in the text; there were many others.

---

[20] A 1941 'feel-good' film about a small-town teacher in the American Midwest whose otherwise catastrophic life is redeemed by the love and respect of her former pupils.

With little German activity to worry about camp life revolved around exercises, training, coping with the weather – and building huts. Accommodation and infrastructure had not caught up with the Clyde defences' rapid expansion.

> *"I'm feeling the slightest bit browned off, chiefly because of bad weather and mounting seas of mud around the camp, a slight cold and a poor light to write this by. Talk about eye strain! It nearly blinds you to read for half an hour. I think I must do my correspondence on my nights off in future and take them to a Greenock canteen.*
>
> *From the above can be inferred that the usual care and attention has been devoted to the relaxations of the gunners. Lady, they may have shot down 600 planes, but that does not entitle them to the blessings of electricity, even if this has been a static site for two years."*

Expecting to be there for some time the troops settled in as best they could.

> *"This seems to be reminiscence night here – every chap is reeling off his gunsite experiences and a fire has been lit and on the whole a more cheerful atmosphere prevails."*
>
> *"… the town canteens are a decidedly bright spot and a great credit to the hospitality of the Scots. It's more like a family circle than anything else, even to cigarettes being handed round at the conclusion of a meal. One is impressed with the sincerity of everybody up here to everything connected with the war effort and the welfare of the services. The south has nothing on it.*
>
> *The night which it is prudent to avoid (as the girls in the canteens assure us earnestly) is Friday, when the navy and the 'Red Duster' boys [merchant navy] come ashore to spend their dough. Then is the air dark with flying bottles and the exciting vision of Glasgow 'going round a' round' merely a preliminary sensation for these*

stalwarts. I don't doubt they frighten the Germans, for by God they frighten us."

"… I visited Glasgow yesterday and had a delightful tour around. There is a beautiful park wherein is situated the University and the Art Galleries – which I just missed. The Kelvin Hall is also an interesting building rather like the Wembley Stadium. And you would revel in Sauchiehall Street – every other shop is a gown shop with some glorious models in the tartan style, modom. There are some good shows on too, 'Fantasia', 'Kipps', 'Pimpernel Smith', stage shows etc; the only string re full appreciation of these being the 9.30 bus and of course, soldiers pay! But the ice rink does make allowances for this last contingency and I think your idea about forwarding my skates a very good one! I should like to visit Glasgow once a week and cut out Greenock as the latter place is a bit of a hole and although my respect for our seafaring men is unbounded, I prefer a place where they don't make themselves so conspicuous and the thoroughfare so dangerous."

"… Oh, by the way again, I'm booking up for evening classes (2 evenings a week) at Greenock and taking a correspondence course in radio engineering. We have had an education officer along to interview anybody interested and the terms are exceptionally good."

"… Unfortunately there are no art classes available but I am taking machine drawing as the next best substitute. There is also a highly recommended French conversational course which sounds rather good. We are getting special time off for this, so it will at least relieve the tedium of our rather dull existence."

In the event the French class got going but there wasn't enough demand for the technical drawing. The urge to self-improvement didn't extend beyond the GL.

"I am rather fortunate in having a few kindred spirits here, and the evening classes are pretty accessible, otherwise life would be still

pretty grim... Do you know that the GL men are the only ones here to avail themselves of the benefits of evening classes?"

War news was still bleak.

"Everyone is rather depressed at the news from Russia. The position is undoubtedly grave, but the Soviet has put up such a marvellous show up to now that they may yet stop the Germans."

In the day-and-night job the steadily deteriorating weather added to the frustration of trying to keep their temperamental – and increasingly obsolete – GL Mk 1 working.

"We are still messing around with this beastly set. The weather has reverted to normal and there is plenty of rain about. I suppose we shall finish it sometime."

Two fruitless alerts on 5th October had gun and radar crews scrambling to their stations but no targets showed up.

"We were just into bed and blessing the fact that we weren't manning when the alarm went. We had just about got our trousers on when it was cancelled. We got back into bed and had barely turned the light out when it rang again and was again cancelled the moment we were outside. This so incensed one bloke that he shouted 'What the B.H. are you playing at' for the benefit of the GPO."

Returning soaked from a dance Eric and some mates found a concert in progress at the camp. It would have been rude to miss it.

"It was only when we were rolling into bed about 3 am that someone casually mentioned that we were on duty at 6!

We had another shock when we groped our way out to the instruments this morning; the rain had started a small spring in the path to the GL, if you please! I can see us hiring a speed-boat yet for alarms!"

Annual inoculations mid-month prostrated so many of the battery's men that all leave was cancelled to preserve some kind of cover. Among other things this interrupted another harvest trip. His own inoculation left Eric weak, shivery, sleepless – and distinctly grouchy.

"The weather is just unbelievably bad. It's been coming down in bucketfuls ever since yesterday morning. It's pretty grim to think that we have to put up with this sort of thing all the winter. The mud around the instruments is nearly a foot deep now, there are no duckboards for a path over the 'mat'[21] so we have to wade around two sides to approach it.

I suppose I'm pretty inured now to official ineptness and indifference, but my God it makes me boil sometimes to see the lunatic way things are mishandled (maybe it has something to do with an inoculation). This gun site was no sooner built than survey… (apparently called in to view the finished article) condemned it as the most waterlogged valley in the district (I think I mentioned the spring).

How the hell *can we expect to win wars with this sort of ghastly incompetence? To join the army is to despair, to stand appalled at this unparalleled exhibition of lunacy.*

We had a colonel's inspection this week with the same old rot, kit stacked up just so, etc. Everybody was feverishly running around tidying up the ground and scrubbing any wood in sight. Of course he wasn't shown the defects of the camp.

---

[21] GL 1 E/F and GL 2 receivers were surrounded by a wire mesh 'mat' to provide an artificial horizon for elevation measurement.

It's going to be a typical gun site winter. The drinking water has been condemned, there is no water, hot or cold, in the washhouse and rations seem to be short all too often. To hell with it, anyway I'm getting out as often as possible. It's like being granted a permanent ticket for the Mad Hatters Tea Party. Why did I ever harbour any delusions about being allowed to fight for democracy?"

A few days later the inoculation after-effects had abated but the weather hadn't.

"The camp is now completely flooded and looks like a cheap imitation of Venice. The spring under the mat is now a river gradually approaching the dimensions of the Firth of Clyde and we've put out submarine nets around the receiver, just in case. They're also useful in case the operators are caught in the rapids. Talk about invasion practice! We were manning again at 6 a.m. this morning and how we got out there was a mystery. Coming back at midday you could at least see to swim. There was a service in the canteen at the time and, so help me, they were singing 'For those in peril on the sea'. We splashed past laughing uproariously and irreverently.

You get so smothered in mud that you can hardly keep a foothold when on maintenance work and unfortunately one of the boys fell off the receiver on Saturday, landed on the concrete and hurt his back. He was taken to hospital and we are all anxiously awaiting news of him. Another of our fraternity, 'Taffy' Roberts, has been taken ill and is now in hospital so there is a kind of gloom around the joint. Everyone has a maddening desire to get hold of the high-up who is responsible for the choice of this site and push him well down into the slush."

With invasion still a concern they defended the site against a mock attack by the Scottish Rifles.

> *"… afraid this is a bit later than usual owing to a 24 hours invasion practice, which has kept us running about in tin hats and respirators all the time…"*

Lessons learnt were built into a revised ground defence scheme. An air exercise (*'Domino'*) was not a success however, and a re-run three days later was little better.

Then – finally – a Mk 2 radar arrived. If ever they needed an instance of the proverb "Be careful what you wish for…" this was it.

> *"I am ever so sorry not to have written before but we are having the very devil of a time here, swopping over a 'Mark 1' set for a 'Mark 2,' amidst indescribable chaos caused by boggy ground and army inefficiency…*
>
> *It's been going on for nearly three days and looks as though it will last another three at least. Luckily it is not raining but the ground is simply terrible. We had to find a fresh site for the transmitter (new) so the owner/farmer of the adjoining field was asked if it could go in a corner of it. He said certainly and then the Army got to work. Great six-wheeled lorries thundered on to the spongy turf, circling round like Spitfires to discover likely places to deposit the transmitter and power unit. They were accordingly dumped after what seemed an exciting game of dodgems but were no sooner left than they proceeded to sink rapidly. It was a genuine peat bog. There were wild SOSs for winches and tackles and the instruments were hooked up just as they were going down for the last time. They were eventually extricated, but not before one of the rescuing lorries was imbedded itself and pulled out with great difficulty. Of course, what should have been done in the beginning was achieved at the finish, a relatively dry spot was surveyed and a groundwork of sleepers placed in position for the instruments. Everybody was so pleased when the instruments were finally in position that nobody paid any heed to the farmer's outcries. One good field ruined.*

You would think that the lessons learnt on this occasion could be applied to the next, but exactly the same thing has happened today, when the receivers were changed. No groundwork was prepared and tonight there is one receiver and one lorry up to their axles in mud, awaiting the dawn and more lorries to pull them out – and a master site out of action. A more pathetic spectacle of brute force and bloody ignorance was never seen. I always like to think of the Iron Duke's description of the Portuguese – 'I don't know if they frighten the enemy, but my God they frighten me…'

Saturday

I couldn't finish this last night as I was summoned to guard the instruments and had to spend half the night in a beastly draughty cabin. Well we finally achieved the changeover and I feel too damn tired and fed up to comment on it.

It is now dark and we've just finished groping for telephone lines and called it a day. I never want to see a sleeper again."

It took until the end of the month to get the new kit bedded in and working.

"Thank goodness most of the outdoor work has been done. We still have to supply our own guard for the instruments and do our night manning. But the instruments are far more interesting now they are in action; these Mark 2s are an enormous step forward."

Newspapers reported the death of Joan Fieldgate, a 27-year-old evacuee escort returning aboard *SS Port of Wellington* when sunk by a surface raider in the Indian Ocean. She was rescued, imprisoned at Liebenau and died of dysentery on 9th October 1941.

"What a terrible place to meet ones end. Her parents must feel pretty awful about it."

HMS Ark Royal was the Royal Navy's first purpose-built aircraft carrier. She had a busy – and successful – two years during which German propaganda claimed her sunk several times. On 14th November 1941 they were right: she foundered after a torpedo strike by U-81 the previous day.

At about this time Eric found a kindred spirit in Len Nash who was already a sergeant. The two remained firm friends for the rest of Eric's time with the battery. They explored the local ice rink together, reviving Eric's pre-war enthusiasm:

> *"Would you like to be an angel and send on those skates sometime? Some of the boys have been to the rink at Paisley which is nearer than Glasgow and pronounce it quite good. So I am planning a visit in the near future."*
>
> *"… I managed to team up with Len Nash for this [24 hours' leave] and yesterday afternoon we looked around Glasgow, and in the evening went to Paisley for the ice skating. It was quite nice (albeit crowded) and quite like old times. I felt pretty rusty and it was Len's*

Figure 6: Eric on ice. These are probably post-war cartoons drawn by a colleague.

*first attempt at this on ice so you can guess that we didn't do anything
very brilliant. But it was very exhilarating none the less."*

In a local innovation the GL crew started overnight guarding with
just two operators instead of the full team. It made for a heavy night
when they were on but – with alarms now rare – a week's respite in
between. Eric used the time to bone up on trigonometry in the hope
of a Technical Instructor's course. Chances seemed good – the
Divisional GL commander had more or less promised he would be
in the next batch.

Rumours of an impending move to Kent raised GL spirits: *"it
would be lovely if it were so wouldn't it? Much as I like Scotland in general,
it is a bit too far away."*

So did a planned outing to see *'The Merchant of Venice'* in
Greenock. Then the move was announced. The radar section – only
– was attached to 359 Battery at a site being built east of Glasgow.

> *"This must be rather a hurried note, dear, as we are moving!
> Not to Kent – yet! We are going to Airdrie, which is just the other
> side of Glasgow. We move out tomorrow morning, and today we are
> having a field check on all equipment, etc. It will be just our luck to
> come to a Mark 1 site and have to erect another Mark 2!"*

So much for evening classes, Kent and *'Merchant'*. When they arrived
it just got better.

> *"Talk about out of the frying pan! Darling, words fail me when
> I try to describe our new quarters. We are actually in tents again –
> tents! – in about the coldest weather we have yet experienced. There
> is a pioneer battery erecting huts on the spot (we are manning GL
> on this site before the camp is finished!) so until these are finished we
> and the equally unfortunate Pioneers have to lump it under canvas.*

Having sworn myself faint last night in common with the rest of the gang, I'm feeling somewhat more philosophical. But don't you think it's the limit at this time of year? It was so cold last night that even my eiderdown and four blankets couldn't keep me warm and the frost looked just like snow. We have plans for a great communal bed if this lasts! We are wondering if this sort of thing is a hardening off process for Russia or a subtle joke of the Ack-Ack Command's…

The Pioneers are a tough crowd on the site and highly diverting. Tea was a bit on the late side tonight, so they proceeded to remind the cooks of this by heaving bricks on top of the cook house. The canteen has quite a Yukon touch to it when the company assembles. I'm very thankful to be with such a nice crowd of operators, they keep very cheerful and we generally manage to make the best of things."

"… There is a great sea of mud all over the site (they've never heard of preliminary concrete runways around here). Scottish gun sites are giving us the pip. The poor devils here spend their lives digging out lorries and utility vans. I've never in all my life seen such a dump – I'm beginning to have an idea what Flanders was like.

We are still living like gyppos (superior ones, of course). We've bashed holes in diesel cans and made braziers, burning coke wantonly despite gentle (more or less) reminders from the site commander about rationing. One of our crew was demonstrating fire lighting in one the other evening by attaching a piece of wire to it and whirling it around his head. Of course it came unput and disappeared into one of the Pioneers' tents, bringing them out like a swarm of angry bees. We all scrammed to the instruments and came back late at night – on tiptoe! You can't stay and argue with those babies! Nothing could convince them we hadn't done it on purpose."

The versatility of HAA guns in North Africa piqued their professional curiosity.

"What was very interesting was a report on the recent Libya

fighting. It seems that in the emergency both British and German AA guns proved excellent anti-tank weapons and were responsible for the majority of tank casualties on both sides… They were also used to shell aerodromes and supply dumps. So this band of 'weary willies' may yet find themselves fighting with the Panzers!"

Jennie was probably less excited about that idea. One of her nephews had already died training with the RAF.

On 7th December the Japanese attacked Pearl Harbour using techniques learned from the Fleet Air Arm at Taranto – and propelled the USA into the war. Like many British people Eric and Jennie greeted this game-changing news with surprising (to us) dismissiveness – almost *schadenfreud*.

> *"The Japs can certainly hand it out – let us hope the Americans can take it. I am surprised to hear the amount of criticism I do of the Americans. I don't think there is much love lost between us really."*

Just three days later came news of the loss of *HMS Prince of Wales* and *Repulse*.

> *"Great blow losing those two ships. Somehow I thought things were going too well with us last week."* (Jennie)

On 18th December, following a week of air raids, the Japanese landed in Hong Kong. The defenders surrendered on Christmas Day after a seventeen-day battle. Relatively lightly defended, it was the first Crown Colony to fall to Axis forces. The invading troops were ordered to take no prisoners and the slaughter was horrific.

> *"The news from the Far East is not so hot – is it? Seems as usual we have not enough fighter aircraft."* (Jennie)

The German assault stalled at the gates of Moscow. Their equipment was unsuitable for the bitter December cold; casualties and exhaustion left the *Wehrmacht* weakened as Russian reserves arrived in strength; and German logistics couldn't cope with the hundreds of miles of scorched and frozen earth between Moscow and the border. None of this was an excuse to Hitler who sacked five generals and took personal control of the army. Operation *Barbarossa* had cost upwards of a million lives in six months.

On the Clyde, camping in foul weather and thinking about Shakespeare may have inspired this pastiche on a certain Scottish play.

WITCHES ROUND THE PLOT!
(Scene: Plotting Tent set amid a Blasted Heath. Enter the Tactical Control Witch, the Gun Position Witch, and the Plotting Witch, with attendant devils.)

TCW	*When shall we three meet again?*
GPW	*At midnight, on the cry of PLANE*
PW	*When the next alarm is nigh*
	When the Hun is in the sky
All	*Able, Baker, Charlie, Dog,*
	Fine or cloudy, rain or fog
	Each to each his task this e'en
	All to plan the shoot unseen.
TCW	*I the duties to allot.*
GPW	*I to bawl!*
PW	*And I to plot.*
All	*Each by both the others muddled*
	Tho' the outcome may be fuddled
	Let's to the occasion rise,
	Synchronise our cues and cries –
	Hurry, Hurry, Toil and Flurry,
	Fuss and Bother. We should worry!

TCW	*Plans are mine!*
GPW	*The guns are mine!*
PW	*Barrage Plots are my design.*
GPW *(nastily)*	*P.L.M. is far too slow.*
PW	*A slight. A dirty crack. I go.*
Devil	*Alarm, you know.*
All	*A plane! A Plane! The Hour! The Hour!*
	We have no light. There is no power.
	Chaos! Darkness! Din Satanic –
	Counter-order…
	Devils Flap!
	And Panic

(Plotting tent slowly collapses)

The cards flipped again. 359 Battery went to Burrow Head Practice Camp at the end of December for live-fire exercises. After that it transferred to 63rd AA Brigade and ceased to be of interest to 60th HAA. In August 1942 the battery turned up in the Falklands where it stayed until early 1944.[xix]

206 Battery in the meantime moved twice in a matter of days, ending up on sites at Kilcreggan and Rosneath commanding the northern entrance to the Clyde – almost opposite their original Gourock posting. If there was a grand plan to all this, the cold, wet gunners couldn't see it. First there was rumour.

> "We have been mucked about in the usual way prior to a fresh
> move. We had kits packed Monday, unpacked today, then they took
> half of us away and I think the rest of us will follow tomorrow.
> Apparently we are in for a real dose of the great outdoors this time.
> We are off to a site with only a GL mat and a few tents (!) to assemble

the instruments. *Happy Christmas! We are all so browned off about it that the subject's not mentioned in the best circles."*

Then counter-rumour.

"After all that mucking about on Tuesday, prolonged into Wednesday, they've decided to keep us here as a team (eight of us). That means constant duty and 24 hours off every week. Six days in this dump straight off! Even one afternoon for bath cancelled.

I daren't try to foretell how long it is to last, except that there are rumours of us going to a firing camp with this mob on the 31st. God knows why we have been condemned to spend our lives with '359' a more God awful bunch I've never encountered...

We had a good laugh over the doings of the bunch that went to fix up the new set. Jimmy Coyle took half a dozen with him and arriving there, found no set or sign of life. They had a conference, then decided to tramp to the village and attend a dance. Soon after they had gone, the set rolls up with a convoy of guards and an officer. It ended with them being hauled out of the joint by the scandalised officer and a ticking off for Jimmy!"

Followed by yet more rumour.

"Well here we are, still in the land that God forgot! It's been blowing a sou-westerly gale for two days and nights, reaching such an intensity at times that we feared for the huts and the instruments! The wireless has conked out and there are no papers, so altogether I am well informed. Have we won the war yet?

We have had some rather vague news tonight. 206 is moving, where we don't know, but HQ is pretty pleased about it and hints that the move is good – Monday's the date – but we don't know whether we are moving with them yet. I hope to God we do. We are all very, very sick of this life and find it impossible to keep cheerful whilst cooped up here for a full week without a glimpse of the outside world. The crowd here, officers and men, are simply foul. The officers don't bother to return salutes so they've had none from us lately."

The joyous epiphany came on 16th December – back to 206 Battery at Kilcreggan, a relatively dry site. With huts.

> *"Well we finally packed up and left Airdrie yesterday and are now established on the above site…*
>
> *We had a most interesting journey via lorry and were very gratified to find the site a decently built one and in particular free from mud, except on the approaches to it. There are a lot of Irish nearby at work on a seaplane base[22] and as there have been several cases of sabotage, we mount a strong night guard, including one for the instruments. I*

Figure 7: Kilcreggan Gun Site in 2011 (Martin Briscoe).

clicked for the first duty and did two spells of 2½ hours during the night.

We seem to have landed into a very inaccessible spot. We are at the tip of a narrow peninsula of land stretching out into the Clyde opposite Gourock and to get anywhere within reasonable time one has to take the ferry to Helensburgh, which saves a walk of some miles by land. But at the moment we are so pleased to get into a decent billet that we are not worrying over much about where we can get to."

Daylight revealed more attractions – and a fix for the transport problem.

"We are on the most picturesque side of the Clyde here. Ben Lomond is due north of us, standing out from a range of hills and mountains that look like the Rockies. There is water on three sides of us and a magnificent view of the harbour and the south side. It's really most exhilarating after Airdrie, especially.

I think I mentioned that the Yanks are here building a seaplane base. They run their own ferry service to Helensburgh and admit servicemen to this privilege. This is very useful as the ferry proper packs up about six in the evening. I came back at 11 o'clock last night in their ferry boat and believe me it was some crossing: they use a fast motor launch that holds about 90 and it swept through the water like a torpedo boat, drenching all and sundry. It's surprising how rough the Clyde is."

The remains of the Kilcreggan site were still visible in 2011.[xx] Christmas brought its own logistic issues.

"We have saved £2.10.0 for a beer fund, but are confronted with the awful prospect of not being able to buy any. A press gang has been appointed to scour Clydeside for the needful. As the boys say, the

---

[22] Rosneath, which was jointly developed under the US Lend-Lease Act of March 1941.

situation is the reverse from the usual, when we generally see plenty of beer but have no money."

Having arranged Jennie's visit for a 48-hour leave at the beginning of January Eric found himself setting up a new site (probably Darnley in south-west Glasgow) with 168 Battery – again. The leave was still on provided nothing else went wrong.

"There are eight of us on the site fixing up a Mk 1 and we haven't the slightest idea what it is to be for, whether for genuine manning or training ATS. There are only two of us from 206, the rest are from 168 including a snooty Bdr [Bombardier]. I realise now why 168 boys at Donnington called for three cheers 'for the only GL Team who mixed in with the boys!' It's only the fact that he has the last say in my 48 hours leave that keeps me on the fringe of politeness.

I have seen the Battery Captain about the leave and it's OK with him as long as I can be spared from the GL for that period. So it's as good as certain!"

It turned out to be a training site.

"We had four trainees arrive three days ago, and expected a T.I. along. But no instructor turned up and so we were told to commence a training programme ourselves. Well, we have had a very enjoyable time, working very hard and combining maintenance with training. We have also, I think, made very good progress."

The technical instructor's arrival left the radar crew with little entertainment.

"We have a set that has apparently been in use in the days of the Flood and just damn all to do. Tomorrow I commence strenuous

efforts to get back to the other section. I do wish to God that something would happen *in this life: I'm not too particular as to what. I can't even seem to start an argument here! No wonder men are flocking to the Commandoes and to the paratroops."*

Boredom, inevitably, bred scratchiness.

"We have had some fun here over the weekend. Had a slight brush with the T.I. over the question of doing instrument guards and parading with the trainees, so had a word with Jimmy Coyle about it – Jimmy's Irish reaction was to go right up in the air and send transport for us straight away! The T.I. refused to let us go, and the officers backing him up, there ensued a hell of a row between the two troops. A compromise was eventually reached. I am to stay here to be in charge of maintenance and to assist in the training and also to be in charge of the blokes on parade... We had to take the 'innards' of the set out with a vengeance yesterday – the slight thaw we had melted the snow on top, it leaked through and absolutely soaked the set; when we switched on there were blue flashes all around reminiscent of a Frankinstein [sic] film, it was shorting everywhere! We went frantically to work and practically dismantled the whole set before we remembered that we ought to have informed the Radio Officer!

... We have shifted the receiver this afternoon to a place nearer the huts – for instructional purposes – and yours truly was the stooge who had to dismantle the aerial array – 'Emma' says he always has fits of giddiness! It's as good an excuse as ever I've heard. God it was cold up there! I came down feeling like one of Timoshenko's[23] *victims.*

---

[23] Semyon Timoshenko, a cavalryman by training, was an early recruit to the Red Army from the Tsar's forces. He was a moderniser and stern disciplinarian. Competence and Stalin's friendship saw his career prosper, though his star faded somewhat with the failure of a counter-offensive in May 1942.

It was rather like a Russian scene afterwards. We had legions of men out on the ropes, hauling, and we were all smothered in snow."

168 Battery's guns were pulled back, raising GL hopes that they would return to their unit at the same time. It was not to be.

"Jack Tullett and I have been having the time of our lives 'vivisecting' the instruments here – owing to the sudden departure of the 168 boys, leaving us here in sole charge until Saturday – for maintenance only! We also have a very affable radio officer here, which helps a lot."

Eric's relationship with the technical instructor went from bad to worse.

"I have my own private 'pain in the neck', it happens to be the T.I. He's a most objectionable bird at times but I'm getting him under control!

The maintenance here is a full time job but he seems to think I can be available at any time to take the blokes on practical instruction. Infernal cheek! He has taken a hut as a lecture room, gets the blokes to light a fire, blathers to them on theory, and then expects to retire to the mess while I try to teach them some practical work between laying cables and generally probing the innards of the accursed thing. Luckily the Radio Officer is a perfect brick and joins me enthusiastically in putting him in his place. To say nothing of two sergeants at left troop!"

"... Had a first class row with this swine of a T.I. this morning and am proceeding to bang in a 'first class' complaint to left troop HQ. Hoping it results in a 'first class' kick in the pants for him. Won't weary you with the details. Complaints are also on their way from the trainees and from the Ordnance Staff Sergeant. He seems an out and out swine. My God, the fellows in this army who get stripes!

Sometimes I think that the only way to 'get on' and live a tolerable life is to adopt a fighting attitude to everything and everybody; be bombastic, make a lot of noise, stir up plenty of s– (army term!) and generally make yourself a much-noticed nuisance. The trouble is I just haven't got it in me, I loathe the noise and fuss, and I suppose I go out of my way to avoid it. A row leaves me depressed and miserable when I suppose it should make me bloody angry.

Before this gentleman arrived I had got these boys pretty enthusiastic about GL and had managed to teach them the simple drills and give them a simple idea of the works. Now they are all thoroughly browned off and two have applied to come off the course. And nobody in authority cares a damn. The officers won't listen to them. The bloke just gets away with it, and knows he can, what's more. Complaints about a senior N.C.O. from a gunner are viewed as insubordination in this democratic institution. The whole thing makes me ill."

"… I feel very browned off at the moment after a week's battling with all the elements possible, with a trainee crew and a lazy T.I. Just a stooge I am! Get called out whatever happens and it's been happening plenty just lately. There is a gale roaring over the camp at the moment. I've just struggled back from repairing a broken upright on the Diesel. To hell with it all – what I want is my leave. And I don't want to come back. God blasted stuff one has to mess around with on this job. I feel more like a navvy than a radio bloke."

The weather at least provided an excuse for a snowball fight.

"The boys had the time of their lives in the gunpits yesterday. The gunners fought the Command Post in a large scale snowballing match. It was very amusing, the GPO was at his post with a megaphone shouting out firing orders as though it was a shoot. The Rad. and I provided additional entertainment by falling up to our armpits in a drift while fixing a cable."

The war paid the occasional visit with a futile 'take post' every couple of days – but too seldom to make sense of what they were doing.

"I missed one bit of excitement. A submarine was reported to have penetrated the Clyde boom last week, also was subsequently sunk (also according to report). Guards here were doubled on instructions from the Admiralty so there must be something in the story."

There is no record of a submarine in the Clyde that month so it could have been a false alarm. Otherwise gun site life was an endurance test punctuated by building, maintenance and training with the odd inconclusive alert. Anything out of the ordinary was a relief.

"We had a little excitement the other night. I was on duty in the instruments and heard a shot fired about 10pm. Reported it and then went to sleep. Was awakened by a second shot, which turned out an officer and the guard. They organised a search party, found no signs of anybody except an American parked in a car (with a girl friend of course!) And as he had no identification card and no driving licence they took him to the camp for questioning! Needless to say he was extremely indignant and the girl said she never had thought much of the Artillery! It didn't clear up the mystery of the shot as he hadn't a gun on him. And it certainly didn't disturb my slumbers."

The 'Arcadia Conference' in Washington ended on 14th January 1942. It was a joint strategy meeting between Britain, the US and other combatant governments. It reinforced the 'Germany first' principle set out the previous year and helped by Hitler's lunatic declaration of war on the US in December; set military objectives for the following year; and created a number of joint command structures. It also produced the 'Declaration by United Nations,' a statement of war aims which contains the seeds of the modern UN.

Developments on the ground were less encouraging. There seemed to be little anyone could do about Japanese advances in the Philippines, Malaya, Borneo, Burma and the Netherlands East Indies. Malta came under heavy air attack and U-Boats found easy pickings in the weakly-defended shipping lanes along the US east coast.

More cheerfully, the Red Army's counter-offensive under General Zhukov took Kirov and Medya, while British forces reached El Agheila in Libya for the second time. That was as far as they got before Rommel's riposte on 21st pushed them all the way back to El Alamein.

> *"The blokes in the hut are discussing the latest withdrawal to Singapore Island, and are taking a very poor view of it. Likewise Rommel's romp into Benghazi – that phantom host which we destroyed in the first battle, according to Cairo."*

Jennie, too, found the contrast between talk and achievement dispiriting.

> *"The Japs seem to be pressing on with their offensive very steadily. The BBC as usual is radiating plenty of complacency and minimising the value of Japan's conquest. Seems to me, as soon as we begin to do a bit of advancing on one place, we have to make another 'magnificent withdrawal' somewhere else. Well thank God for the Russians and their leaders.*
>
> *I wish they would get on with winning the war instead of talking about punishing people after it's won."*

Vile weather and a steady drip of loss did nothing to improve their mood. Sad observations like this were repeated thousands of times across the country.

"It's very tragic about poor Bill – what an awful end to a healthy life. I suppose the interval in the water and exposure did all that."

Roosevelt's State of the Nation speech on 6th January committed the US to arming the United Nations – and when possible the occupied countries – with overwhelming superiority in *materiel*. He set production targets for 1942 of 60,000 aircraft (45,000 of them combat), 45,000 tanks, 20,000 anti-aircraft guns and six million tons of shipping; with further increases planned for 1943.

"America's plane and tank output for '42 sounds pretty colossal doesn't it? 60,000 planes ought to make some impression on Berlin... And the Russians are still advancing, bless 'em! I see Molotov has issued a lengthy atrocity list. I certainly should not care to be a German soldier on the Eastern front. No wonder the Russians aren't taking prisoners."

"... There seems to have been a lot of American officers around here lately looking at our AA Defences."

A Russian delegation toured Britain at the invitation of the TUC Anglo-Soviet Trade Union Committee. While in London they met the Prime Minister and made a BBC radio broadcast. Jennie observed, *"The Russian Trade Union delegates seem to be getting a great welcome don't they. I'll bet 'Red' Clydeside was glad to see them."*

Richard Heydrich called the 'Wannsee Conference,' a brief meeting in the suburbs of Berlin, on 20th January to initiate the 'final solution' – extermination – to the 'Jewish problem'. The focus of the meeting was administrative: 'how,' not 'whether' or 'why.'

Cosmo Lang, Archbishop of Canterbury, announced his retirement on 21st January. His term in office brought limited approval of contraception, condemnation of Nazi anti-Semitism, opposition to the death penalty and tireless work for unity and rapprochement between churches. However, he pressurised Edward VIII to abdicate and made an ungenerous broadcast when the decision was announced. He also supported the government's pre-war appeasement policy. Both issues placed him in the opposite camp to the *Mirror* and *Sunday Pictorial*. Jennie was scathing.

> *"I notice in a brief survey of his activities they carefully omitted to mention that he was chiefly instrumental in getting Edward VIII hounded out. The narrow minded old bigot. Said he took up Holy Orders on account of his interest in the poor of East London. Fat lot of good he's ever done for them."*

Constant privation and bleak war news brought public morale – and Churchill's reputation – to a low ebb. In a February reshuffle Clement Attlee became Secretary of State for Dominion Affairs and Deputy Prime Minister. Kingsley Wood left the War Cabinet but remained Chancellor of the Exchequer. Arthur Greenwood, Minister without Portfolio, left the Cabinet. Lord Beaverbrook became Minister of War Production (from Minister of Supply) for two weeks before resigning. Oliver Lyttleton became Minister-Resident for the Middle East.

Sir Stafford Cripps had just returned from a stint as ambassador to Moscow. He made a wildly popular speech in which he described the war as a struggle between freedom and tyranny, and appealed to workers in occupied countries to sabotage production in any way possible.[xxi] He was appointed Lord Privy Seal and Leader of the House of Commons.

> *"Cripps' speech seems to have made a good impression – his hint about India was very welcome."*

In March he went to try and secure India's commitment to the war effort in exchange for the promise of self-government after the war.

His proposals were neither radical enough for India nor conservative enough for the Cabinet and the mission failed. Gandhi's reaction was *"If the Congress President asks my advice I will say that the British proposal form* [sic] *a post-dated cheque. Accept them or not."*[xxii] Eric had astutely observed a couple of months earlier.

"Not a very dignified spectacle, is it? Trying to strike a bargain with India with the Japs almost knocking at the door."

The two of them were otherwise encouraged by the shake-up.

"What do you think of the Government changes? The new additions seem to be very much welcomed. I still think there are a few that could do with clearing out."

"... Still with further government changes and Dr. Temple as Archbishop of Canterbury I begin to have a few hopes of this country after all."

"... Quite a good debate this week, wasn't it? Let's hope the new Cabinet will get on and get something started. I think everybody is 'fed up' with hanging about, with nothing happening."

At windswept Kilcreggan the troop found humour where they could.

"There was a most amusing 'ten minute prayer session' – the parson's Scripture reading coincided with a bloke's attempts to get a telephone call through in the phone box installed in the room. The resultant blend had the room in fits – it might almost have been a stage turn, it worked out so perfectly. 'Joseph said unto her – I want a trunk call, Miss!' 'They came nigh to Jerusalem – it's near Warwick!' Even the poor parson saw the joke."

The German battle-cruisers *Scharnhorst* and *Gneisenau* and the heavy cruiser *Prinz Eugen* were trying to repair weather and battle damage under constant air attack at Brest. Hitler ordered the ships home by the shortest route – straight up the Channel – with heavy escort between 11th and 13th February. In one of Britain's greatest humiliations of the war they completed the Channel dash unscathed, though *Scharnhorst* and *Gneisenau* later hit mines. The three ships achieved little for the rest of the war.

Singapore fell on 15th February; General McArthur was ordered to evacuate the Philippines on 22nd. The Japanese heavily defeated Allied forces at the Battle of Java Sea on 27th then overran the Dutch East Indies. Early in March they completed their conquest of Java, Burma and New Guinea. They now threatened Australia, making the point with a surprise air raid on Broome. Jennie wrote:

> *"We still seem to be doing very badly in the East. Let's hope we manage to do something a little more in keeping with the traditions of this country soon."*

An RAF raid on Essen was notable for the first operational use of the Lancaster – one of the new four-engine bombers which would change the balance of the air war.

On 5th March 1942 the *Daily Mirror* published a Philip Zec cartoon of a merchant seaman clinging to a life raft. Its caption: 'The price of petrol has been increased by one penny. Official' was a reminder that fuel came at a high cost in lives. Churchill, Herbert Morrison (Home Secretary) and Ernest Bevin (Minister of Labour) furiously misread it as telling merchant seamen their lives were being sacrificed for petrol companies' profits. There was talk of closing the *Mirror*.

Jennie was outraged.

> *"Have heard tonight that they propose to ban the Daily Mirror unless it comes to heel. Nice people. I'm waiting to see the reaction of*

Figure 8: 'The price of petrol has been increased by one penny. Official'
(Trinity Mirror)

the Press to this latest move of our friend Mr. Morrison – quite a nice
bloke he's turned out to be."

As was Eric – this crossed in the post.

"What do you think of the proposal to ban the Daily Mirror?
The blokes here take a very poor view of it. I am sure the Government
would love to stamp it out of existence. Over our dead bodies!"

Depriving the armed forces of 'Jane' (a comic strip about a beautiful,
intelligent woman who invariably lost most of her clothes in the
course of a story) would have been the last straw.

The columnist William Connor ('Cassandra') who was jointly responsible for the cartoon left in disgust, writing *"The government are far too glib with the shameful rejoinder that those who do not agree with them are subversive – and even traitors."* He joined the army, where he worked with Hugh Cudlipp on the forces' paper *Union Jack*.

"I suppose you have also heard that Bill Connor (Cassandra) has resigned from the Mirror. I consider it a great blow to journalism and the most severe blow to the Services. He certainly put their point of view better than anybody. I look forward to his reappearance after the war. Good old Cass! I like a bloke who chucks a salary because he won't be censored. I dislike witnessing the obliteration of a sincere writer who could be one of our leading propagandists, shortly to be subjected to Army discipline and gagged like the rest of them. I dislike most of all to see people get away with it, including the administrators of this noble army."

The *Daily Express* on 18th March named two men convicted of lying to obtain extra petrol coupons, and predicted coal, gas and electricity rationing – retrospective to the start of the year after the coldest January and February for 45 years.

An attack on St Nazaire, five miles up the Loire estuary, avenged the humiliation of the Channel dash. A destroyer laden with explosives rammed the gates of the only battleship-sized dry dock on the Atlantic coast while commandos demolished port installations. This 'Greatest Raid of All' was an outstanding success – the dock was out of action for the rest of the war and without it the *Kriegsmarine* dared not use *Tirpitz* in the Atlantic. 169 of the 622 men taking part were killed and 215 taken prisoner when most of the un-armoured motor launches supposed to bring them home were sunk. Five VCs and 84 lesser decorations were awarded for the action.

In mid-March the Scottish weather finally improved. It drew out senior officers from Brigade to visit the battery on 2nd, 14th and 26th. Perhaps coincidentally there was a new impetus to training.

> *"Life seems to be bucking up no end here, it must be the spring. Parties are being send down to the local rifle range to polish up their marksmanship (those for instance, who have never yet fired a shot in this war, like the old Territorials!) And we have started a special session of P.T. including daily basket-ball. It's grand but it has made me as stiff as a rake!"*

Trade examination – at last – gave Eric formal recognition of his skills.

> *"I am really 'aving a go' at my wireless theory, determined not to be put off however bloodily the situation develops. The big wigs from Brigade sang more songs to us of great opportunities etc, big developments and so on and so on. It's getting to be rather like that 'Wolf' legend."*
>
> *"... Only news here is that we are all being Trade Tested on Thursday [12th March] – undergoing a severe inquisition so that a grudging army council can make sure that it is not throwing an extra 1/3 a week away on an unskilled man – after being bullied into making some sort of a cash grant. Such breathtaking generosity makes one all the keener, of course, to pass the wretched test. I have been entitled to draw Trade pay for over a year now. Niggardly swine!"*

Even social life began to wake up – as did Eric's journalistic instinct.

> *"I was voted on to the Entertainment Committee on Friday and undertook one or two jobs that specially interest me – a library, weekly debate or 'Brains Trust' and a chess club. I went over to Greenock*

yesterday and was promised 120 books from the Public Library, also 200 books for £2.10.0. from Boots. Not a bad start.

I am also starting a 'News of the Week' board which will present items of special interest to the men, clippings from our press and from the Soviet War News (good opportunity) also, I hope, a few contributions from the men themselves. It will take the place of a weekly magazine.

The Mayor is coming down next week and I think I am booked for an interview with him. So that may get me somewhere. I am keeping up my policy of frequent agitations!!"

Eric co-opted four gunners to help set up the battery library, and the Brains Trust launched in hilarious chaos.

"Then impromptu questions were asked for and Emma ambled to the front in his usual dreamy manner and mumbled something about 'could anyone tell him what lay beyond the universe' to which Len retorted 'you ought to know – you seem to be there more often than not!' – the sergeant superseding the professor! The meeting broke up arguing violently about the wheels of railway coaches! I really think this sort of thing should be broadcast – it's funnier than anything on the wireless."

He and Len responded enthusiastically – but without much hope – to an advert for Ordnance Radio Officers. He had to scratch around for his birth certificate and two testaments to his good character: something the army couldn't be expected to know after only a year and a half. At first the prospects looked hopeful.

"The officers here seem to take our going to OCTU [Officer Cadet Training Unit] for granted, so I can only surmise that both Len and myself have been given good recommendations by Regt. And

I understand that I'm due for promotion when Jimmy[24] has passed and is 'off the strength' of the Battery. So that even if this falls through I shall have the opportunity of applying for a T.I.'s course or ordinary commission."

Things seemed to be moving.

"I haven't any more news of the application I am making. We have (Len and I) to be interviewed by a selection board when the applications have been considered – in London! But that may not come off yet awhile.

In any case I have the T.I.'s course as a 2nd string, and am assured I shall click for one or the other. I hope so."

Then came disappointment.

"Another thing that hasn't added to my cheerfulness is the Radio Officer's announcement – in response to another very earnest enquiry – that he thinks that T.I.'s courses are being discontinued! Wham!"

And again.

"I had an interview with the Major yesterday. My RAOC [Royal Army Ordnance Corps] application has fallen through, lack of suitable qualifications the reason. However, he hinted that promotion was due for me shortly, when he would recommend me for an RA commission. Of course, you have to hold 'stripes' before you can apply, but he is starting me off on gun drill and instrument drill right away. He's a hell of a nice bloke, quite young and very efficient."

---

[24] Jimmy Coyle had just left the section for OCTU.

Eccentric but surprisingly effective, Operation *Outward* began on 20th March: unmanned balloons were launched from Felixstowe to blow over Germany on the prevailing winds. They were armed either with a trailing wire to short-circuit power lines or with incendiaries to start forest fires, and worked often enough for the *Luftwaffe* to put a lot of effort into shooting them down. The launch crews were WRNS (Women's Royal Naval Service, or 'Wrens'). Unlike their army oppos, they were given machine guns for self-defence and trained to use them.

On the night of 28th March the RAF attacked the city of Lübeck in its first experiment with 'area bombing' techniques. The raid on a city which Arthur "Bomber" Harris describes as "built more like a fire-lighter than a human habitation" destroyed or seriously damaged a fifth of its buildings and killed 300 people. Hitler was furious and demanded retribution.

Over two years before D-Day, the battery began to see what lay in store.

"You remember the Battery invasion exercises in the lochs last year? Well they made a film of the whole proceeding – to be shown only to the units concerned, I think. It was good, demonstrated the landing of a complete force, paratroops, shock troops, engineers, artillery etc. By the way we are the invasion Regt – last medical was to relegate all under A3 to mixed batteries. However, to proceed. The sound track broke down and the boys supplied their own commentary. When the battleships appeared – 'Hi, this must have been taken when we still had some!' Great roar of laughter heralded the appearance of our own crowd with the mobile ack ack. It is really amazing how this sort of thing gets such a humorous reception – especially from men who might be doing it all at a very early date."

Jennie observed: *"I see Bevin says we shall be starting something soon – so I suppose things will get a little more exciting."*

– then, as his words sank in, *"And what exactly do you mean by writing 'We are the invasion regiment'?"*

Training tempo stepped up another notch in mid-April.

> *"Our team has been split up and half the men sent to Right Troop to man the instrument there. Result is we have had scarcely any leave, this also coincided with a lot of aircraft co-op. We have also started hard training in real earnest. We had a 3 hour PT session yesterday which beat anything previously experienced, including boxing, unarmed combat, a sort of all-in Rugby and pretty strenuous road work and PT. Everyone's in it, officers, cooks, GL(!) etc. Four instructors from the army school of PT administered it and we had no difficulty in believing them when they told us it was Commando training!"*

As ever, it was a mystery what they were training for. The return to France was still some way off but, unknown to the troops, there would be combined operations in North Africa, Sicily and Italy first. Eric at least knew they were training for something definite and worthwhile – Jennie didn't have that compensation for the uncertainty.

> *"We are still proceeding with our PT. We had a two mile run yesterday and are promised more intensive work this week. There is a rumour that we move out in about five weeks for more mobile training, the ATS* [Auxiliary Territorial Service] *to take over the site."*

At the end of April the battery's other troop disappeared to Combined Operations Training Centre Toward (a second school to supplement Inveraray) for five days' systematic torture.

> *"The toughening process is continuing and still varies in manner.*

Right Troop were whisked away by boat and had to land gear on a hitherto unlandable beach."

Eric was broadening his skills with an eye on that elusive promotion.

"Len has to take a three days motor cycling course, which has left me here as No. 1 and which, of course, has come at the most awkward time. The major had to interview me on my 24 hours leave last week, which cut down my visiting time, and we are so damned short handed that time off is nearly impossible at any other period – typical of the army...

I 'start' on the guns next week, and will receive regular training in the art and practice of gunnery from now on. It will certainly be a nice change from the present routine. I am also booked for a session on my old friend the predictor.

We also seemed to be 'booked' for a lively training programme as regards our 'toughening' training. The cookhouse will proceed to go out of action occasionally and we must cook our own grub as best we can! I can foresee some cases of stomach trouble."

Eric was invigorated by activity and a revived sense of purpose, and impressed by Major Andrews the new battery commander.

"Been going 'great guns' on the gun drill. Quite a pleasure getting off the instruments on to the guns for a change.

I don't think you need worry about lack of a 'second front' – that deficiency seems about to be remedied in the near future. I dislike writing too much about military matters on principle, but it's been dawning on us recently that this army of ours ain't shaping up half so bad. I never thought I should ever be particularly proud of the army, but we are certainly experiencing many changes and gaining a refreshingly new outlook.

Am particularly interested in our major. He's quite young, and was a sergeant at Dunkirk. Must have had pretty rapid promotion since. He's doing a lot of much needed cleaning up, and certainly knows his stuff."

"… We are still working pretty hard and I'm doing my mobile training. It's surprising how gun drill requires different 'technique' from instruments. It's very lively and interesting."

Not everyone was as enthusiastic.

"Met Johnnie Teagle and Vic Boyes yesterday, and had some amusing conversations. Vic was openly scornful of the recent manoeuvres, and was expressing his opinion too loudly for Johnnie's comfort."

In the Pacific Lt Col Doolittle led 16 Mitchell bombers, taking off from *USS Hornet* on 18th April, to attack Tokyo. The aircraft carried on to land in China (or in one case Russia) as returning to the carrier was impossible. The raid had little physical impact but gave American morale a big boost and demonstrated that the Japanese home islands were not invulnerable. Most of the crews survived but the Japanese troops looking for them killed an estimated 250,000 Chinese civilians.

The RAF bombed Rostock on 23rd, 24th, 26th and 27th April. While the official target was the aircraft works there, the attacks were effectively an extension of the area bombing techniques tried out at Lübeck. Hitler ordered retaliatory 'Baedecker' (tourist guide) raids on targets of more cultural than military value. They started at Exeter on 23rd and 24th; Bath, Norwich and York followed in quick succession. One of the Bath attackers found himself over heavily-defended Bristol by mistake. He dropped his bombs and retreated rapidly.

"Did you hear anything from your people about a raid on Bristol

at the same time as Bath? Reg Honeywell was on leave and lives near Brislington – I think it's St Anne's. He says they had it pretty hot; it was sandwiched between two raids on Bath.

We seem to be giving Germany a good dose of bombing these days. That Rostock raid must have been terrific. The RAF is certainly showing 'em something."

On 30th May the RAF's first 1,000-bomber raid hit Cologne in a concentrated 90-minute strike.

It is sad to reflect that both sides were drawn into targeting civilians when the experience of the Blitz could have – should have – shown that it would not have the intended effect on their morale.

Early in May Eric and Jennie spent a blissful seven days' leave together, first sightseeing from Dumbarton then at home west of London. While he was away the regiment was busy shuffling guns around and acquiring transport to bring itself to a full mobile scale. On his return Eric found himself at yet another site near Kilmacolm.

"We are here for intensive training and may shift south at any time. This last period is supposed to be the last 'polishing' and training will commence each morning at 5 a.m. starting Monday. So we are expecting the worst...

We joined the Battery section when they disembarked at Gourock, and were conveyed by lorry to our present abode. The Battery is liable to move at any moment, and all leave has been stopped indefinitely, even 24s. Men already on leave have been recalled. Jones (the Bombardier) has been notified, presumably. Vic Brushett and myself are acting NCOs as 'Smut' is under arrest! – for lying in bed until 9 o'clock one morning. Bright lad! It looks as though he is going to get it rather heavy.

We have a grand complement of brand new lorries, about 25 for this section alone. There is no lack of drivers, as a considerable number were drafted in recently,"

"… We are definitely due to come south, darling! Our ultimate destination appears to be a training camp somewhere near Southampton… The training will be an intensive mobile and combat course, including mobile GL.

We are rather unfortunate in having a set on the site here, so we operate as well as take part in exercises. The gunners are 'non-operational' and go out in the evenings!"

"… Our destination seems to be Shoreham, near Brighton… We are going fully mobile for a period of intensive training.

Len is starting out with the advanced convoy. We shall follow in about 3 or 4 days time. We were up at 5.30 this morning dismantling the sets – in rain! Brrr!"

"… Len and myself are the only GL men left on the site. The rest have departed to Right Troop, to take over the set there."

From the end of March 1942 small numbers of fighter-bombers carried out steadily increasing attacks on southern coastal towns: so-called 'Fringe Targets.' They approached over the sea, very fast and low, dropped their bombs and disappeared. In May there were 23 widely-scattered raids on militarily insignificant targets which usually had no AA defences at all. That had to be fixed.

After Japan's entry into the war the few available reserves had gone to British garrisons in the Far East or to help the Americans. General Pile also had to find 120 heavy guns to cover assembly areas for Operation *Torch*, the Anglo-American landings planned for late autumn in Vichy North Africa. The only way to defend fringe targets was to reduce cover in the north, which seemed less threatened for the time being.

"A great trek down South seems to be in progress. We are only one of

many involved… Then there is the prospect of action in that part of the country, very welcome after such a long interval."

Personal kit was limited to 56 pounds (25 kilos) per person so Eric had to abandon his library and send his accumulated comforts back home. They shipped out on 1st June.

The previous night 25,000 people had gathered on Glasgow Green to hear speakers of all parties call for a Second Front in 1942.

GROWING CONFIDENCE

Beside the Seaside

The radar section arrived at Hove in early June 1942, a few days before the guns. The weather was fine, they were a lot closer to home, the site had a sea view, and there was a chance of action.

"*Well we are on the sunny south coast, on a site with a lovely view of the sea. Have been too busy erecting our instruments to do more than just glance at it occasionally…*

We are billeted in empty houses, hence the address. Cold running water and the usual amenities, my dear. Oh, no beds, but of course that's a minor detail by this time. I'm acquiring a torso like gun-metal… The 'war' atmosphere is very invigorating, we have had four alerts and the sight of one hostile (while we were busy on erection!) And it's nice to be sitting on a set with command of the Channel.

I felt so grubby this morning that I was glad to draw off a bath of 'cold' and jump into it. We hope to get the boiler going today."

However the beach was still littered with invasion defences so they couldn't take advantage of the sea, and eight months of Glasgow's brisk ways left them ill-prepared for southern reserve.

> *"We have had a boring interval at the camp waiting for the guns to be placed in position before commencing gunsite routine and full manning. The atmosphere is not too congenial – everybody feels cooped up in the place and I loathe this Brighton district – especially after the friendly and informal ways of the Scots. Brighton is certainly in a class on its own – thank God. Its only saving grace – the sea – is quite inaccessible."*

Jennie didn't quite pick up on that point.

> *"It must be jolly nice to have a bath on the premises and the sea within handy reach in this weather. Have you been for any swimming yet?"*

On 4th June Reinhard Heydrich, an architect of the Holocaust, died from injuries received in a Special Operations Executive (SOE) ambush in Czechoslovakia. At least 1,300 people were killed and 13,000 arrested, deported or imprisoned in the brutal reprisals that followed. The villages of Lidice and Ležáky were obliterated.

Twenty people were killed and 59 injured when an undetected German bomb went off at the Elephant and Castle on 6th June. Tube train vibration from the nearby station probably set off the bomb, which must have fallen over a year earlier.

> *"That explosion at the Elephant seems to be a peculiar affair – wonder what was behind that?"*

The loss of four Japanese aircraft carriers for one American at the Battle of Midway between 4th and 7th June decisively tilted the balance of naval power in the Pacific.

From time to time the *Luftwaffe* gave the battery (now fully operational) some night amusement; but friendly fighters too often cramped the gunners' style.

"We were turned out of bed at two in the morning (today) on account of planes crossing the coast – sirens and all! Quite like old times. It's very perplexing trying to find one's way in the dark on a new site. I just couldn't be bothered about paths and charged through a field of cabbages! Then found nearly everybody had done the same.

We were very successful in locating and 'holding' three hostiles for some time – but no guns fired as the fighters were up. Then some local enthusiasts fired a Bofors at a friendly plane, after which we went back to bed."

Which perhaps inspired this:

"REALISTS

They spring to their posts at the peal of the bell
The telephones ring and the officers yell:
And Plotter, Predictor and Radar combine
To calculate angle and tangent and sine –
Though which plane to tackle it's hard to decide
For a 'doubtful' in searchlight is promptly espied
Whilst a gunner is busily chalking the runs
On an oversized board, of more probable Huns.

but

Down by the guns there is infinite calm
For it always is thus with an Ack-Ack alarm
Down by the ammo the minutes will drag –
So down by the guns they are playing at Brag!

Now Radar's on target, all set to engage
And Number Four scans the appropriate page
Of the data Book, shouting the fuze and what-not
And someone says READ and another bawls PLOT

Predictor's O.K. and the pointers are steady –
And never an instrument there but is ready
To play its devoted, meticulous part,
And all that they lack is PERMISSION TO START.

but

> *Down on the guns there is never a flap –*
> *There's a mug at each elbow, a book in each lap:*
> *As to what's in the wind they won't stoop to enquire –*
> *For they know bloody-well that the guns never fire!"*

Eric managed a weekend trip home, returning to find the regiment on the move again. At 5:30 AM, in the middle of packing, a *"Messerschmitt came over low level and bombed Shoreham. No sites had opportunity to engage."*[xxiii] The incident was treated rather more colourfully on the ground.

> *"There has been an awful row over a plane that suddenly appeared over Shoreham and dropped a bomb without being identified. It was the day we left. The Major has been reduced to Captain's rank and the officer on duty placed under arrest for negligence."*

The battery left their very temporary home from Hove for Eastleigh near Southampton.

> *"We have moved from the operational gunsite and are now billeted in a girl's school (minus girls) until the morning, when we move to the training camp."*

The camp was at Hiltingbury, Chandlers Ford. It was a training establishment at the time, a concentration area for the Normandy landings a couple of years later, and a Polish resettlement camp after the war. It was big, housing some 10,000 troops and their vehicles in the run up to D-Day. Today it is a housing estate.

> *"Well here we are at last, a very weary company just parked at the training camp. It seems quite a good place, reminiscent of North Bot* [Northumberland Bottom], *the quarters are very good. We are in a large hut with about twenty of the old gang, so we feel quite at home.*
>
> *Eastleigh seems to be a short distance from Southampton and near to Twyford and the 'battle training area'."*

They were in for a gruelling mix of operational manning, battle exercises, mobility training in the surrounding country – then back to camp for parades and inspections.

> *"Although the training is very hard and exacting it is invigorating after such a static existence – and I think we would have been happier if we had tackled this sort of thing earlier. Bringing the GL station into action and dismantling same we can now accomplish in about 12 minutes each way, and so far nobody has collapsed in the process. To think we used to consider two hours very good time! The secret is in working by numbers – at the double – and in perfect unison."*

This was a Damascene conversion: just four months earlier he wrote; *"I have never seen anything so damn silly as the drill book that someone has been ingenious enough to invent for the benefit of the GL. A lot of damn rigmarole about erecting the instrument by numbers which we have to learn by heart. Wonder who draws a salary for concocting this sort of rubbish – such as numbers 2 and 3 unhooking the power unit from the lorry, no.3 orders 'Drive on' and the lorry moves forward ten yards and halts!! (it generally gets bogged anyway). There's a hefty book crammed full of this 'bull'."* In 1942 the description must refer to Mk 2 gun laying (GL) radar with its separate transmitter and receiver cabins, large antennas to go on the roof of each, and separate generator trailers. Twelve minutes was quite an achievement.

"Then there is convoy training of which we had a lengthy experience yesterday. We had a specimen battery move and it really was immensely exciting and certainly very funny at times. Orders were issued from Regt giving details of an enemy landing in Dorset, and our job was to proceed to a rendezvous to give air protection to the reinforcements. Maps were issued giving reference squares of the route and the rendezvous in the New Forest. We then essayed to get underway and the fun began!

A 'Pathfinder' lorry goes first, dropping off men at 'awkward' turnings etc to direct the convoy. The first man was dropped at the exit, and blowed if he didn't direct the first gun towing vehicle the wrong way! First mess up in fifty yards!

Then the 'Pathfinders' were told to watch for a blue flag on the last lorry, which would pick them up on being hailed – their own lorry (the first) showing a green one. Half way along the road it was discovered that the flags should be the other way round, so they were reversed! – with the result that the 'Pathfinders' ignored the green flag on the last lorry and were left behind – all dead men, as the instructor informed the officers afterwards.

Anyway, we reached the spot assigned to us, and after some camouflaging of guns and vehicles and lessons in personal concealment (the officers by this time looked anxious to dive down rabbit holes) we had a lecture which was followed by supper – very nice too. At 11.30 pm we had orders to move – our forces were retreating (loud, long sardonic laughter) the enemy had cut the road to the south so we had to go back by a different route. At this point the GL guardian spirit put in a timely intervention. We were ordered to change lorries, moving to one lower in the convoy.

We moved off again, had a lovely two hours run through lovely scenery, being hailed at every turn by mistrustful Pathfinders not relishing the prospect of a night in the New Forest. Then just as we were 'dropping off' the convoy halted amid a lot of shouting and we baled out to discover the former GL lorry on its side blocking the road. It had wavered at a farm road turning, run up a steep bank, snapped off a telegraph pole and overturned! Nobody was hurt, the lorry was empty save for the driver and the officer in charge, and they weren't scratched.

By the time we had winched it up and reached camp it was five o'clock, and so help us, we were on parade at 8.15! Hardly worth while disturbing the kit layout! And we are off again tonight! What a life!"

Southampton suffered its last big air raid on the night of 21st June. About 50 aircraft attacked the city, killing 14 people. Two planes were lost.

"We had rather a hectic night. There was a raid on Southampton and Eastleigh and of course we all had to arise and stand by. I was compelled to do this, otherwise I don't think it would have even awakened me."

His aunt in Arundel wrote *"I suppose you didn't happen to get any of those 'blighters' down on Sunday night, eh?"* Unfortunately not.

Training, drill – and accidents – continued unabated.

"I have been appointed No.1 in charge of a lorry and half a troop detachment, which should make life fairly interesting. We stayed in camp today – the drivers having a rest. About time too! Three more accidents have occurred, and they've come to the conclusion that drivers need a little rest occasionally. Some of them must have been driving with their eyes shut. One of them piled into another telegraph pole

yesterday when doing only about fifteen miles an hour. What with the air raids and the ack ack the local services must be in a hell of a state!"

"… We have been proceeding almost non-stop on these 'flips' getting some awful 'telling offs' despite all our efforts. Must admit that most of us are feeling rather flat by this time. So far the physical aspects haven't affected me much but I get periods when I suffer from a surprising lack of enthusiasm, and wish for nothing more than to fly straight home and to hell with everything else."

The Battle of Gazala, a four-week bloodbath, ended with the fall of Tobruk on 21st June. British armoured forces were outgunned, outwitted and decimated. Despite brave delaying actions at Mersa Matruh and Fukah, it took 13,000 casualties at the First Battle of El Alamein to blunt Rommel's advance.

"The war news is still very depressing. There is a perceptible effect on the spirits of the men when we strike a patch like this – more that I should have thought possible. Petty jobs become absolutely unendurable. Noticeably Blanco-ing![25] *We have been ordered to do this for the second time within ten days. Jimmy Coyle writes and says that at the OCTU tables are scraped with razor blades until they are white! Oh my God!"*

Tobruk should have solved Rommel's supply problems but the Bletchley cryptanalysts routinely read his radio traffic, allowing the Royal Navy and RAF to wreak havoc with Axis supply convoys. The

---

[25] Blanco was a cleaning and colouring compound used by the Army since about 1880. Keeping webbing up to scratch was a tedious and time-consuming job as old Blanco had to be scraped off before applying the new coat.

violent stalemate was eventually broken by the Second Battle of El Alamein in October.

On 23rd June Oberleutnant Arnim Faber returned from patrol in his Focke-Wulf FW 190, did a victory roll, and landed – at RAF Pembrey. He had mistaken South Wales for France and so presented the RAF with a gift of the best fighter in the world at the time. A thorough evaluation didn't make the FW 190 any less scary but produced advice for Allied airmen to go like the clappers if there was any chance of meeting one.

Bomber Command staged their third thousand-bomber raid, on Bremen, during the night of 25th June. The Focke-Wulf factory there was seriously damaged but the RAF had to mobilise every available aircraft, including training units who suffered losses of over eleven percent.

On 27th the ill-fated convoy PQ17 left Iceland for Arkhangelsk. It was spotted almost immediately and came under attack from 2nd July. Disastrously, the convoy was ordered to scatter on fears that the *Tirpitz* was out. Single, unescorted merchantmen were easy meat for the *Luftwaffe* and U-Boats; only 11 arrived of the 35 who had set out. After this experience and the previous PQ16 (which had lost eleven of its thirty-five ships) the Royal Navy suspended Russian convoys for the rest of the Arctic summer.

At Eastleigh the training lurched between farcical and fearsome.

"Right Troop (Tekel, Vic Bryan and co) are an amazing bunch. The greatest excitement yesterday was caused by the discovery of a glow worm… It was carried over to the gun team which paused to examine same in the middle of going out of action. Another thing which always tickles me is the enthusiasm with which the blokes go and hide themselves when ordered to do so as a routine – they do it so thoroughly that they are never on hand when the next job is to be done. But in between these spells they put in some remarkably good

work. One team put their gun into 'action' in five minutes fifty seconds, which is the record so far."[26]

Camp routine was irksome for people who in the first place had trouble thinking of themselves as soldiers, and in the second were working up for active service.

> *"We are fully prepared for hard training here, but what is increasingly maddening is the red tape and spit and polish nonsense around the camp. It makes everybody so thoroughly depressed and apathetic that no interest is taken in the ensuing training...*
>
> *We now have to stand to attention at all bugle calls, which practice I honestly believed had perished with the Boer War. And after hard exercising we were turned out of bed at four o'clock this morning to wash the dust off the lorries because some nincompoop of an official was inspecting them. Actually the slightest breeze would cover them again, the dust here blows about like a sandstorm."*

The course climaxed in two days of independent and two of combined battery exercises, three days at regimental level and two of the whole brigade.

It was a rough inauguration for Captain Reeve. He had joined 206 Battery as a second Lieutenant at the beginning of 1941 and was pitched into temporary command for the exercise. He was promoted to Major later in 1942 and stayed with the battery for the rest of the war.

> *"This morning's attempt comes to you from under the greenwood tree – and a particularly wet one. We are on a four day exercise, and*

---

[26] In contrast, the 25-pounder field gun could be set up in under a minute.

judging by the way we feel this morning, we are wondering if we can go the distance.

Of course it would set in damned rainy for the show. I suppose it adds to our stock of experience, but anything more hellish than a night in the forest with an amateur mobile battery I have yet to imagine.

Of course the inevitable mess-up occurred. The two sections were to combine at a rendezvous to put the last site in action, scheduled for 11.30 pm. We went to the wrong one. So about midnight we pulled out for the right one. Then when we got to the right one it was discovered that the lorries were short of petrol – why only then, God only knows. So they went off leaving us in pouring rain and taking our auxiliary kit – blankets etc. We simply had no time to do anything about it and nowhere to sleep. I remembered seeing a house in the trees on the way to the waggon lines, so I collected our clique and headed for that in desperation. It seemed deserted, so we decided to force an entrance into the shed nearby. We hoisted one bloke through the window and he succeeded in bringing down a pile of empty cans with him. However, nobody raised the alarm, so we made ourselves as comfortable as we could and did our best to get some sleep. We were off again at 5 a.m. and have now put another site in action, had breakfast and feel comparatively cheerful. But the complete lack of organising ability on the part of some of these officers really makes me tremble for the safety of the rank and file. They were quite content to see men going off to sleep in the wet grass without lifting a finger to find alternative shelter. God knows what would happen in hostile country."

"… We are concluding the exercise today and returning to camp to take another turn at duty battery before going out again. On the whole it hasn't been too bad after that foul start. We had two very good nights in the open. Some of us bunked up on a bed of ferns and it was like a spring mattress, besides being warm. The only trouble is the place is infected with gnats which make things rather uncomfortable. But we have slept more comfortably than at that wretched camp. I am

only sorry that we are going back to it. The actual job of 'reccing' for suitable sites, which I have been doing on the 'flip', is very interesting and certainly more to my taste than rotting on a static site. The only thing I have to complain about is some very bad organisation.

The meals have been very good indeed. Right Troop is fortunate in possessing a good cook. The field kitchen is a very interesting one. They put a large pressure blow lamp at each end of a line of square cooking tins and thrust wood in between, along the trough. It does its job in no time.

It gives me a very 'active service' feeling to view a harbouring convoy at night or in the morning, the camouflaged lorries, cooking fires, little map conferences, and men washing or eating, generally in the middle of a wood. This camouflage business gets quite an instinct – you feel quite naked if you stand up or make yourself conspicuous while in the field."

Back pain kept Eric out of the regimental exercise and on guard duty instead. That put him in a foul enough mood for a blazing row with his mate Len.

"Nash seems to be ambitious of acquiring the real Drill Sergeant manner and bawling the crew out on the slightest excuse. I suppose as I am (or was!) in line for promotion I should adopt a like manner – instead I have a thumping row with him on the subject. But if to be an NCO one has to adopt the prevailing habit of sitting down hard on all concerned, I must forego that pleasure. I think that persuasion and encouragement is the thing that everybody stands in need of – the life itself is pretty bloody without making it unnecessarily more so."

The exercises were followed by two days' cleaning and packing for the next move, rumoured to Middlesex – an exciting prospect for Eric who would be able to nip home when off duty. At one AM on

17th July the weary soldiers climbed into their trucks and departed. For Kent.

On 18th July 1942 the Messerschmitt 262 first flew under pure jet power; earlier tests had included a backup piston engine in the nose. Two years later, after a long gestation, it became the world's first operational jet fighter and moved the goalposts for Allied fighter pilots and AA gunners alike.

Kent – Again

Their new post wasn't home but it wasn't bad. Eric's troop found itself just south of Maidstone at Boughton Monchelsea, replacing units of 90th HAA who were off to the joys of mobile training.

> *"We are in a pleasant enough spot near an orchard, the GL sharing three tents, well away from the rest of the camp, and the voice of authority, and we are doing 24 hour shifts which lets us out of camp fatigues, parades and other abominations."*
>
> *"… The situation here is pleasant enough, we are surrounded by orchards and I hope to bring some fruit home with me – strawberries perhaps…*
>
> *This site here is a 'master' one which means we are constantly plagued with manning, exercises, red tape and occasional alarms. Still it helps break the monotony."*

A local resident remembered passing the site.

> *"Coming back from Chart Sutton, the long, straight road from Boughton Monchelsea ran beside a wood which concealed an army camp of Bissen [sic] huts and anti-aircraft guns. If there was a raid on as we passed by, and there were German planes overhead, these*

guns would often open fire. The noise was so deafening we would
put our heads down and pedal like mad!"[xxiv]

While the regiment worked up to its full mobile allocation of
vehicles in July and August the GL team earned their keep by
keeping lookout from the antenna as 206 Battery raided the
strawberry fields. There were also technical talks:

> *"All number ones (GL) were summoned to King's Hill*[27] *this*
> *morning to hear a secret lecture on recent enemy 'jamming' devices,*
> *also some particulars of the progress of enemy GL."*

And, of course, some running about.

> *"We have been launched on an infantry training programme,*
> *dashing around in battle order with fixed bayonets just like soldiers.*
> *Don't get me wrong, I'm not claiming to be one, but it looks awfully*
> *realistic!"*
>
> A bit of air activity brought *"… the unfamiliar experience*
> *of quite a long night action. We didn't fire, of course, as this area gives*
> *priority to fighters but we were supplying data to fighter command*
> *which made things more interesting."*

The 'Baedeker' campaign was fading. Canterbury suffered a heavy
raid on 31st May 1942 followed by smaller attacks the next two
nights. Ipswich, Bury St Edmunds, Nuneaton, Great Yarmouth and
Weston-Super-Mare were hit in June but that was the end of it. Very
low-level attacks by fighter-bombers continued unabated. They
were tricky for the defences because they arrived with very little

---

[27] Probably RAF West Malling.

warning at widely-scattered coastal targets. The fleeting engagements demanded fast, accurate aircraft recognition.

"I arrived here yesterday just in time to see a security film and some aircraft recognition films, shown at the camp. They were all very good especially the recognition stuff."

Allied aircraft were forbidden to cross the coast at less than 1,000 feet unless they had their undercarriage down as a distress signal. Mistakes still happened.

AA Command eventually met the threat by vastly increasing the number of light guns around the coast, keeping them permanently manned in daylight and installing direct lines from radar stations to give the gunners as much notice as possible. This was yet to happen.

"We have been very busy for the last few hours; we have had three alarms during the night and consequently I feel somewhat dopey."

Another *Luftwaffe* innovation was to use unarmed Junkers 86 bombers specially adapted for very high altitude. One such dropped a 250 kg bomb on Bristol from 40,000 feet on 28th August killing 48 people and seriously injuring another 26 in Bristol's worst single-bomb incident of the war. By mid-September the RAF had a flight of modified Spitfires and the Germans thought better of the idea.

By now fears that Germany would quickly knock Russia out of the war were obviously wrong, and American troops were arriving in ever-greater numbers. Allied commanders switched their focus from invasion defence to a second front in Western Europe. AA Command had to create eleven mobile brigades and give seven of them to Home Forces. General Pile, whose job was to defend the UK, agreed but observed:

> *"Who can doubt, in view of our shortages and our ever-increasing commitments, that it was an incredible and undeserved piece of good fortune that the German forces were so tied down in Russia as not to be able to concentrate on us?"*[xxv]

Churchill lost patience with Auchinleck's command in North Africa, replacing him with General Alexander as C-in-C Middle East Command, and with General Gott as commander of the Eighth Army. Gott was killed when his plane was shot down returning to Cairo from the battlefield. His replacement was General Montgomery.

On 18th August 206 Battery moved to Gibraltar Farm and Twydall near Chatham in a shuffle of static and mobile units. Taking over a permanent site had a definite upside.

> *"This site has a marvellous situation. We are at the mouth of the Medway and can view Allhallows and Fenn across the water. And the camp itself is very well laid out, with a nice canteen and wash house, showers etc."*

The disastrous Dieppe raid launched the next day. Its objectives were to prove it was possible to seize a port, to destroy military installations, gain intelligence and boost morale. All failed. Over 6,000 men (largely Canadian) were put ashore of whom nearly 60% were killed, captured or taken prisoner. The RAF lost 96 aircraft to the *Luftwaffe's* 48; the Royal Navy lost a destroyer and 33 landing craft.

> *"We are also invigorated by the news of this invasion. Let's hope it is the real thing at last. Hundreds of fighter planes have been flying over since dawn – and looks like a real heavy concentration on Dieppe. And what do you think of Churchill's visit to Moscow? Is it possible we are getting a move on at last?"*

Churchill flew to Moscow, straight from sacking Auchinleck in Egypt, to tell Stalin there would be no second front in 1942. His reception was glacial: Stalin already knew it from his sources in London.

British and American opinion deeply appreciated Russia's hardship and sacrifices. Public enthusiasm for early landings in Western Europe matched that of President Roosevelt and General Marshall (US Army Chief of Staff). Roosevelt had earlier told Molotov, the Soviet Minister of Foreign Affairs, he was willing to put six to ten divisions ashore in France even if it meant losing 100,000 – 120,000 men; a conversation which Molotov gleefully relayed to Churchill. British commanders were nervous of upsetting the Americans but understandably leery of a massive sacrifice of British life for doubtful and temporary relief of the Eastern Front. In July the war cabinet formally rejected the American proposal. Roosevelt and Marshall reluctantly accepted the alternative of joint landings in French North Africa. This plan became Operation *Torch* in November.[xxvi]

The failure at Dieppe made the point that we were not yet ready for a European adventure. Lord Louis Mountbatten, lead planner of the operation, later observed that every life lost at Dieppe must have spared ten in Normandy. The statement in a 1948 speech to Canadian war veterans is widely quoted and widely disputed.

The gunners in Kent were preparing for whatever joy might fall out of the orders lottery. In between alarms (mostly futile) they practised with rifle and bayonet, swimming in full kit, mobile deployments, snap shooting, unseen target shooting, barrage shooting, and heard lectures on the French Colonial Empire and the USSR.

"We did a Commando PT today in battle order. Kilner and Sgt Wyrill both became stretcher cases, the former cut his leg on a bottle and Wyrill's blood pressure became too much for him and he passed completely out. Prayers were offered up by the Heightfinders but he

subsequently regained consciousness! Johnnie Tekel was quite beside himself with excitement, he is now drinking steadily in the canteen."

"… They have a delightful variation of the usual charging, crawling and diving for cover. Large V-shaped tank traps have been dug around the camp about 15ft in depth and we have to take them in our stride, which with a rifle is none too easy.

You sort of ski down it and climb up same with the technique of a spider. Johnnie Tekel looks very comic doing this – has the appearance of a galvanised rifle with something on the end of it. He is particularly 'explosive' about this sort of thing. Another of my worries is that when doing this my trousers always work down – quite a Mack Sennett[28] touch. Still I hope it will eventually put the fear of God into the enemy.

We are reduced to a pitifully small crew – only five of us counting Len Nash. 'Geordie' is in hospital with stomach trouble and another bloke is attending a funeral, besides the leave men. And we are moving one of the instruments tomorrow…

We have had an alarm tonight, but nothing came of it. Apparently they fired at Maidstone after we left and put the village into a proper state.

I don't think we shall be left in peace tonight somehow, the guns are banging away on the Essex side, so methinks I will get a little shuteye."

"No news of promotion yet! The tempo of this army calls for the deepest admiration."

In fact Eric was already a paid, acting Bombardier; he just hadn't heard yet. Nor had anyone else.

---

[28] Mack Sennett was a pioneer of slapstick comedy, and founder of Keystone Studios.

"On Monday I was ushered into the presence of Kilner and asked if I'd ever considered a commission!

I decided to be tactful and just say 'yes' and subsequently I was interviewed by the Adjutant… He wound up by saying I would stand a poor chance as a gunner!"

The daily round of maintenance and training began to pall. Eric scratched around for a new direction.

"No news worth mentioning from here, except that we have just started 'calibration' which means being cooped up in the cabin for an awful long spell…

My word this is a dull life.

To keep my hand in I am giving a series of wireless theory lectures for an hour every day. First one was quite successful."

There were inspections.

"We have had any God's amount of big wigs visiting the site today also the Brigade IFC (Major GL) consequently we have had a terrific Blitz on the instruments – polishing up and all that sort of thing. There's also a bunch of trainees which should never have been passed out of Div School, which we have to somehow turn into operators."

And more inspections.

"I was due to take the adjutant of the Regt. last night, and was in the set with one of our own officers when he arrived. He appeared slightly huffy because we weren't waiting to receive him with open arms, and suggested that we finished what we were doing and he would wait outside.

I suppose we were longer than his Majesty bargained for because when we finally 'finished' he was nowhere to be found!

Subsequent enquiries proved that he had summoned his driver and driven away! Kilner was in quite a fright about it and took a poor view of Mr Knight and myself being rather amused. However, I hear that he is having another 'go' tonight."

A mobile exercise came as a welcome change.

"Our 'toot' went off all right – can't say it was very exciting or gave us any hard work. Sleeping out was rather a cold business, but we piled bracken on to the floor of the lorries and made the best of it. Generally speaking, the whole atmosphere was rather a 'holiday' one – must have been a reaction from having no examiners about."

September was also enlivened by firing practice at Bell Farm, a coastal site very close to Eric's birthplace.

"We had a good shoot yesterday – I think everybody enjoys a firing camp – despite the fact that we had to arise at the crack of dawn – brr! … GL was very much commended, needless to say."

Their training included exposure to 'harassing gas,' a non-lethal irritant that the Germans were expected to use. It temporarily causes acute distress and reduces troops' efficiency by forcing them to wear respirators.

"We all had a dose of 'D.M. [Diphenylamine-chloroarsine]' – the harassing gas – yesterday. Five minutes in the van altogether – two with respirator, two without and one 'with'. It seemed to affect some more than others – nerves chiefly I think, although the sensations were unpleasant enough. All this on top of a lovely dinner! Pork chops and really posh ones at that."

And so back to the infantry exercises.

> "... we are building a bridge across a tank trap, which at the
> moment looks pretty precarious. Trigger is having great fun sending
> Emma backwards and forwards over it with various odds and ends
> – the poor chap is terrified of anything resembling danger."

They did at least get to a dance, described thus:

> "... we spent most of the time in the canteen. Biggest joke was
> coming back afterwards – a couple of BHQ Bombardiers were 'tight'
> and were very amusing – sat on the floor of the lorry and sang happily
> all the way back. The joke is they are both rather austere fellows in
> the usual way."

The Battle of Guadalcanal had been grinding on since the second
week of August. Eric and Jennie didn't discuss the brutal six-month
struggle which saw the Allies seize the initiative in the Pacific
campaign. The parallel maelstrom at Stalingrad did catch their
attention.

> "Isn't it marvellous about Stalingrad? It's almost a miracle how
> the Russians have been able to withstand those attacks. It doesn't look
> as though we are going to do much about a second front this year,
> despite Churchill's promises. Well it had better be in the spring."

Rommel returned to Germany for medical treatment. The Afrika
Korps would feel his absence in the approaching Allied offensive,
which also gave the Russians some relief by drawing off *Luftwaffe*
forces from the Eastern Front.

Mysterious Cornwall

On 21st October 1942 a vague order sent advance parties scurrying to collect mobile guns from various places and move them 'to locations at present unknown.' Three days later, after a rushed handover, the rest of the battery headed west. Haste and secrecy inevitably made for mistakes: with one troop of '206' going to Barnstaple and the other 70 miles further on, Eric's convoy went to the wrong place.

> *"This seems to be the most appalling mess up on record and so much appears to have gone wrong that it is difficult to sort it all out.*
>
> *In the first place it's the wrong site for us. We arrived there in the evening and found Left Troop in possession and Right Troop somewhere down in Cornwall! Left Troop advance party are presumably taking their gear down there so we left our equipment here last night. We finished unloading in the small hours and then repaired to a local BHQ. We weren't expected, got no food and had to bed down in the lorries. This morning we are about to try and discover the whereabouts of Right Troop.*
>
> *It isn't the fault of the Battery or even the Regiment but of the so-called organisers who move us. It really is a shambles, and nobody knows a thing about what will happen next… But it looks as though we shall be down in Cornwall some time today. It's been quite an eventful trip taking it all round – we lost a gun and towing vehicle somewhere around Newbury, and I had to go back and look for it with a three ton lorry! We found it after a lengthy process of elimination, and caught up the convoy past Andover. We passed Stonehenge and stayed at a transit camp at Taunton. Then the authorities gave us an alternative route and we made a detour north and were in sight of Minehead."*

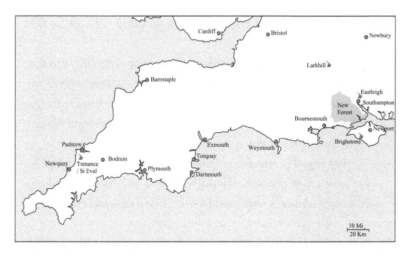

Map 4: South-West England. Showing locations mentioned in the text.

Amid intense security outgoing mail was censored before posting and the regimental war diary gives little idea of what they were doing. Eric's troop was at Trenance near RAF St Eval south of Padstow; they had to collect their post from Bodmin.

"*The only thing we know ourselves is that we are here on an important job, and that leave will be resumed as soon as possible…*

We have certainly worked harder than at any other time during our lives, but I must wait until I come home to tell you much about it.

It's rather a good thing we have no time for anything but work, as comfort is non existent. One just finds a dry place and goes to sleep at the end of the day. We get a bath by courtesy of the RAF in the vicinity. Primitive as our accommodation is, it's heaven compared with the lot of some others. We saw quite a lot on our way down.

I have been on 'general duties' with a vengeance. We have no 'instruments' with us, consequently we are not 'OFC' – I have been Orderly Bombardier, predictor number and Guard Commander…

123

Permission is not even granted to leave the camp – except for the aforesaid baths.

The thing that was most enjoyable, speaking personally, was the trip down, which left me unscathed. Some of the boys suffered in comparison – Reg West contracted a cold which left him croaking, and plenty were upset by the continuous travelling and petrol fumes, but we had plenty of fun at the same time.

Reg begged permission to leave us at one town saying he had to buy some cough mixture. We walked into a pub later to find him consuming whisky in large quantities! It's been a stock joke ever since."

At some point Eric underwent parachute training with the idea of deploying 3.7s by air. The thought of supporting airborne forces with a serious gun capable of anti-aircraft, anti-tank and field artillery roles must have been very attractive. There was just one snag: the mobile 3.7 on its carriage weighed over nine tons but the maximum *all-up* weight of the largest available glider was seven tons. With no other evidence we can guess that the training happened here and there was a failed attempt to develop a lighter mount – but that remains speculation.

"I've done a succession of arduous duties, and now, to my great horror, am in the middle of a short, intensive small arms course at a local aerodrome...

There is still a great deal of tension in the vicinity, with continuous manning and all signs of something in the wind...

We are spending our evenings by candlelight and there just isn't anything bloodier. But thank God we have a Nissen hut. The interior would look quite picturesque to an artist in search of life in the raw... But the grub continues to be pretty good after a shaky start and there's surprisingly little moaning. The reason, I think, being that everybody knows that they have done a real good job of work,

*real active service stuff under damned difficult conditions, and it does
make you proud of this lot to see how they have pulled it off. It must
needs be unspectacular on account of 'security' but I think it ranks
with the best any of the services can do, Air Force included.*

*... I am trying to give the short course a bit of attention, as it covers
all small arms training, bayonet, grenade and field observation work,
and the inevitable assault course – a sort of nightmare obstacle race. The
instructors are all RAF – and quite good too – except that they will call
me 'Corporal' – usually in terms of gentle admonition. I must admit
that my bayonet work could do with a lot of improvement. Urged to
'put some devilment into it' today I engaged an instructor with the
utmost fury, the sheath came off and he had to jump for his life!*

*... Personally, I like grenade throwing best. It has all the dignity
of distant relationship to the enemy."*

The radar turned up at the end of October so they designed barrages
to protect St Eval airfield, where American anti-submarine
Liberators had just arrived.

The Second Battle of El Alamein – the turning point of the
desert war – had been in full swing since 23rd October. After so
many false dawns and disappointments hope seemed presumptuous.
Jennie wrote on 4th November:

> *"The news has been a little better of late. I notice the Press reports
> the doings of the Eighth Army very cautiously – no doubt they have
> had enough of making themselves look cheap with a lot of ballyhoo."*

'Emma' Tullett, Eric's oppo in 168 Battery, was equally cautious.

> *"The news from Egypt sounds surprisingly good and everyone
> here is quite happy about it, maybe we shall hold the Afrika Korps
> back this time."*

By 11th November the German and Italian forces were in full retreat. Rommel, hastily recalled from Germany, had no answer to overwhelming Allied numbers and air power; the 37,000 Axis casualties were about 30% of their total strength. Hitler's inevitable order to stand firm for victory or death was pure fantasy: this was indeed the end of the beginning.

The US Navy suffered heavy losses in the Solomon Islands between 12th and 15th November. The Japanese nonetheless failed to destroy the American air base or reinforce their doomed forces on Guadalcanal. This was one of only two occasions when battleships fought each other in the Pacific (the other was the 1944 Battle of Leyte Gulf).

In Britain, travel time was removed from the leave allowance of soldiers stationed up to 400 miles from home.[xxvii] A daylight attack at Canterbury on 31st October killed thirty-two people and injured 116, with further casualties in a second raid that night. 'Emma' wrote:

> *"Jerry machine-gunned the street and did a bit more low level bombing.*
>
> *Jean's mother had been in there shopping and had only been back for half an hour when the raid started.*
>
> *A lucky break eh?!"*

168 Battery was with the other half of '206' near Barnstaple. After the initial confusion – and having to build their gun pits – they had an easier time of it.

> *"I might add that I have thought of an idea to replace string on the Range Converter...*
>
> *We look after this phone from seven AM till ten PM and in the morning one fellow does cookhouse, and all spare men go on parade. The main consolation is that we get out in the afternoon till midnight,*

and a secondary one is that we go just over the road to a house to get a bath though naturally there is a rota."

Eric's hectic West Country stay finished with a short leave. Then back to school.

Radar School

He was cynical when told about this at Twydall in September:

"I'm down for a course sometime in November; something to do with management of GL sites, it sounds very interesting, also very far away. So much can happen these days. It will probably be cancelled by infantry training!"

In fact the course booking held up and got him out of Cornwall a week ahead of the troop. He reported to the Wireless Wing, 6th AA Division School at Buckhurst Park, Withyham in Sussex. Like Southover Hall it was a stately home borrowed by His Majesty. Unlike Southover it still exists. The estate includes the Hundred Acre Wood immortalised by A A Milne in the 'Pooh' stories.

"There are only eight of us on the course which is for NCOs and it includes two ATS. It is fairly comprehensive and takes up most of the day with very short breaks for meals. It appears to be a 'Unit Instructors' course which means me delivering plenty of lecturettes.

The school itself is not bad, except for a preponderance of Red Tape and a host of Parades, but one expects that sort of thing here. It is also like Burwash in a pretty inaccessible spot. However, we have beds, good food and a pub about ten minutes away where one can get a good supper...

I don't think much of the new brand of T.I.s, they appear to be word perfect on drills but not so hot on theory, and generally not a patch on the old Burwash crowd. They also appear to be frightened to death of the ruling authority. I hope Watchet [School of Anti Aircraft Artillery, Radar Wing] *is an improvement otherwise I shall be changing my mind about an instructor's course.*

Buckhurst Park is the home of the De La Warrs – can't say I've heard much about them, but the church is full of their memorial tablets."

Herbrand Sackville, 9th Earl De La Warr, was a Labour politician who held a number of government posts in the 1920s and 1930s but was dropped from Winston Churchill's administration. As MP (and mayor) of Bexhill-on-Sea he persuaded the council to construct the De La Warr Pavilion there. It is now an arts centre.

The course was frustrating for one of Eric's experience.

"What does annoy us is the confounded red tape around the place. They have co-operation every night for the Trainees, but the basic course breaks up before the next weekend and the major insists on us providing a team from among just ourselves. Just as though we want experience on the damned exercise. So there's danger of the next weekend being mucked up, but it will be only after a first class row."

"… Well, we definitely have to leave a team in during the weekend but those who cannot get home have very kindly consented to remain behind and do the needful. So all things considered I should be able to get home alright.

I forgot to mention that there is officially no rail travel allowed for students – which is another snag as one has to circumvent authority by trekking to another station. Damned silly isn't it? But it's typical of the things they think up here. We have also got to dodge a staff bloke who waits at Victoria in the hopes of catching somebody. On the whole it should be most interesting. I'll have to put over my best fieldcraft…

Drills are as boring as hell. Mobile drill is a half baked sort of affair which consists of dismantling a set by a method that takes twice as long as the way we did it at Eastleigh. On the whole the course isn't so hot, but I suppose it's useful as a refresher."

"… we really are having things chucked at us now, and it seems lecturette session is impending, with Major and Captain in attendance. My advanced theory certainly needed a brushing up but compared with the rest it's not too bad.

I wish we had more exercise here. I think that's the reason why we get so cold. If there was a moon I'd go for a run of an evening but it would be asking for a broken neck as things are."

He gained confidence with both content and fieldcraft as the course progressed.

"We all got back safely last night. At the last moment we decided to alight at the station before Withyham, to avoid any 'Gestapo' on the gate. We reached the 'Dorset Arms' in time to hear most of Churchill's speech, which seemed to go down well, particularly with the Canadians. What went down far better with me was a pint and a cheese roll…

We are supposed to be having lecturettes tomorrow, so there is great preparation and swotting tonight.

I suppose I must get down to it myself some time."

It was all right on the night.

"I got a 'very good' from the major and a 'quite OK except for so and so and so and so' from the instructor. Only two of us out of six have emerged intact so far, the rest have been somewhat flayed."

The Bletchley cryptanalysts finally broke the U-Boat 'Shark' code, ending a ten-month intelligence blackout due to improved Enigma machines. In Chicago Enrique Fermi's team initiated the first nuclear chain reaction. Both successes were deeply hidden but appreciably shortened the war. In (almost) equal secrecy the V1 flying bomb took its first powered flight and Hitler authorised development of the V2 rocket.

On 17th December Anthony Eden confirmed press reports of mass executions of Jews. The previous day Hitler had extended the killing programme to Gypsies.

Eric went back to Iwade for a few days after the course.

"You would have laughed at one unfortunate incident this morning. We had another 'alarm' after a short 'stand down' and found when we reached the receiver that the door was locked and the keys missing. There was supposed to be gas, tanks and dive bombing and there we were, sitting on the steps like mugs while brass hats raved! No it wasn't me!"

The regiment left Cornwall at the beginning of December and scattered: 168 Battery back to Crewe, 169 to Formby and 206 to Blundellsands near Liverpool. The Regimental Cadre of Battle Training Instructors had disappeared a week earlier; anyone who thought that ominous would have been right.

Battle School

Eric caught up with the battery just in time for a round of medicals and inoculations. He spent a day fixing a recalcitrant radar then packed it for the move back south, to Hertford.

"We have been reformed in infantry fashion – company, platoons etc. I'm a section leader (sounds like the ATS, doesn't it?) in charge of about ten men, with such sinister names as first and second rifleman, bomber, machine gunner etc. I've even got a second-in-command in case I drop dead – which to judge from the accounts of the assault course is no unlikely possibility.

This is 'the' Battle School, of which a writer in the Express stated that he preferred Libya every time!

But I do take a poor view our doing this in the season of peace and goodwill to all men, and a damned cold season anyway. I understand that wading through rivers is just a sideline."

On 24th December 1942 the Resistance assassinated Admiral Darlan, whose orders had led to the slaughter of the French fleet at Mers-el-Kébir. However, he prevented the Germans using French ships, refused to provide conscript labour, and protected Jewish war veterans. Coincidentally in North Africa when the Allies landed, he negotiated the surrender of Vichy French forces there. He was little missed. Jennie commented: *"What do you think of the news this morning? Well it has solved the problem of Darlan."*

With no hope of Eric getting back for Christmas, Jennie arranged to join her family in Bristol for the celebration. It was just as well: training started on Christmas Eve with a one-day break, which Eric didn't see, for the festival.

"Some Christmas here! Yesterday we commenced some very realistic assault stuff – scrambling across a varied countryside, a wonderful pot-pourri of ponds, brambles, ploughed fields and thick wood. I needn't have worried about those blackheads – I think I've left them all behind on the blackberry thorns.

Oh and you know that second-in-command of mine I spoke about? Well, I haven't got one now! He happened to be Jack Hobbs and during a 'take cover' he dived into some long grass and landed on a tree stump. Rather a silly thing to do to my mind – I always pretend to get down quickly and then have a good investigation!

Anyway, the next few minutes resembled that famous picture of the Death of Nelson and he was eventually carted off to the Medical Post.

When we got home in the evening I scraped off the mud and did a double-quick change in an endeavour to acquire something of the festive spirit. Then to my utter stupefaction I was detailed for Regimental Guard Commander. It was a real piece of dirty work of which more anon. I raged and protested but all to no purpose, so it is my bitter lot to spend Christmas Eve and most of today in the b—y guardroom. It is a guardroom too! This is the HQ of the local yeomanry and the guardroom is complete with prisoners' cells with little peep holes in the doors and massive keys hanging in a row in the passage. And I have one prisoner! A most fantastic bloke. He is Lord Howard of Effingham[29], a descendant of the illustrious person of that name, a personality well known in the 60th, at present awaiting trial for six months desertion! He is a very nice chap too and knows all there is to know about guard reports! In fact he filled mine in for me!"

Guard duty meant missing the Christmas celebrations. He didn't miss them that much.

"They got the men up at six for Church Parade at light, which infuriated them. Dinner was arranged in the drill hall in the middle of the town which involved a march from the barracks, which would have been all right if they hadn't let the men loose when they returned

---

[29] Mowbray Henry Gordon Howard, 6th Earl of Effingham (1905–1996) descended from a fleet commander who faced the Armada. He married Malwina Gertler, a Polish émigré and suspected spy, who was interned in 1941.

from the Church Parade. Of course, they all flocked to the pubs and when they got them together again they were in an awful state. The officers did a bunk and left it to the sergeants (who were as bad as any) to march the men down. I don't think the storming of the Bastille had anything on that march out! I was on duty, but were I ever so tight I should still have been ashamed to have been in it. They created enough noise to wake the dead, and the townspeople must have taken a poor view of it."

Training restarted after Christmas with the intensity turned up.

"I feel amazed that all my life I have walked round hedges instead of putting my head down and bursting through them. In battle training, gaps are disallowed on account of they will almost certainly be covered by machine guns. And there is generally a deep ditch the other side which you can't avoid owing to your momentum. Being now quite heartless to the sufferings of my fellow men I must confess that I have seen few funnier sights than a bloke impaled half way through a thick hedge, or hanging upside down from the last six inches. One man had the courage to protest violently, saying he was born in the ordinary way, not assembled in a tank factory. As the whole regiment is practising here it's quite commonplace to turn a corner and see gunners hanging from barbed wire or intricate hedging. They are greeted with sardonic cries of 'Oh, well done that man!' 'Tons of guts' etc.

Well, sitting here and writing about it afterwards one can see the funny side, but my God it does seem a half-witted proceeding when you are at it. War reduces us to a level where animals appear highly intelligent – the way cows stop and look at us gives me the feeling that they are sizing us up for a lot of bloody maniacs."

The course culminated in large-scale exercises.

"We finished our training yesterday with a regimental contest in which all troops of the Regiment participated.

It was quite the most strenuous day we have had, but most enjoyable. Our troop did very well indeed, we came second in the Battery and fourth in the Regiment. Our troop was also listed as having 'the best section commanders in the Regt' which is rather sweeping but very gratifying.

There was a complete tactical scheme for the day, and you may be interested in the details. There was first a 'pursuit course' in which we had to pursue a body of paratroopers and destroy them – this was a most exhausting affair as there were relays of them! Then we did a tank ambush and were then supposed to have gained information to the effect that a body of the enemy were established at a certain map reference. This necessitated a 'troop in the attack' and an uphill charge! Then we did wood-clearing – which somewhat resembles tiger hunting – then a 'defence of a vulnerable point', after that 'section in the attack'! – a series of mopping up operations, then a troop attack on a machine gun post – across a stream! After that they took us back in lorries, thank God!

What was pleasing was the way in which the whole troop rose to the occasion! We were especially complimented on our speed, which was described as 'really magnificent'!"

Eric learned he was to be a father and, unsurprisingly, that the regiment was slated for overseas duty.

"I'm glad I broke the news about our overseas service and that you take it well. The thought of leaving you at this time rather terrified me – I wouldn't care a rap as regards myself."

The battle of the capitals had been quiescent for some time. It flared up again in January 1943 when RAF Lancasters and Halifaxes raided

Berlin in a mission noted for the first use of 'Target Indicator' marker bombs and an attacking force made up entirely of four-engine bombers. Casualties and damage were both light.

> *"The raid on Berlin seems to have been pretty effective. I notice that war correspondents flew on the raid for the first time. One of them had a good story in the Mail."*

London's first major raid in some time prompted Jennie's seasoned comment: *"The wireless went off badly and then all the local guns opened fire with much rattling of windows. However it soon got quiet again locally. But it seemed quite like old times for a bit. We had another alert about 5 a.m. Lasting an hour so I'm told though I didn't hear the all clear being fast asleep."* In the city people had lost the habit of diving for shelter and went out to watch the display: a bad move. Over a dozen were killed by falling AA shells and splinters.[xxviii]

On 20th January a low-level attack by fighter-bombers caught London's defences unprepared. At Sandhurst Road School in Catford six teachers and 38 children were killed; sixty children and a number of teachers were injured. Seven aircraft were shot down on the way home.[xxix] Jennie heard the fuss but the raid didn't get as far as her area;

> *"We have an 'alert' and quite a spot of gunfire at dinner time, but nothing else exciting. It is a very dull day with plenty of cloud cover – just right for a 'spot of bother'. I expect you wish you were in action and could have a pot at some of these Jerries."*

A Berlin rally on 30th to mark the tenth anniversary of Hitler becoming Chancellor of Germany was just too tempting. RAF Mosquitoes repeatedly disrupted it with low-level nuisance attacks.

> *"I wonder what the effect of the daylight raid on Berlin was?*
> *Well timed anyway."*

They kept Göering off the air for over an hour and interrupted a speech by Goebbels. One aircraft was shot down.

The Casablanca Conference ended on 24th January with a declaration that the Allies would accept only Germany's unconditional surrender.

> *"I notice that Stalin refused to join in the Casablanca meeting.*
> *I wonder if he was too busy?"*

Though intended to reassure Stalin (who was indeed fully occupied with Stalingrad) that the West would not make a separate peace, the declaration was heard in Germany as a fight to the death. Hitler replied that there would be no victors and defeated in the war, only survivors and annihilated.

As he spoke the final destruction of von Paulus' Sixth Army was under way at Stalingrad. The strategically pointless battle cost between 1.7 and 2 million Axis and Soviet lives between August 1942 and February 1943. 91,000 Germans were taken prisoner, of whom fewer than 6,000 ever returned to Germany – some not until 1955.

On 18th January the Soviet Army succeeded in opening a supply route to Leningrad (now St Petersburg), which had been under siege since August 1941. The siege was not finally lifted for another year and caused millions of deaths, mostly from starvation.

Casablanca also produced a strategic directive to British and US air force commanders for joint operations against Germany. The overall objective was *"the progressive destruction and dislocation of the German military, industrial, and economic system, and the undermining of the morale of the German people to a point where their capacity for armed resistance is fatally weakened."*[xxx] The whirlwind gathered strength.

On the Beach

The 'Fringe Target' raids against harmless coastal towns intensified in January 1943: they were among the few ways the reduced *Luftwaffe* could still hurt Britain. The main defences against fast, low-flying fighter-bombers were our own fighters and the astonishing mix of light AA guns being shifted south from wherever they could be found. The heavies were not exempt even though there was little a hand-cranked 3.7 could do against the threat.

After Battle School 169 Battery was split between Worcestershire and the Mersey. The other two moved to the Isle of Wight which had been raided three times in three weeks.

> *"We were originally due for leave tomorrow but this new development of air warfare seems to have altered the whole scheme. Our original destination was the Midlands… We haven't the slightest idea where we are going"*

Eric's troop found themselves at Brighstone on the Island's south-west coast, occupying a permanent site with two fixed, two mobile

Figure 9: The coast at Brighstone

3.7s and a Bofors light AA gun. Leisure travel to the coast was still banned as an invasion precaution so the gunners were among the very few 'foreigners' there.

> *"We had a very nice, comfortable journey down, travelling by train instead of lorry and landed on the island about one o'clock yesterday.*
>
> *The island has impressed me very favourably, it is far more hilly and picturesque than I had imagined. And the situation of the camp is magnificent, right on the cliffs with a lovely view of coastline and sea. And the camp itself is very comfortably equipped so there is really nothing to complain about at all – which is a change!*
>
> *… It is certainly pleasant to get back to technical work after so much running, wading and falling, particularly in such surroundings."*

Eric quickly found one drawback to the site:

> *"Half our time is spent keeping mud out of the works. The approach to the set resembles Wembley ice rink."*

He then discovered southern zephyrs can be a bit – shall we say – brisk?

> *"For the first time in my life I have actually experienced being blown across the road. I was wearing a gas cape at the time and for a minute I thought I was going to take off."*

A stream ran through manning hut and gales made the rations run so hazardous that they drew lots for the privilege. The radar crew gratefully used a lull in raiding to bring their drills and equipment up to scratch.

> *"Well, so far the time we've spent here has been rather dull as regards action. I'm rather glad about that as it has taken us all our time to get*

things straight. The teams were acutely browned off and very indifferent
as regards their drill and it's been a case of pushing them hard all the
week. I fear I'm a wee bit unpopular as a result! But we are reasonably
fit now in the event of a spot of action – which is a load off my mind."

Not that the enemy was wholly absent. 168 Battery shot down one
aircraft and engaged another without result. '206's other troop, on
the Island's north-west coast, fired 'pointer' rounds (to draw
friendly fighters' attention) at a pair of FW 190s.

> *"Life has been complicated by official visitors and by Jerry, whom*
> *we like much better… The raids aren't very satisfactory. They consist*
> *of two or three raiders coming in at very low level, doing their stuff*
> *and buzzing off again before we can do much about it. They also use*
> *fighter bombers which are as fast as Spitfires, so I'm afraid it leaves*
> *us standing still mostly. Right Troop did 'have a bash' the other day,*
> *Kilner took the shoot however, so he may have fired at one of ours!"*

Jennie picked up the flippant tone.

> *"Sorry to hear you did not have any luck with the Jerries. I think*
> *they had better hand you out some rifles if they come so low. Otherwise*
> *the best thing will be to take a pot at them as they leave France."*

She remarked more seriously about wide-ranging raids on 10th
February in which 77 people were killed and 123 seriously injured
in attacks on Berkshire, Hampshire and Sussex. Over half (41) of
the fatalities were in Reading. Newbury, Midhurst and Chichester
were also badly affected.[xxxi]

> *"We had the sirens yesterday about 4.30 or so. I understand Reading*
> *caught most of the bombs. There was plenty of gunfire round about."*

A spot of sunshine finally put a more cheerful complexion on the coast.

> *"It's a treat to come down after a night's manning to the rest camp and have a good wash, then sit at the table in the canteen facing the sea and write a letter."*

Even with Goering's attention elsewhere, Eric had plenty to keep him occupied.

> *"The Brigade instructor is here on a comprehensive training programme, and in addition to that I have five new recruits on my hands who, as GL recruits go, are pretty deadly. And unfortunately the only NCO here besides myself is worse than no NCO at all, our bright Bdr Jones about whom something will have to be done shortly, because in all my life I have never met a lazier devil. And in addition we have had fairly heavy manning periods so my spare time has been nil... as usual, GL is very unpopular in the cookhouse on account of not observing* [meal times].
>
> *One of the highlights of gunsite life is my morning row with the catering corporal who is just as cussed as I am first thing in the morning. We both accuse each other of having the easiest job on the site – 'pity you don't do my job for a change' etc! At any other time of the day we are quite good friends, and he sends corking suppers to the manning hut."*

Anti-Aircraft Command had trouble throughout the war recruiting and retaining good people. Although a specialty demanding physical fitness and mental agility, the rest of the army treated it as a reserve of trained men and a dumping ground for unemployables. General Pile put it colourfully in his book: *"Out of twenty-five who arrived at a fairly representative battery, one had a withered arm, one was mentally deficient, one had no thumbs, one had a glass-eye which fell out whenever he doubled to the guns, and two were in the advanced and more obvious stages of venereal disease."*[xxxii] Pile addressed the issue by the innovative use of women, Home Guardsmen and automation. The problem still affected the men on the batteries.

> *"I think I mentioned that I have been given five men for training: the best of them is none too bright and the two most hopeless have been drafted from latrine duties, if you please.*
>
> *I am booked for a working interview with the Troop Commander tomorrow on the subject of these last two, he is going to have them back or have the matter referred to Regiment. I'm damned if I'm going to waste any more time with them."*

Guadalcanal fell to US forces in February after a six-month fight. The Japanese lost 24,000 troops killed but managed to evacuate 10,000 after a deception convinced the Americans that a counter-attack was imminent.[xxxiii] The Russians recaptured Rostov and Kharkov. German forces withdrew from Libya to the fortified Mareth Line in Tunisia but still had a sting in their tail: they inflicted heavy losses on Allied forces approaching from the west at Kasserine Pass. Jennie couldn't resist a little *schadenfreud*.

> *"What splendid war news again – especially from Russia! The Americans don't seem so hot though. Must say I feel a bit pleased that they are being altogether eclipsed by the Russians and the British. Might stop them saying they won the war this time."*

On 15th February 1943 relief troops arrived on the Island and, with no warning, '206' packed their bags; they were on the move again.

Spartan

The first step was back to Kent: Margate on the Isle of Thanet. The position covered approaches to London, Canterbury and RAF Manston so offered the prospect of action. The battery re-equipped with updated guns in reasonable comfort.

> *"Of course we were up at the crack of dawn, travelled all day on two sandwiches and a few cakes and now we are manning for the night. Time is 3 a.m., and all's well, so far.*
>
> *Margate looks like the deserted village but the site has its compensations. We are billeted in houses – plenty to choose from too! – and the ground is nice and chalky and free from mud. And by all accounts there is plenty of firing, so the boys shouldn't be too unhappy."*
>
> *"… we are due to move again in ten days time. This time we shall be 100% mobile and go chasing around the coast, if rumour is correct, with our own gear, including a signals group.*
>
> *… We are billeted in private (empty) houses here and have settled in quite comfortably, got organised on the fires and have plenty of hot baths. The GL has a house all to itself (of course a notice has already appeared outside 'GEE HELL, WATT AN OHM!') We are taking the second floor for the short duration: the only snag is no beds, but we are too used to that to worry. It is really grand to walk into the bathroom for a shave in hot water in the morning."*
>
> *"… We are now polishing up our drills and equipment in order to take the field as a unit of the 'home forces' and nowhere do I see any outward manifestations of joy. The Os.F.C. [Operators, Fire Control] loathe the idea and view me with deep distrust and misgiving in view of my recent 'purge' and the fact that I welcome the change. I think there certainly will be periods when we will all loathe it, but it will be a more stimulating way of living than the present life, besides contributing more to the war effort."*

In fact they had a week before moving to Northampton for the start of the show.

Spartan from 1st to 12th March 1943 was the largest offensive exercise ever carried out in Britain. It involved ten divisions: six on the 'Allied' side and four on the 'German' in a dress rehearsal for the break out from Normandy. The attackers were mostly Canadian under General McNaughton and the defenders mostly British under General Gammell.

> *"The last few days have been so chaotic that I don't remember clearly just what has happened except that we have been moved from place to place collecting new equipment and working on it day and night.*
>
> *Yesterday we set out for our base here, we left at 7.30 a.m. And reached base at 2 a.m. this morning. One becomes quite immune to loss of sleep. It's Eastleigh again plus a little more...*
>
> *We are now part of the artillery arm of the Home Forces, so you can guess that the training is somewhat rigorous. It is officially described as Spartan – much more picturesquely described, of course, by the rank and file.*
>
> *We passed through London yesterday and it broke my heart to leave it behind."*

By 1st March he was in the Aylesbury area.

> *"We are having a breather here having accomplished our job of invasion, and before the opposing army tries to chuck us out. Thank God for the first part of 'mission accomplished', I had the first good sleep last night for a week."*

The Northampton start in fact made him part of the 'German' force. The attackers assembled on the south coast and advanced north, with much of the fighting along the Thames and Kennet. Three days later, still in Aylesbury, he wrote,

> "… *the situation at the moment is a static and very boring one, and I'm hoping that some side will secure a 'victory' very shortly and allow us to proceed on leave. This business may be very interesting to those blokes who fly around with maps, but personally I'd far sooner be digging the garden…*"

On 5th March the battery moved to Biggleswade, "*a delightful little village which is very well disposed to us,*" losing a gun with a broken mount on the way. While there they took seven "prisoners." Next day brought a change in fortune from 'somewhere in Bedford.'

> "… *we have pulled in for breakfast and eaten it on the village green and are now awaiting developments. I am sorry to add that we are retreating, the enemy is making an attempt to pincer us after a successful breakthrough!*
>
> *It's certainly like the real thing when you get the order to pull out, which we had at 2 a.m. this morning. The roads were packed with all kinds of transport. We passed everything from tanks to Jeeps. The fact that Canadians are after us adds zest to the scheme – we are not quite sure how we would be treated if captured! The boys thought that it wouldn't be a bad idea, they had visions of having a good meal and being sent home. The officers have hastily warned all and sundry that capture might mean road making and trench digging, however, so I don't think there is much chance of anybody taking the wrong road on purpose!*
>
> *There are some very attractive villages in this part of the Midlands and the countryside is very pretty, though rather flat. Of course we are invaded by scores of kids – nearly all running surreptitiously errands to replenish cigarette stocks…*

Hallo, we are off again. There must be a second Timoshenko[30] *commanding the other side. Well, good luck to him. The sooner he finishes, the quicker we get leave."*

The gunners had their usual trouble taking the whole thing seriously.

"Last night the GL boys got wind of a social in the village so we decided to do the rash thing and go along for a slice of night life, and chance the battery moving out on us!

It turned out to be in the vicarage (!) and we all bowled in with our escort of villagers to find a couple of our officers there! I was so tickled I just stood there and roared, they looked like a couple of schoolboys caught in the act.

… They asked for 'songs from the visitors' and after the first couple the vicar and his spouse beat a hasty retreat, on the plea that they had to count the money! Thereafter the entire entertainment was provided by the artillery!"

Spartan finished with the 'German' forces on the verge of destruction. Despite winning, General McNaughton was judged to have done poorly and was sidelined in favour of General Crerar, one of his subordinates.

"You will be pleased to hear that after more pushing around an armistice was signed and we are now preparing to toddle back to Margate, and are we glad! There is an indication that leave starts as soon as we get back, though knowing this outfit I would be rather surprised – but anyway it couldn't be far off."

---

[30] Semyon Timoshenko was a senior, modernising Soviet commander who commanded the Stalingrad front during the battle for the city (Wikipedia).

Another unit on the 'German' side was 49th (West Riding) infantry division. 60th HAA were to work closely with the Yorkshiremen the following year, doing the job for real.

Ramsgate, Larkhill

Back at Ramsgate Eric spent a few days drawing up a section training programme then shot off as soon as leave restarted. In his absence the battery's guns were sent away, two at a time, to be fitted with anti-tank sights.

Eric was still in contact with 'Taffy' Roberts and Jimmy Coyle.

> *"I was very pleased to hear from Robbie again – he does have a grand sense of humour and always tickles me immensely. He is on embarkation leave and thinks it is North Africa. He is as pleased as punch. No ties, of course, except a genuine old school one, in Robbie's case. I wish there was another Roberts in the section, or another Jim Coyle. Very stimulating both those boys."*

Early March brought a double raid on London, largely ineffective but close enough for Jennie to notice the AA fire.

> *"We had quite a lot of gunfire last night. There was quite a volley as we came out of choir practice and went down for the train. We had another alert and a lot more firing in the early hours of this morning."*

Tragically the sound of a new 'Z' battery firing its rockets near Bethnal Green tube station, used as a deep shelter, triggered a mass rush for the one entrance. A woman carrying a baby slipped in the press and her body became a trip wire for those following. 173 people, 62 of them children, died of suffocation and crushing in the human avalanche.

*"What are the details of that shelter disaster? Were there actually
170 people killed in a panic? We don't know the story, but it sounds
incredible."*

An Afrika Korps assault on Medenine in Tunisia met superior, alert,
well-dug in British and New Zealand defences and failed badly.
Rommel left Africa for the last time on 10th March, passing
command of the remaining Axis forces to General von Arnim. The
Mareth Line was eventually taken by combined frontal and flanking
attack on 26th/27th March.

A German counter-offensive recaptured Kharkov. In the
numbing scale of slaughter there the Russians lost some 45,000
dead. Jennie summed up the popular view:

*"Yes, the war seems to be going pretty well in Tunisia but not so
good in Russia. I wish we could start more of a counter offensive to
take some of the strain off the Russians."*

At Ramsgate the regiment trained with its normal enthusiasm.

*"The Brigade is carrying out an ambitious GL routine and I've been
marked down for practical instruction. Also as usual a complete set of
amended drills has come out, which necessitates a bit of preparation…"*

*"… The GL training programme is proceeding very well. It is
a Regimental stunt and I am doing the practical. We have a
Withyham T.I. for the Theory…*

*We have had some fun 'erecting and dismantling' today. Most
of the trainees have never been up a ladder and a few had extreme
attacks of 'vertigo' which caused quite a lot of unkind amusement.
My 'do you know what' Davey was quite paralysed and announced
that he would ask to be taken off it. Len replied that he would fall off
before he was taken off, and he was nearly right."*

Gun crews tried out their new anti-tank sights, firing offshore from about three miles inland, then had to clean down and pack up for the next move.

> *"Most of the Battery is away this afternoon practising a tank shoot – out at sea!"*
>
> *"… we had one day to prepare for moving to Salisbury which of course meant a complete overhaul of the equipment, then at the last minute it was decided not to take the GL. So of course we just had to unpack and settle in again."*

The battery set out for the School of Artillery at Larkhill on Salisbury Plain.

> *"As camps go it's pretty good. It is the size of a small town and contains a theatre and cinema besides universal canteens.*
>
> *The one snag is the wind that sweeps across the plain, raising a terrific sandstorm. A truly military environment…*
>
> *There are also 'druids at the bottom of our garden' – namely Stonehenge, visible about two miles away. Now all we want is a bit of leave. There is an excellent train service to London.*
>
> *We harboured late last night on a spacious common near Dorking… It was a lovely night for sleeping out, but we rose again at five, which made the night a bit short.*
>
> *My face feels baked to a cinder with the wind and this everlasting dust should give us quite a Middle East completion.*
>
> *The battery is here to practice anti-tank shooting, but I believe we shall continue with our own training."*

Eric missed one 'toot' as he was instructing at the time.

"We commence our GL training programme tomorrow and it looks as though we shall be left alone."

"… The training course is proceeding quite well. I have been able to fix up a room with tables and forms and have secured a blackboard. I do most of the theory which interests me more than drills and there is a fairly appreciative class, so I feel quite happy about it."

He couldn't get out of the next two though.

"We have been out on a day and night exercise which started yesterday and on the whole was quite enjoyable, except for the heat. It was in the nature of a demonstration for officers doing mobile training, and by the time I had rushed around the site and helped with the erection I was perspiring so freely that I could hardly see.

We have been tightening up today on the practical drill, as it was rather less of a demonstration than we had hoped for!"

"… [Len] is in a stage of acute unpopularity as he always is when a training programme is in progress. He really is the limit when it comes to handling men, he treats them like kids. Constructive suggestions re a cure have ranged from stilettos to rat poison."

"… It hasn't been a very inspiring day, we have been mucked about a bit by our 'officer trainees' but on the whole it might have been worse…

One great attraction of the exercise is the lovely country and villages we pass through during the runs around the Salisbury district. The houses in the villages are nearly all perfectly thatched and in beautiful setting of trees. We must have a ramble around here together some day, providing we don't venture too near Larkhill."

On 16th April forty-seven single-seat fighter-bombers attacked London and the Thames Estuary at night. Bad idea. With no navigator, the pilots were disoriented by darkness and ground mist. Their bombing was off and no fewer than three picked up a British searchlight beacon and tried to land at RAF West Malling. One undershot the runway under fire; one was shot down trying to take off again; and one captured intact. All three pilots lived. The unlucky pilot of a fourth FW 190 baled out nearby, too low. He did not survive.

'206' in the meantime was off to the seaside. Again.

SERGEANT

Good Morning Campers

2 06 Battery rejoined the regiment at Butlin's holiday camp, Clacton on Sea. There was just one snag: it was the 16th Light and Heavy Anti-Aircraft Practice Camp for the duration and the only visible red was on staff officers' collars. The good news was Eric's third stripe coming through at last.

> "Well, life is certainly brightened up considerably when one is 'granted the privilege of the mess'. No stacking of kit, marching in the ranks, and other obnoxious practices which one gets rather tired of after all this time! And what is rather satisfying is to stroll into meals and eat 'em off a tablecloth! Honestly, the sensation's terrific!
>
> What is also terrific is the pace of the training here. I've just finished 24 hours continuous duty, including the training of three teams from early afternoon to midnight in the set. I was as hoarse as a raven this morning – and recommenced at 8.30. It's lucky my drills are up to date, there are any amount of staff officers wandering about waiting to pick you up on small points."

The camp was one of several coastal training bases set up for the gunners to keep their hand in with live-fire practice. A scheme to try radar-directed fire against a towed target provoked derision, and sympathy for whoever flew the tow.

> "The training plane tows a 'sleeve' behind it and there's terrific

competition to shoot it off the tow rope. Up to now nobody's hit the plane.

Our turn is coming when we do GL shoots next week. God help the pilot! It'll be the first time anybody has attempted to shoot off a sleeve by GL, so I hope he's insured! Of course there's much cynical laughter by the gun sergeants at the prospect."

Their cynicism was rational; the towing aircraft would have given a much stronger radar return than the target. In the event weather, equipment and butterfingers thankfully aborted the exercise.

"Of course the firing programme was thoroughly mucked up owing to the weather. We tried again today and just when we'd got cracking the set packed up. So we dismantled, and in the course of that the prize idiot of the section dropped an aerial and broke it…"

The training was no joke – especially not to the unfortunates who fluffed it.

"We are passing through a rather severe disciplinary stage, there is a list up tonight, quoted from Regimental Orders, of ten NCOs reduced to the ranks as a 'result of the firing results' and that is our battery alone. So the atmosphere isn't exactly cheerful."

Gunners with live ammunition to hand weren't about to ignore a passing enemy plane. 168 Battery blazed away at a Junkers 88 on 8th May with no visible result.

"We are operational, thank God – that is to say, the GL, so we are relieved of guard duties. We are manning continuously and nothing could be better."

On 9th the RAF received yet another present – deliberate this time – when the crew of a Junkers 88 night fighter defected with their aircraft to RAF Dyce (now Aberdeen Airport). In the early hours of 20th May yet another FW 190 on a night raid inadvertently landed at a British airfield – Manston in Kent.

Firing camp ended on 12th May. The regiment returned to Ramsgate with Eric bringing a rear party back by train.

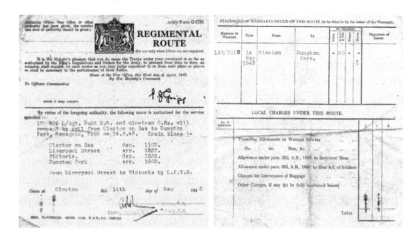

Figure 10: Movement Order from Clacton to Ramsgate

The twelfth also brought an end to fighting in North Africa when General von Arnim and 230,000 Axis troops – the remains of the Afrika Korps – surrendered in Tunisia. Von Arnim wound up at the Combined Services Detailed Interrogation Centre (CSDIC) at Trent Park near Cockfosters, where he and other senior prisoners were treated with impeccable courtesy and their conversations systematically eavesdropped[31]. Jennie observed:

---

[31] See Helen Fry; *'The M Room: Secret Listeners who Bugged the Nazis'* (CreateSpace, 2012) for a full account.

*"Poor old Von Arnim! I'll bet he would rather be in our hands
than Hitler's at the moment though!"*

On 16th May the RAF carried out the famous 'Dam Busters' raids,
breaching the Möhne and Eder dams in the Ruhr. The raid
disrupted production for months, diverted building and repair effort
from the anti-invasion defences, and killed about 1,600 people. Over
a thousand of them were foreign prisoners-of-war and forced
labourers.

At Ramsgate the regiment spent five days shooting against sea
targets. Two FW 190s rudely interrupted practice on 1st June by
strafing the area from rooftop height, too low for the guns to reply.

Orders to mobilise for overseas launched a scramble to come up
to full mobile scale, including rifles for the gunners and the
infamous 'Sten' for NCOs. This British derivative of the Thompson
sub machine gun was simplified to the limit for ease of manufacture.
Its great virtues were cheapness and the ability to use magazines
from the Royal Navy's Lanchester or the German MP-38. Its infamy
came from its habit of jamming at inconvenient moments or firing
when it wasn't supposed to.[xxxiv]

> *"We had a rather hilarious evening yesterday cleaning our new
> issue of Sten guns. They look most rough and ready things and come
> to pieces like a Hornby train. We had springs jumping all over the
> room when we took them apart to clean and everyone was getting
> their bits mixed up and trying in vain to put them together again.
> One bloke made a heap of his bits and shouted 'Salvage, Salvage'. It
> was well after midnight when they were all finally re-assembled.
> Now we'll have to learn to fire 'em!"*

Eric seized the chance to acquire a new battledress blouse and
watertight boots.

On 11th June the regiment, still not up to strength, left for a week's ground firing at Redesdale in Northumberland setting up overnight at Catterick. The exercise thus combined long-distance convoy, rapid deployment and field artillery practice. The GL had nothing to contribute to ground fire, so carried on north after Redesdale, lodging with 357 HAA Battery at Thompson Park in Sunderland.

"It has been rather a gruelling trip, easily the longest we have ever done.

We started out on Friday at about 2 a.m. and our first halt was at 1 pm Saturday, somewhere in Herts. Then we proceeded to Bedford where we deployed the GL. After a very hasty meal we came out of action, proceeding north again (this was about ten o'clock at night) and then I just lay down on the floor of the lorry and slept. When I awoke it was getting light, we had halted for a few hours rest. We were in North Lincoln.

We had about four hours sleep in blankets, then breakfasted and were off again. We travelled through Yorkshire most of the day, halting for meals, and we anchored up at Catterick in the evening, and spent the night there. Then the following morning we journeyed through Durham and Northumberland arriving at Reesdale [sic] late at night.

Well we are off again now darling – just the GL – to some site near Newcastle, so I'd better end this for now and drop it out on the way."

"… When we moved out yesterday we thought we were destined for Newcastle but we have proceeded a stage further.

We are only here for a few days, we leave on Saturday for Ramsgate and while we are here the section is attached to a static site while the rest of the Bty does some ground target shooting. Grand life this static stuff. Nice orderly routine and good messing…

Sunderland is a dirty but very friendly town; we have been made very welcome all the way through Yorks and Durham. Passing through the latter town we stopped for ten minutes and immediately received trays of tea and cakes."

The 'Fringe Target' attacks continued at a 'nuisance' level, unless you were under them. Some had much greater impact: Sunderland was recovering from a night raid which killed 69 people.

"They had a bad blitz here about three weeks ago and the townspeople are still talking about it – as usual the bombs have missed the works and hit the houses. The streets are particularly ugly and dirty and even the pubs are depressing! No, I don't like the industrial north much."

Other May raids leaving forty or more dead hit Great Yarmouth (49), Chelmsford (46), Cardiff (43), Bournemouth (116) and Torquay (40).

… Marched Them Down Again

The regiment convoyed back to Ramsgate from 20th to 23rd June. Next day the guns set off back to Larkhill, the only HAA regiment taking part in exercise *Fortescue* which tested camouflage, anti-tank and yet more field gunnery. The GL team, once again irrelevant, was left kicking its heels.

"Main thing is to keep the blokes busy on something, otherwise they talk of nothing but their ain folk and the next train out of Ramsgate.
… I'm getting down to driving again – I'm glad to have something like that to get my teeth into. We are roaming around tonight for a short spell."

Fortescue was "… deemed a success for all concerned"[xxxv] when the troops returned on 3rd July. There was suitably enthusiastic chat in the Sergeants' Mess afterward.

> *"I found the Battery back when we got home today. They have been having a pretty exciting time doing a 'concentrated' shoot on Salisbury Plain – a sort of 'El Alamein' affair in which all sorts of guns took part and fired for about an hour non-stop. They say the target area was a real spectacle – just covered by a mass of flame."*

Artillery was a conspicuous Allied – and specifically British – talent in the approaching North-West Europe campaign. Planned barrages and the ability to call down accurate fire at short notice spared many infantrymen's lives. In the absence of a serious air threat ground commanders cherished the 3.7s' long range, high rate of fire and plentiful ammunition.

In 1943 that was still to come – but Ramsgate was on 'Hellfire Corner': within range of German coastal guns at Batterie Lindemann (Sangatte) and Batterie Todt (Cap Gris Nez).

> *"We had a spot of shelling again last night – it didn't last long and was directed at the other end of the town, and eventually the sirens started up. It's really quite fantastic to think of the Germans shelling us direct."*

Eric visited the guns after the siege of Calais and was duly impressed by their scale.

July passed with more firing practice from Ramsgate seafront, replacement of their 3-ton lorries, and introduction to the new GL Mk 3 radar set.

> *"Our preliminary Mark 3 course is in full swing and I am busy preparing graphs, diagrams and typed summaries for the benefit of*

the officers. The new instruments are very interesting indeed, and an enormous advance on the Mark 2."

On 9th July a lone raider bombed and machine-gunned a train and a crowded cinema in East Grinstead killing over a hundred people. The month also saw the first appearance of the Messerschmitt 410 (*Hornisse*) over Britain. This fast, twin-engine fighter-bomber gave British fighter and anti-aircraft crews a headache because it looked uncannily like the Mosquito.

General Władysław Sikorski was Prime Minister of the Polish government-in-exile and Commander-in-Chief of the Polish Armed Forces. On 4th July his plane crashed just after take-off from Gibraltar killing everyone aboard except the pilot. At the time Sikorski was loudly demanding a Red Cross investigation into the discovery of 20,000 bodies of officers, police, intellectuals and other dangerous Poles in a mass grave in the Katyn forest. The Germans and Russians blamed each other for the massacre but the Allies' dependence on Russia and admiration for their wartime sacrifices tilted public opinion against Polish suspicions.

> *"Yes, the Russo-Polish affair looked like being a first class political mess, but I think Stalin's May Day message did a lot to clear up the position. Rather silly to let Goebbels get away with it, to my mind, but the Polish fraternity here must be a pretty reactionary lot."*

The timing of General Sikorski's death raises speculation to this day that his aircraft was sabotaged. It certainly damaged Polish influence in a Britain already paying more attention to its new superpower allies than the country in whose name the war started. The government-in-exile was eventually sidelined in favour of a Stalin-appointed Committee of National Liberation (PKWN).

Russia admitted responsibility for the Katyn deaths in the 1990s.

In the east three spookily quiet months ended as the Battle of Kursk flared on 5th July. A long-expected German offensive foundered on Russian defences in depth and massive numerical superiority.

> *"Yes, the Russian front has flared up again, I wonder if it's a new offensive? We shall soon see. Well, they've had two years and I don't suppose they will be any more successful this time."*

In the middle of the month Hitler halted the attack and transferred reserves south to face the British and American threat in Sicily, where landings had started on 10th.

> *"News looks good from Sicily, doesn't it? How it will shake Musso if we make a clean sweep of it. What a boomerang his declaration of war has proved to be. I don't think that country will ever make a flippant declaration of war again in its lifetime."*

Mussolini was sacked on 24th July and arrested on 25th in a coup organised by King Victor Emmanuel III, a necessary but not yet sufficient condition for the country's surrender.

A Soviet counter offensive delivered a strategic victory at Kursk with the searing human cost routine on the Eastern Front.

Crammer

On 23rd July Eric joined 232 AA (OFC) Training Regiment at Arborfield, the Army Technical School near Reading,[32] for a two-

---

[32] Earlier in the year Mary Churchill – Winston's daughter and a newly-commissioned ATS officer – did a ten-week posting with 205 (Mixed) HAA Regiment there.

week total immersion course. The timing makes it likely it was on the Canadian GL 3 Mk 1, which was available slightly earlier than the British Mk 2 the gunners eventually took to France. The censors cut out of the letters (literally) any reference to the course content so it is impossible to be sure.

> *"The new equipment we are learning to handle is very involved but very interesting."*
>
> *"… they haven't half slammed things on to us since we've been here. Yesterday we went out on a 'siting exercise' and returned at some unearthly hour…*
>
> *The course is proceeding quite well. Captain Kilner is with us and amuses every one with his gesticulations of despair when the instructors delve into things…*
>
> *We are out again this evening until about ten pm so you can see we haven't much time to spare. Still, I think it's damned ridiculous to keep us at base all these weeks, then to cram everything into a fortnight. Typical of the army way of doing things. The RAF operators have as many weeks as we have days learning this sort of thing."*

The GL 3 trailer with its built-in transmitter, receiver and generator was a vast improvement on its predecessor but a tight fit for the crew sharing it with hundreds of valves in the July heat.

> *"Working on the instruments in this weather is something akin to murder. There is in particular a horrible little room into which about four of us have to squeeze and we generally come out as potential stretcher cases."*

The unrelenting pace made no allowance for rank, prior knowledge, or lack of it.

"When I think of the old static GL days and consider what we are doing now, it seems incredible. The officers cut a really pathetic figure – they are expected to get a grasp of it all, and of course, they haven't the 'background experience' that most of us have.

Tonight all the Troop sergeants are going out on a night exercise and then have to be ready to take their own troops out at 6.30 a.m. And then an exam in the evening!"

"… Yesterday we did our first real Troop scheme – the ones before have been in the nature of NCOs practices – and things went remarkably well, except for the fact that the predictor we were carrying overturned in one of the lorries and of course bashed itself up a bit. Needless to say there will be quite a row about it. Fortunately I agitated about a box for it before I went, and removed the telescopes as an extra precaution, but I'm principally worried in case there's a Court of Inquiry, which may postpone leave again. I'm now awaiting a report from workshops, and doing a great deal of swearing – and sweating – ! in the meantime."

With their first child due any day he was less than pleased that all leave was stopped for the course.

"… this, I trust, will not affect a spot of 'compassionate' during the happy event."

He got his compassionate leave – 24 hours' worth – the day after his son's birth. He then had to dash back to the course and leave Jennie to deal with the paperwork. That couldn't be let drift as the baby's food ration depended on it.

"Yes, I have had the book for the extra 10/6 from your pay. I have instructions to hand in my books at the GPO next Monday and get a new one including 8/6 for the expected child. Of course, by *now they have the doctor's certificate to say the expected child has arrived, so I suppose there will be another slight alteration. The baby need not be registered immediately – the only reason for haste is that in these days you can't get a ration book for the child until he is registered."*

So that was the first thing she had to do when she escaped from the nursing home.

"I have been over to Ruislip Manor this afternoon and got H.R. duly registered and collected his ration book, clothing coupons etc."

Apart from tracking the boy's progress daily Eric followed the Italian government's collapse with interest.

"Italy is really boiling up, democratic papers are making their appearance and there are reports of strikes and rioting. I don't think there will be many Germans left there in a few weeks."

"… Italy seems to be heading for revolution. Fascists are being shot at and besieged in their local HQs and generally having no end of a poor time. There are also reports of Germany moving large forces through the Brenner to occupy North Italy."

That was a portent of very unpleasant things to come.

The RAF and USAAF attacked Hamburg repeatedly from 24th July to 3rd August causing over 42,000 civilian deaths and almost completely destroying the city. On the night of 27th ideal conditions led to the first artificial firestorm – a fire so intense that it creates its own tornado. The trick was repeated at Dresden, Tokyo, Hiroshima and Nagasaki.

The raids also escalated electronic war by the first operational use of 'Window': metallised strips dropped in bundles to confuse enemy radar. Each side had tested the idea over a year before but avoided using it in the belief that the other hadn't thought of it.

On the Road Again

The regiment dispersed as the course finished: 169 Battery back to Larkhill replacing 168 Battery who moved to Ipswich. Eric rejoined '206' at Colchester for a short stint at an operational site where, despite little enemy activity, the battery managed to pop off nine rounds at a passing plane.

Army postings were still infuriatingly fickle.

> *"Len Nash called me up today literally choking with rage. He has been after a T.I.'s as long as I have – and that is now some time – and now it appears that Regiment have nominated Bombardier Strudwick to go to Watchet to take the course. Of all people he is the last person to either want the course or derive any profit from it – so of course he goes on it! We are thinking of putting up a spot of passive resistance. I can't say I'm surprised, this idiotic case is typical.*
>
> *At the same time the three trainees (GL) have been posted to us in case they are needed. The people who chose them (for a mobile Battery) have picked two men of about forty, and the third man, who is eighteen, has nil intelligence and a double rupture! Needless to say we are attending to their return tickets with the greatest possible speed."*

The battery left for Ramsgate on 1st September and got as far as Dartford before it diverted to Oxford with no word of explanation.

> *"There is no GL for us here, we are giving a hand generally, but anything sooner than Regimental Guards at Ramsgate. The site is a lovely one, on a golf course near the town and the weather perfect."*

'Giving a hand generally' meant all the fatigues going so Eric was grateful to move on with the GL team to a nearby rocket battery. Better yet, it was a permanent site with decent facilities.

> *"I have just arrived at the 'Z' battery site and it is a real blessing to find a decent bed, showers and mess awaiting me. I am doing a training programme as well as the usual manning."*
>
> *"… The 'Z' Battery sergeants are a jolly crowd. They were formerly with an anti tank regiment and consider it rather a come down doing this work! – and they do work hard.*
>
> *The Home Guard man the guns at night and seem very keen. Their duty comes round about every eight days. I consider it rather lucky to be here at least we don't live 'messy'."*

Of course there was a downside.

> *"I am afraid that while we are here we shall not be very lucky for any short leave, darling. The trouble about all this static work we are doing is that it has to be done on our mobile establishment, which employs far fewer men than the static one. For instance we have to supply a plotting team, which is never required in a mobile role."*

Four men on long leave, one on compassionate leave and two seconded to telephone duties left him seven plus himself to man the GL and semi-automatic plotter; luckily the *Luftwaffe* was still keeping its head down.

The army laid on extra entertainment to stave off any chance of boredom.

> *"We are having a very varied training programme on this site. We are doing signalling, and rocket and Bofors gunnery in addition to our usual work, and tomorrow we are doing motor cycle*

training. Looks as though the GL section will be extremely versatile soon."

"… I have been pretty busy these last few days. Have evolved a mobile drill for the plotter and forwarded it with necessary diagrams to Regiment. Then we are proceeding with our very full training programme."

Exercise *Harlequin* in summer 1943 had two objectives: to practise deploying large forces for an invasion; and to convince the Germans that it had started, drawing them out to fight on Allied terms. It morphed into *Starkey* on 9th September, when a dummy invasion fleet set sail for Boulogne. The Germans weren't fooled and ignored the whole thing.

On 3rd September Allied forces crossed from Sicily to the Italian mainland, landing in Calabria (the 'toe' of Italy). The Italian capitulation was signed on the same day but not announced until 8th to allow time to prepare for German reaction. Poor planning and communication allowed the Germans to take control of most territory not already occupied by the Allies, and some Italian forces remained loyal to the Axis. Most of the Italian Navy escaped to Egypt or Malta, or was destroyed, but fighting in Italy continued almost to the last day of the European war.

"Italy's surrender is quite magnificent news isn't it? I've saved a copy of the News Chronicle of the historic morning and I do feel persuaded at last that we are beginning to see the end, though it looks as though plenty of fighting is still in store for us in Italy.

What a wretched position that country is in now and what a just retribution, when you consider the way in which they trampled on France and Greece, to say nothing of Spain and Abyssinia. I can't visualise the Germans clearing out before they have transformed Italy into a battleground."

The Allies landed at Salerno on 9th September. Determined German resistance came worryingly close to winning the ten-day battle. They were able to fall back in good order on a succession of prepared lines which turned the occupation of a supposedly defeated country into a prolonged nightmare. Churchill's 'soft underbelly' of the Axis proved, in the words of General Mark Clark (Allied commander at Salerno), 'one tough gut.'

The endless, bloody grind left the troops on the ground weary and cynical – especially after the Normandy landings drew public attention northward. Their cynicism found perfect expression in a song written a year later by Lance-Sergeant Harry Pynn, to the tune of 'Lili Marlene.' One verse is enough to give the flavour:

> *"We landed at Salerno, a holiday with pay,*
> *Jerry brought the band down to cheer us on our way*
> *Showed us the sights and gave us tea,*
> *We all sang songs, the beer was free.*
> *We are the D-Day Dodgers, way out in Italy."*

On 12th September German paratroops rescued Mussolini from prison at the Campo Imperatore ski resort in the Appenines. He remained puppet leader of the Fascist rump of Italy until his execution in April 1945.

On 11th 206 Battery took part in Exercise *Blitz* to test defences under heavy air, ground and gas attacks.

> *"We have had a weekend exercise-cum-air co-op which has been rather arduous and boring."*

Then after three weeks at Oxford two batteries ('169' were still at Larkhill) moved to Braunstone Camp at Leicester. A spit-and-polish posting, it at least offered new toys.

"However there are some consolations here – we have a wealth of new equipment to practice on. We have a searchlight GL when we can get it working! – a Mark III and a 'light warning'[33].

In addition, to instructing on these, I am immersed in M.T. [Motor Transport] work – doing everything I can on the lorries and driving at least once every day. So I shall hope to emerge from here the complete driver!

It's really good when you begin to feel your feet on driving and there's a lot to learn about maintenance and checks etc.

We had an amusing afternoon yesterday. We took our searchlight lorry out to fill up with petrol. I drove her out of the camp and was doing, as I thought, quite nicely. Approaching the main gate I changed into lower gear to take the exit slowly, but had a job to get the gear in. Beckerman, who was 'watching over me' said 'All right, I'll put it into gear' – did so, and when I let in the clutch the lorry shot backwards – he had put it into reverse!

Funniest thing was, the relieving guard was marching along behind us – all very Regimental and proper, and they scattered in all directions. I laughed about that all the way to the petrol dump."

Playtime finished nine days later when Eric set off with the 206 Battery advance party to take over two operational sites at Great Yarmouth and Oulton Broad, near Lowestoft. 168 and 169 Batteries reunited at Norwich.

"There seems to be action in plenty. The guns here fired 20 rounds last night, one of several occasions. The Battery will move in

---

[33] Possibly 'local warning:' a radar scanning a wide sector at maximum range to cue in the gun-laying set on an approaching raid. Obsolescent GL sets were often used for this.

on Wednesday and we are busy checking all accommodation, stores, etc. There's plenty of that to do."

"… The place we have arrived at is so badly equipped that we in the advance party have spent nearly every minute dashing around for coal, bath facilities, laundry arrangements and a dozen and one other things. In the early hours of the morning we guided the convoy in (six a.m. to be precise) and now everybody is settled in, cursing heartily and cursing the move that took them out of Leicester.

I have since taken myself and four GL men out to a mixed static site (much to their delight!) We are here in charge of the plotting control, as the 'F' troop site has no GL and as they fire nearly every night here we should get some action. But I shall probably be over at 'E' Troop shortly as there is a Mark II and a Mark III there."

Luftwaffe activity was light overall but East Anglia came in for a fair proportion of what there was. '206' saw sustained action during the nights of 7th, 23rd and 24th October.

"We had actions on Wednesday night, and on Thursday. The last was pretty hectic. I was on the mixed site on that occasion, when we passed through barrage plots to 'F' Troop, about a mile away. About eight 'hostiles' attacked a nearby aerodrome, and the firing was fast and furious. The mixed site were firing electrically operated guns, each gun firing at the rate of one round every 2½ seconds, and with our guns joining in about a mile away it sounded like Alamein!

I was rather bucked by the proceedings as our effort was an all GL one, with [Eric] as Plotting Officer! In fact we opened the ball with a barrage at long range. I hate to add that we didn't hit anything, but we meant well…

Well, we finally retired to bed, and then to my astonishment I was awakened and told to pack my things and report to the Lowestoft site. It transpired that the GL there was out of action, Len Nash away on a course, they hadn't fired and Kilner was throwing forty fits. The amusing part was that this site had a Mk II and a Mk III!

There was plenty of trouble to clear up, mostly on account of the damned radio mechs, who I am suspecting more than ever of being saboteurs. Of course no checks had been made worth mentioning, with the inevitable consequences, and of course Kilner went completely off his nut, and dashed around making things worse.

I've only been off the set for meals for the last 48 hours and feel pretty weary tonight. However, things are more shipshape and we ought to be able to put up a show in the event of a return visit."

The night of 7th also brought the *Luftwaffe's* first use of 'Düppel,' their equivalent of 'Window,' in a raid on London. A Putney dance hall was destroyed with the loss of 76 lives.

On 18th November the RAF opened an all-out assault, lasting four months, on Berlin. Some 2,000 people were killed and 175,000 made homeless the first night. Hitler demanded revenge.

Final Preparation

206 Battery moved to Ullesthorpe in Leicestershire on 2nd November. This was their home for nearly four months, though they didn't have time to get comfortable. They spent the first half of December practising anti-aircraft shoots at Tonfanau firing camp near Towyn on the mid-Wales coast. After three days to clean and repair the kit they went back to Redesdale for a week (including Christmas) for field gunnery practice on the Otterburn range. Eric in the meantime spent three weeks mastering the AA No 3 Mk 2 radar and rejoined the battery at Otterburn.

In early November RAF reconnaissance confirmed intelligence reports of peculiar facilities going up in France. Each featured a building shaped like a ski on its side (hence 'ski sites') and a ramp pointing towards London. New evidence connected them with the pilotless aircraft under development at Peenemünde. Energetic bombing successfully delayed the start of the now-imminent V1 campaign. The press published garbled reports of pilotless bombers, secret rockets – and British jet fighters – from early January 1944. The V1s got here first.

The Tehran Conference between Churchill, Roosevelt and Stalin took place at the end of November. They agreed on support to Tito's partisans in Yugoslavia, attempts to draw Turkey into the war on the Allied side, and – at last – a commitment to landings in France the next year. Stalin's allegedly joking proposal to execute 50,000 – 100,000 German staff officers after the war was unceremoniously rejected but he came away with agreement to a westward expansion of the Russian border at Poland's expense. The Poles would be compensated with an equivalent area of Germany.

On Boxing Day *Scharnhorst*, perhaps the *Kriegsmarine*'s most successful capital ship, sank off North Cape while trying to attack a Russian convoy. With her forward radar disabled by the convoy escorts she didn't know she was running onto *Duke of York*'s 14-inch guns. There were just 36 survivors from a crew of 1,968.

In January 1944 the *Luftwaffe* began the reprisals Hitler had demanded for the RAF Berlin raids. Operation *Steinbock*, known in Britain as the 'Little Blitz,' kicked off on the night of 21st with the heaviest attack on London since July 1942. Despite several weeks' preparation, new electronics, tactics and aircraft (the Heinkel 177 four-engine bomber) the early raids achieved little and took heavy losses. Results improved as the campaign continued into February and March, but it remained expensive; around 8% of sorties did not return. Londoners on the other hand did not relish having to dive for the shelters again and it was a doubly anxious time for 60th, busy elsewhere.

"... I must say I was feeling rather worried at the news. I don't know if I was just stupid to imagine that nothing serious in the way of raids would occur again, perhaps it was wishful thinking..."

January took the regiment to the Bedford area for a week-long exercise (*Bloomer*) and a two-day Exercise (*Watling*) at Daventry.

"Johnnie Tekel said he could imagine a certain sergeant who lives for mobile drill taking his kids to the country after the war and getting them to remove the wheels in record time, also jamming the car between trees and camouflaging it."

The guns went to Yorkshire for Exercise *Eagle* in February leaving the radar teams behind. The entire regiment then concentrated at Grimsby, where it remained until mid-April. Now part of 21st Army Group, it was temporarily reassigned to Air Defence Great Britain (ADGB) because of the renewed threat. This triggered a move back to operational sites in the Great Yarmouth/Lowestoft area. Passing through Beccles High Street Eric noticed a shop called "Geoffrey Nudd" and thought the name had a nice ring to it; Jennie was pregnant again.

Over fifty planes attacked London on the night of 18th April in the city's last major raid by manned aircraft. Thirteen of them – almost a quarter of the raiders – were lost. The *Luftwaffe* then turned its remaining strength on the build-up of forces for the approaching invasion. On 30th April the Fritz-X radio-guided bomb was used over Britain for the first and only time in an attempt to sink a battleship at Plymouth.

The government knew however that the assault of the robot V-weapons could not be long delayed. Luckily the more alarming casualty predictions were unfounded.

Press reports in April describing the murder of 70,000 Jews in Odessa gave a further clue to the scale of the Holocaust.

Figure 11: Sergeants of 'F' Troop. Eric is third from left. The next two (kneeling and seated) are Tommy Adams and Sammy Beckerman. The location is probably Evenley Hall, Northamptonshire.

Amid tightened security, the troop's address became 'F Troop, 206 HAA Bty RA, 60th Regt RA, Army Post office, England.' Formal group photos were taken for the record, to be used in the event of triumph or disaster in the coming battle.

"We were dished out with the 'tam o'shanter' hats early in the week, and then subsequently we had a photographer down to take pictures of groups. I have ordered quite a collection, one of the Battery, one of the Troop, another of the GL section and enclosed is a picture of the Sergeants of the Troop."

"… I'm afraid all these are very unimaginative 'collective' ones. Funny how there is generally only one idea of taking a picture of a number of people. Old Frank Charman[34] would doubtless be excessively pained at the sight of them."

---

[34] A news photographer noted for his 'creative' approach to assignments.

On 10th May they pulled back to concentration areas in Northamptonshire for repairs, loading trials and to waterproof their vehicles for landing.

> *"Well, nothing even remotely exciting is happening to us – except that we had to do our own cooking today and even then nobody was taken ill...*
>
> *Have been doing the usual spots of mending and washing. I was forced by a domestic state of emergency to do a spot of darning and got into rather a tangle. I thought it might be a good idea to pad out the sock with another one – and inevitably, of course, sewed them nicely together."*

Route marches and the occasional exercise kept them from going stale.

> *"We revived a bit of our Hertford infantry training yesterday with a spot of 'Troop in the attack' – which was taken with the usual lightheartedness. You can never persuade gunners to take an infantryman's job seriously. In one particular case a troop making the final assault wiped out their own rifle group giving covering fire. If ever we undertook this role we should probably finish up by attacking an American unit – or a Canadian, which would be suicidal. Probably 206's only success in the assault role was that battle with the Home Guard at Ullesthorpe."*

The countryside crawled with servicemen of all natures.

> *"Some of us walked down to the local pub for a drink the other night and found it full of the RAF. Eventually one of them approached us and intimated that he would like to buy us all a drink. Needless to say, we didn't say no! He proved to be a most interesting bloke. He was an American who has joined the Canadian Air Force and*

> *he has fought in the Spanish Civil War – for the 'Reds' of course!*
> *Naturally the conversation turned on 'For Whom the Bell Tolls' and*
> *he didn't think much of it!"*

After a command conference with General Montgomery the regiment came to six hours' readiness from 28th May. With unfortunate timing Eric chose that weekend for a quick run home in borrowed army transport.

> *"The trip created quite a sensation in the mess. Of course everyone was very envious and a few quite annoyed about the chance they had missed…*
>
> *I managed the business in quite good time and was back about 1.30 p.m. I did enjoy the opportunity of driving such a long distance, and the return trip went particularly well."*
>
> *"… I'm being watched by the mess after that last effort – in fact Tommy Adams declared he has two men trailing me."*

On Sunday 4th June an Associated Press operator mistakenly fed a practice tape into the live teletype feed to America. In the five minutes it took to retract the flash announcement of Allied landings in France hundreds of radio stations picked up the news, bells were rung and prayers said.[xxxvi]

Two days later it was true and the troops' boredom instantly dispelled.

> *"Well, what do you think of the news? Needless to say there hasn't been much else talked about since Monday – or rather Tuesday – it already seems a long time ago. Funny enough, we were talking one day before about running an 'invasion sweep' and of course it got cracking too fast for us."*
>
> *"… The mess is getting to be a bit of a nightmare. They are all*

practising French as hard as they can go and with the wet weather we have had today they are all in tonight, jabbering away in a most horrible collection of accents punctuated by fierce arguments as to who's saying it right. I think Sammy Beckerman must combine his French with a bid of Yiddish."

In an echo of the invasion fears a couple of years earlier, newspapers warned their readers of a possible airborne counter-attack to disrupt Allied logistics and reinforcements.

That didn't happen but a test salvo of V1s hit London on 13th June. The assault began in earnest with 120 launched on 15th. The attacks were expected and the ADGB guns moved promptly and efficiently to their planned 'Diver' (anti-V1) sites. The new targets were very difficult to hit: they flew too fast for a manually-trained 3.7 to track, and at a height just between the effective envelopes of light and heavy guns. The gunners had to learn fast: better equipment, tactics, skills and siting increased the kill ratio from 17% of those crossing the gun belt in the first week to 80% by late summer.

It was frustrating for gunners trapped in rural concentration areas.

"I know most of the fellows here are thinking of the people at home. The Kent men are, of course, particularly concerned. Len Nash reports some damage to his house, and there are one or two other cases in his district."

"… To be quite candid, I feel dreadful about the raids and the circumstances and feel particularly awful about being away from you at this time. I suppose there are others in the same boat but it doesn't help with the immediate problem. The only consolation is that the prospects of us clearing the Germans out of France seem pretty good, and we won't be bothered with their damned inventions much longer."

168 and 169 Batteries moved up to their marshalling area at Wanstead Flats in London as the first flying bombs landed. They loaded their vehicles on 15th; troops boarded on 16th and sailed for Normandy on 17th. They were trapped aboard by heavy seas and couldn't unload until 22nd.

206 Battery in the meantime kicked its heels in Northamptonshire until 27th when it moved up to the Tilbury marshalling area, boarding at Tilbury on 29th and 30th.

The gunners of 60th were on active service.

NORMANDY

Arrival

Courseulles-sur-Mer, Juno Beach, Sunday 2nd July 1944. The June storms had abated but the weather was still wet and blustery.

Somewhere in the seething mass of transport, yet another landing ship dropped its ramp. A wiry sergeant splashed ashore leading a five-ton lorry and its clumsy radar trailer; the rest of 206 Battery followed. Eric, like most men crossing the beach that day, was on his first trip abroad.

"The arrival and landing were quite a thrill. We had an absolutely marvellous crossing – it was calm and just like a pleasure cruise – the blokes gambled in francs all the way across and either became broke or made fortunes. Otherwise it was uneventful – except for a couple of depth charges dropped, causing a bit of a commotion. Then eventually France hove in sight and the rain and mist cleared away and we had a view of the most enormous collection of ships imaginable – it seemed you could almost walk ashore on them, and not a hostile plane in sight."

"We didn't land that night. We were ordered down below, and then there was some slight enemy action – and of course the Navy blew away ad lib at what must have been a couple of planes. It sounded like a battle royal under hatches, and we didn't like the idea of remaining there much, and a smoke screen they laid down didn't help – for a few horrible moments we thought the ship was on fire!

However the night passed and in the morning we were bunged ashore bright and early. Mine was the first vehicle of Battery to come ashore, me guiding it in in eighteen inches of water! Brrr! The atmosphere was very hearty and congenial, as Vic Boyes remarked, even the MPs were smiling at us."

Since 6th June the Allies had poured 177,000 vehicles and nearly a million men into a beachhead much shallower than expected. Seventy miles wide, it was nowhere more than twenty-five and in some places only five miles deep. Caen, a day one objective, was still in enemy hands after the bloody failure of three assaults.

The planners assumed a need for dense anti-aircraft protection of the beaches. In the event USAAF daylight bombing had destroyed much of the *Luftwaffe's* fighter strength and fuel reserves, allowing the landings to proceed with little air interference. The German army's angry refrain throughout the coming battle was *"Wo ist die Luftwaffe?"* Even so, by mid-June their fighters and fighter-bombers were raiding the beachhead and front line by day, with fast medium bombers taking over at night.

By 24th June a protective Inner Artillery Zone (IAZ) covered the coast from Port en Bessin to Ouistreham. The 136 heavy guns' range extended north over the vulnerable sea approaches and south over the front line. 270 light guns, 44 searchlights, 30 smoke units and a line of barrage balloons along the coast completed the ground air defences.

60th HAA Regiment's 168 and 169 Batteries finally unloaded on 22nd June after four days bouncing around in weather too rough for landing. They took up position to defend temporary airfields near Martragny and Basly.

RAF airmen were naturally keen to operate over the bridgehead without being shot at by their own side. Anti-aircraft batteries' rules of engagement were thus so restrictive that the gunners must at times have wondered why they were there at all. Despite this 169 Battery shot down an enemy aircraft on 25th June.

Tension between airmen and gunners came to a head on 27th June, when three of 60th's four landed troops moved to fill gaps in the beach defences with a secondary field role as needed. The order explicitly stated that airfield commanders "have NO power to restrict fire."xxxvii

Over time ground and counter-battery fire, including suppression of enemy air defences, came to dominate the gunners' work. Two other regiments earned their keep by tracking enemy aircraft mining the sea approaches. As well as engaging the minelayers directly the radar crews plotted mine release, telling the Navy sweepers where to look.xxxviii

The first order of business for '206' was to catch up with the regiment and leave a spot known precisely to German gunners. The battery set up shop at Esquay-sur-Seulles about ten miles from Bayeux, to defend the city against air attack.

> *"We moved inland very early the next morning and in one small village an elderly couple came to the window in their nightshirts to wave to us and there were plenty working in the fields who gave us some very cheery greetings, and so very few signs of the recent fighting except a building damaged here and there."*
>
> *"And there it is. We are just doing our old job now, and it might be a site at Lowestoft or Ullesthorpe, very English little fields and roads and tons and tons of mud!"*

On the day '206' landed Hitler sacked his Commander-in-Chief West. Field Marshal von Rundstedt had committed the sin of asking to withdraw after the 'Scottish Corridor,' a salient west of Caen, held off his counter-attack.

On 7th July the preliminary bombing started for Operation

Charnwood, a new assault. Four hundred and fifty heavy bombers dropped 2,500 tons of bombs on Caen, but released many well back from their targets for fear of hitting friendly troops. The city took far worse punishment than the German defences.

> *But anything the Germans have ever done to us pales beside the kind of raid the RAF can make nowadays. I saw one in progress here and was almost shocked at the ferocity of it. It was absolute hell, one incessant rumble of bombs that could be felt even at a good distance. You could see the ack ack defence gradually go to pieces and it was pretty awful to think of any human beings having a taste of it, even the Huns."*

Charnwood launched on 8th July and over two days succeeded in taking the northern ruins of the city as far as the banks of the Orne. The assault also took Carpiquet Airfield – another D-Day objective – but failed to capture the whole city and the southerly heights (Bourgébus Ridge) as hoped. Hill 112, a critical high point west of Caen, was briefly retaken before succumbing to a counter-attack. Casualties were appalling; most infantry battalions took 25 percent losses. Two more equally savage battles were needed to bring the whole city under Allied control: Operations *Jupiter* (10th July) and *Goodwood* (18th – 20th July). Even then, Bourgébus Ridge remained in German hands.

The long struggle for Caen illustrates the brutal, static early campaign. The German defenders were of roughly equal strength at first, well dug-in, skilled, equipped and motivated. The *bocage* countryside – small fields divided by the high earth banks and hedges familiar to Devon folk – strongly favoured them.

Repeated, bloody assaults for what looked like pitiful gains on a map must have felt like a re-run of Flanders thirty years earlier. The crucial difference was that the Allies could replace their losses; the Germans could not.

Bayeux Holiday

Meanwhile, perhaps as much as ten miles from the fighting, life settled into a routine.

"I haven't really adapted my nature to war. But then neither have the majority of us. We are a conglomeration of placid inoffensive fellows guided and directed by the people whose minds can cope with these gigantic efforts, and who possess the suitable outlook. Nobody really wants to stick his neck out for anything, but when he is trained and directed to do so he does it with surprising efficiency and his thoughts are more with his family than with the tactical situation unless he happens to be an immediate part of it.

I have hated the Germans for the first time since I have been forced to read about the flying bomb attacks on England… Sometimes I have been impelled to urge you to go down to Bristol. If the raids get worse please do so…

Life proceeds very calmly and rather monotonously. We do our spells and rest in the interim and don't feel particularly heroic. The French kiddies swarm around the place and say 'Thank you very much' when they relieve us of our chocolate rations. To our 'Bonjours' they always retort 'Good morning' and there we stick. Oh. There's another one; 'Cigarette for Papa, please' and away goes another Naafi doofer. I think half the little devils smoke them themselves."

"… As regards the personal angle; well there is not such a great difference in our living conditions now as when we used to be in England, on an ordinary site. We are in tents and live on 'compo' rations, which means everything out of tins plus a staple diet of biscuits. It's not very exciting and one misses the 'bulk' but it seems adequate at least, and there is a surprising variety in the menus. Better than bully beef all the time, which was the lot of the soldier in the last war.

When we first came here we were issued with 24 hour ration packs, plus a small Tommy cooker, which supplied porridge, stewed meat, oxo, tea etc. But we were on the move so quickly that it was a miracle if you managed to get anything ready. It invariably ended with me eating some chocolate and getting to hell out of it. But the idea was pretty good. It all really depended on how quick you were. Some blokes who have to be dragged up to do some normal work are greased lightning when it comes to filling the stomach."

There was time for a spot of sightseeing and shopping. The relative normality of Bayeux made a stark contrast with the vicious contest for Hill 112 a few miles away.

"The country resembles an enormous army camp. One can't move for troops and vehicles, field after field and road after road, a never ending procession. It's about as interesting and varied as Salisbury plain.

I have visited Bayeux and it's the same thing there. The whole city is just a mass of khaki all prowling around like hungry wolves in the hopes of finding a stray cafe open and selling food. I had two drinks – the first was watery lemonade, the second something like a mixture of weak peppermint and vivid green ink. I don't know what the hell they called it but of course we found a name for it. I think a shipload of beer to restore army morale is indicated.

The cathedral however is worth seeing. They are displaying a copy of the famous tapestry, which gives an account of Harold's visit to Normandy and William's subsequent invasion: great bursts of irreverent laughter because the boats depicted there looked exactly like tank landing craft!"

"… I sent off three little children's books to you today – they are very attractively printed and illustrated. We can also send food to the

Figure 12: Two postcards of Bayeux

amount of five pounds weight, so I hope to procure cheese (a very nice creamed variety) and some butter – about all they have to offer in the eats line here…

Pleased to hear that Hugh Robert's progress in the sitting up line. I don't suppose the trouble with his teeth will last long."

"I went into Bayeux again recently, and bought some postcards, not a good selection, but perhaps they give you an idea of the place. It really is quite an attractive town but utterly spoilt by the number of soldiers tramping around… We managed to get something to eat this time, after queuing, nothing very brilliant, just meat and cabbage. Potatoes are rationed, and it must have been a potatoless day! Bought about four more books, mostly for children, which I will send with the next parcel.

The people strike me as the most realistic bunch I have ever encountered. I think they prefer us to the Germans, but apart from that they are not demonstrative. The blokes who thought they would be putting garlands of flowers around their necks are slightly bewildered. But De Gaulle is very prominent in all the shop windows, no doubt about what they feel about him.

One can't help being struck by their lack of undue sentiment, and a pride in themselves. There's certainly no inferiority in their attitude, which, considering their four years under German rule, speaks a lot for their strength of character. I like the sophistication of the children. There were two little girls of about eight in that café who looked after the door and saw to it that the place didn't get too full, and did it very well.

I was also amused at a selection of German books tucked away on a lower shelf in one bookshop. One could imagine them saying 'Ah well. New customers, better put up a new selection, something more to the English taste.'"

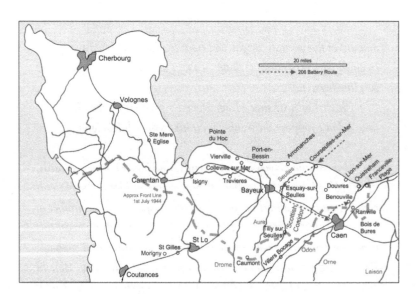

Map 5: Courseulles to Bénouville

A 'Party Conversation' epigram in the *Sunday Express* of 2nd July read: *"It's no use blaming the French if they're a little cool towards the invaders. It's difficult to love a man who has just blown your home to bits."* Rex North wrote in the *Sunday Pictorial* on 18th June that over half the civilians he had met in Normandy had no particular wish to be liberated, that the Allies' most urgent task was to convince them that *"… we are not bombing and blasting their cities just to save ourselves."*

General de Gaulle visited Bayeux to a tumultuous reception in mid-June. He arrived with far more people and luggage than expected (exasperating Montgomery) and left behind four officials as the nucleus of a provisional government.

Mail delivery home was intermittent, though it could get to the troops from Britain in two days when all went well. Generally, however, Allied logistics worked peerlessly. Most of the 400 British tanks lost in Operation *Goodwood* were replaced within 36 hours, and even the beer shortage was eventually sorted.

"All our wants are fairly well catered for. The cigarette supply is quite reasonable, and one gets soap, razor blades etc. And the first supply of beer arrived last week. I also collected a bottle of whisky for 8/6[35]. Amazing isn't it? I think I shall broach it on the occasion of Hugh's birthday, only don't tell him that's only an excuse."

"… It was funny when that beer arrived last weekend. There was all of a sudden a great shouting and bawling and running to and fro and I made a dive for my Sten under the impression it was a Rommel breakthrough. There were already some guns blazing away quite near and some engineers letting off some explosive a couple of fields away but the row 206 kicked up surpassed both. It even brought

---

[35] The *Evening News* on 6th July reported from a Normandy recreation area where whisky was 6d a nip but beer cost 1/6d a bottle.

the Troop Commander out of a private place in a great hurry, looking most hurt and very undignified."

"The variety of canned foods is really amazing. We had meat pudding the other day – some of the best I've ever tasted. Some of the fellows think their wives will get wise to it after the war – or hand a 48 hour ration pack to their husbands and clear off for the weekend."

Despite the reassuring tone of the letters it wasn't all safe. On 8th July, at the height of *Charnwood*, 206 Battery supplied working parties to bring ammunition up to the front.

"We have also paid a visit to the front line on an ammo replenishing run. It was most interesting to proceed right through the areas of the recent fighting, but very depressing to see the extent of the devastation. One small town was literally razed to the ground. As one person said 'Cor! We've liberated this place all right. House by house' which about puts that overworked expression where it belongs. The Germans are fighting for every yard of ground."

Otherwise the camp was fairly comfortable.

"Although life isn't so exciting, there is plenty to do. Re-organisation, re-painting of equipment, training, etc. takes up most of the time we have. The men have a football pitch and we have rigged up deck tennis in place of that murderous basketball, which nearly deprived us of half the NCOs for the invasion!"

"… Field life isn't so bad, really, it is surprising what dodges you can get up to. We rig up a bath with a waterproof sheet tied up at the corners, make a shower with a tin with some holes in it. The generator dries all our clothes overnight when washday comes round. Everybody is most noticeably healthy. There is a craze for shaved

heads, some of the blokes look really dreadful, but it's recommended as being more hygienic. I'm not that hygienic yet."

Further west, on 11th July, the Americans launched their advance toward St Lô and Périers. Field Marshall Rommel's career ended on 17th when two Spitfires attacked his car and drove it into a ditch. Rommel was thrown from the vehicle and suffered head injuries forcing his return to Germany for treatment. Marshall von Kluge succeeded him, taking command of Army Group B while remaining Commander-in-Chief West.

On 20th July *Wehrmacht* plotters tried to assassinate Hitler and stage a coup. Lieutenant Colonel Claus von Stauffenberg planted a bomb at a meeting chaired by Hitler in his field headquarters. The explosion injured Hitler but did not kill him. Believing they had succeeded the conspirators showed their hand by launching the next phase of their plan; nearly 5,000 were executed in the subsequent round-up. Rommel knew of the plot but argued against assassination, and was too famous to disgrace publicly. He was 'invited' to commit suicide.

"The 'purge' in Germany caused great excitement. Any news suggesting an ending to the war is good news to the troops. But I think it is premature to expect an early collapse."

Too right.

Back to Work

The relaxed life was too good to last. The end of *Goodwood* prompted a move east; in the words of the regimental war diary for 24th July *"Leave Bayeux area for Caen area."*[xxxix] From Eric's point of view:

"We have been thrust into very sudden activity, and it has rather upset my schedule.

The weather has been awful: we have been moving and digging in torrential rain which has poured down without stopping. I have found that the only way to keep myself dry on these occasions is to strip down to a pair of pants and just work through it – and as I demanded that all the rest did the same we had a nice collective bath.

Well, the Battery is seeing some real action now, and acquitting itself very well. The shooting is very fast and straight, and we appear to be appreciated, by the way we move about. My section is grand. I've never seen a bunch work harder and keep so cheerful. Just like the old Estuary days."

Action and its aftermath brought mixed emotions.

"Caen is an awful mess. The fighting there must have been extremely bitter, and every yard bears the marks of it. What amazed me was the presence of civilians there, one just couldn't imagine anyone left. And what is more, they gave us a really warm reception – it seems that the more these people have to suffer, the more warm hearted they are. I tasted my first glass of French wine there."

"Funny you mentioning the flying bomb in connection with the feeling of hatred it arouses. I feel exactly the same as you do, but I'm sadly afraid that the mischief has been done as regards any feelings of clemency towards the Germans. The men really hate them for this last business. Their attitude to the German prisoners that pass leaves one in no doubt about that. But I don't know about it causing another war. The Russians will certainly take no chances and I think the handling of Germany can safely be left to them. I know that even to mention 'a square deal' for Germany is to provoke a howl of

*Figure 13: 3.7-inch gun being towed by an AEC matador lorry
through the ruins of Caen
(Photograph No. B 8768 from the Imperial War Museum
collection No. 4700-29)*

*indignation. The flying bomb is obviously a party propaganda
weapon and anybody who uses it to kill civilians wholesale for mere
publicity, to give the Germans something palatable to read, is pretty
low in the scale. After all, we do go for the munitions centres."*

A *Sunday Express* editorial on 2nd July argued for massive
destruction of German cities in revenge for the V1 attacks.

*"As one who has always taken the view that Germans have been
forgiven and let off too lightly too often in history, I am all for making
the lesson this time a memorable and final one."*

Eric's view was less vindictive, more practical and widely held in the army:

> *"What we all want now is a good hard drive up the Channel coast to those damned flying bomb bases – which would be the most popular offensive of all time."*

Despite the *Luftwaffe*'s dismal showing on D Day itself – and the hard-pressed *Wehrmacht*'s complaints – it could still make its presence felt.

> *"There is intense competition between Len and myself (several miles apart) to see who can spot and fire on the most raiders. It generally evens itself out, sometimes he is lucky and sometimes we put up the most rounds. There is a terrific jibe the next morning on the phone if either of our particular units has missed a chance of firing, and it adds a great zest to routine.*
>
> *There is an enormous improvement in the handling of the equipment by the ops. We get on to a hostile so quickly now that the gunners complain they fall over themselves to get the first rounds off. Still, it has vastly increased their respect for us. One hears no more about the 'fish and chip shop' or 'the box of tricks that never works!' We contemplate going round with a hat now at the conclusion of an engagement."*
>
> *"… Despite lack of sleep and more work that we have ever done we are feeling exceptionally well and all keeping very fit. We don't feel so much the poor relation of the artillery who practice a lot of complicated things and do nothing. The period just after we had landed was very flat. The deterrent effect of heavy ack ack fire is most noticeable, and we seem very much in demand, thank goodness."*

German air raids and the nearby front line concentrated minds wonderfully.

"We are all 'funk hole conscious' now – which means digging oneself in to obtain a rest free from all anxiety at night. The initial attitude to this was one of contemptuous indifference – until we moved up and found things going 'boomp in the night' all around. The next morning there wasn't a spade or a shovel to be had for love or money. Blokes generally fiercely averse to burying a bit of rubbish looked set to be going down about twenty feet. The joke is that the opportunity of using them is pretty rare – but I lay in bed and laughed last night! Well, smiled grimly anyway! Mine is quite a posh affair, five feet deep with a box cupboard let into the wall, interior furnishing from a German dug out whose late occupant must have persuaded his French girl friend to part up with some curtaining and such like material. I did a quick recce as soon as I arrived on the scene, and a collection of officers inspecting the dugouts later were somewhat astonished to find large placard which, instead of 'Achtung' etc read 'Booked!! Sgt Nudd'. They got the idea pretty quickly and feverishly inscribed similar notices.

Life is beautifully democratic here. They tried to persuade their batmen to dig their holes for them and the noble fellows said to hell with that – they had themselves to think of. And the things a gunner said to an officer when he caught him furtively walking off with a piece of his corrugated iron simply can't be repeated. 'I didn't know it was yours' said the officer meekly at the finish. 'Well, you bloody-well know now' said the gunner, on his dignity."

Deference was an early casualty of the workload, which stretched the usually cordial relations between battery officers and NCOs.

"Sgt Lake (whose Sten I pinched that time) has a most acid tongue and knows his drills backwards and another Sgt., Anton, narrowly missed becoming a gunnery instructor, and also knows his stuff pretty well. The three of us push 'em around something cruel, it's comic to hear some of the back chat over the phones some nights."

Eric was particularly sore about missing his son's first birthday. He had to track the lad's development remotely as best he could.

"I hope Hugh's birthday went off OK. I daresay there was quite a collection of people there today. We toasted him tonight in the instrument while in action, and celebrated also the firing of a record number of rounds during an air attack. A rather mixed toast, but at least it may be that the more we can do in this respect the sooner we shall all be together again."

"... It was lovely to hear all the news and to receive that super picture of Hugh. Doesn't he look cute? The best picture yet. I think all the boys vote him a corker."

"... Len saw Hugh's picture for the first time yesterday and was very impressed."

"... I shouldn't worry about Hugh taking an occasional tumble. It must be rather a shock but as you say he will have to take a few of them as he begins to get about."

"... So poor old Hugh was stung. One thing about him – he seems to weather all these little complaints and accidents beautifully. Probably thinks the equivalent of 'I can take it'."

... (from Jennie) "Late yesterday I received a notice to take Hugh to Eastcote House by 10 a.m. today to be immunised. Of course the perishing notice had been delayed in the post since Monday. It wasn't very convenient to go but I decided I had better as I have to take him again in a month's time for the second injection, and that will be plenty late enough for me to trail over there. He was very good, in fact he was the only one who didn't 'set up a howl' and the doctor said 'Good chap'.

... This week he has found out how to stand up by his own efforts. He did it first in the play pen and now in the cot and pram. I even found him swanking, holding by only one hand. He will be letting go altogether soon I think"

… (from Jennie) "Hugh is getting more brown than ever. Yesterday as I had washed his sun bonnet I tied one of my coloured scarves on his head to protect the top of his head and back of his neck. He looked like a little Pirate of Penzance. He is getting quite a little tough guy and these last few days has developed a new chortle which suggests that he is going to be a bass baritone – he sounds quite like the villain of the piece."

"… It is grand to hear about Hugh. Your descriptions of him are perfect and give me a very good idea of his progress. Of course the photograph helped as well. Incidentally, I sent the rough proof to Len as he wanted to send it to his wife.

I'm glad he continues to be happy and full of fun – he certainly is a baby to be amused. He ought to be grand fun as he gets older."

"… I couldn't help feeling a bit amused at Hugh's near fatal experiment of eating the soap. I bet he did take a poor view of it! He seems to be fond of playing you up a bit in the shelter, the young devil. Just wait till I get home! Glad to hear he is 'finding his feet' so well. We'll make a skater of him yet."

"… I find it more than exasperating and maddening that I can only sit down here and write about what I feel should be done, without being able to take the least positive action."

His frustration was compounded by knowing that their second child's arrival grew closer by the day.

"It's exciting to contemplate the second, isn't it? Whether, if a boy, he will be like Hugh, or have a different personality, and of course a girl would be very exciting indeed. I rather like 'Geoffrey Alan' for the boy's name – very phonetic!"

Clearing weather on 25th July allowed the Americans to launch Operation *Cobra* on the Allies' right flank. Six days of heavy fighting brought them to open country at the end of the *bocage* – and the Germans to the end of their tether in South West Normandy. The resulting break-out allowed the Allies to close the gate on the 'Falaise Pocket' in late August, trapping the remaining German forces which were then destroyed by air attack.

That outcome was difficult to imagine at Caen; German high command concentrated on the British sector which they thought the greater threat. Consequently the battle there remained static and the beach head crowded.

> *"There is a host of RAF personnel over here, of course. We met some of their wireless men near our site a week or so ago. They were suffering somewhat from near proximity to the Army. They moved hurriedly away from us after our guns had fired a few salvos and then some tanks ran across their new position and cut their cables to pieces!"*

Slow progress brought on criticism from high command and politicians. To put this in context Antony Beevor describes a Red Army liaison officer's visit to 7th Armoured Division HQ. Comparing notes, it turned out that the Russian's sector engaged nine German divisions on a 600 mile front whereas the British in Normandy faced ten divisions (six of them armoured) in sixty-two miles.[xl]

On the Eastern Front a Soviet offensive, Operation *Bagration*, retook vast swathes of land and virtually destroyed one of the three German Army Groups there.

> *"Despite my respect for the efforts being made on this front, the Russians seem to be the main hope of the war finishing quickly. What a sensation if they get to Berlin – it is not beyond the realms of possibility, and soon at that. It's the only possibility the men are really excited about."*

The Red Army entered Poland on 17th July, arriving at the eastern outskirts of Warsaw on 29th. Hoping for imminent liberation the Polish Home Army (resistance) launched an uprising on 1st August which lasted until the end of September. For whatever reason the Russian offensive halted, leaving the Poles to their fate. Some 16,000 Polish soldiers and upwards of 150,000 civilians lost their lives. The Germans then evacuated the city and razed it. Warsaw's remains were eventually 'liberated' in January 1945.

The tide was clearly running in the Allies favour. Turkey broke off diplomatic relations with Germany on 2nd August; Romania switched sides on 24th and the Spanish Government began to assert its neutrality by interning German ships, troops and officials.

The American advance reached Avranches on 30th July and Rennes on 3rd August, threatening to cut off German forces in Brittany. In the meantime Montgomery moved forces to the less heavily defended western end of the British sector and launched Operation *Bluecoat* towards Vire. Low on resources and still focussed on the eastern flank, the Germans were slow to react. Both British and American attacks made rapid progress despite fierce resistance by overwhelmingly outnumbered defenders.

At noon on 1st August General Patton's US Third Army formally came into being. His boss, General Bradley, became Commander-in-Chief of 12th Army Group and thus no longer subordinate to Montgomery.

As American forces besieged the Brittany ports and turned east toward Paris the Germans mounted a strong counter-attack toward Mortain and Avranches in the American rear from 7th to 11th August. The attack was defeated by stubborn fighting on the ground and RAF close air support but there were heavy casualties. Mortain itself was flattened.

7th August also saw the start of a joint Canadian and Polish push, Operations *Totalize* and *Tractable*, toward Falaise. Canadian troops knew that 19 of their countrymen had been shot after surrender by members of the 12th SS Panzer (*Hitler Jugend*) Division. Few prisoners were taken from 12th SS after that.

The beginning of the month was a quiet time for 60th HAA, still defending Caen with little enemy air activity to worry about. E Troop (Len's) deployed on 6th for a ground shoot which was cancelled as the target area had already been captured. On the 10th, 169 Battery moved east of the city to complete its defensive ring.

"We have had quite a long breathing space. The battle has drawn away from us and the gunfire died away to a rumble. Just the back room boys once more! Still long periods of watch, but more fatiguing than exciting. It doesn't help the night pass quickly when nothing happens. Gives the fellows off duty a quiet night, of course.

Some of the interim is being spent in constructing really palatial dug outs. Some of them only require a neon sign and commissionaire to blossom out as night clubs.

Some of the German communal ones are very well constructed and so well reinforced that it must have been the devil of a job to get them out."

"… Will certainly do a sketch of the dug out – which I have since boarded and made more spacious. You would laugh at the recent work on the dugouts. They were only about 3 or 4 feet deep at first, then their owners started to make improvements and since they were boarded over it meant going down. So all over the place you could see showers of earth vomiting out of trap door entrances, for all the world like a colony of moles at work. Then two men built a little chalet half way down an enormous bomb crater, like something out of 'Rio Rita'[36]*"*

---

[36] 'Rio Rita' was a 1929 musical comedy set in Mexico.

His letters ooze reassurance and no doubt understatement. In one passage for example:

> "I hope I haven't given the impression that we are in any danger, darling, because really there isn't the slightest ground for it. We run no more risks in our role than we were exposed to at home – in fact, the periods of real action are so short that they are not even to be compared to the old Estuary days. We had the opportunity of firing quite a bit at first, but it was in our usual role and we didn't receive any personal attention from Jerry. He has more to worry about than our insignificant selves. Now, just in case you imagine we are dashing about doing 'Troop in the attack' and knocking tanks about I must tell you that part of the unit is engaged in gathering in the harvest locally!! There! What a come down! No medals for the likes of us – but may be you won't worry about that!
>
> We could best be described as a 'support arm' of the army. As soon as positions are taken all branches of the Artillery are moved up to provide the necessary barrages for the next attack and for defence of VPs (vulnerable points) – which range from aerodromes to crossroads and ammo dumps etc. So things are liveliest for us when we take up a new position after which we find the 'noise of battle' receding and we are once more all alone – and there is a beautiful calm wherein we sunbathe and devise wonderful dug outs and say what a dull thing life is! Then we get 'Prepare to move' and we all curse like hell!
>
> It's really vastly different from all previous conceptions. I didn't think we would be doing things [in] this quiet matter-of-fact way. Compared with this Eastleigh was a Ypres! But I suppose it is all the immense amount of training we have had that makes things so. It makes you realise why we were moved around so often in England.
>
> It's just the same with everything over here. There is great road courtesy and no breakneck hurry, loads of MPs to direct traffic: every mile

of the road is labelled like an underground station, movement control know precisely which unit is travelling, and to where, and only an utter fool could go wrong. 'Tidiness' is the best word to describe it. The organisation has had my unstinted admiration ever since I've been over here."

Jennie wasn't fooled; she wrote shortly after the landing:

"The idea of you going into the actual fighting zone, although expected, comes as something of a shock to me. Somehow combat seems so very foreign to your nature that I just can't get used to the idea of you being engaged in it. I feel very thankful that you are in the artillery and a more or less technical occupation. First and foremost because it seems to me safer, and secondly because it seems to me a more impersonal way of waging war."

At home, local scouts installed a Morrison shelter for her.

"We still get troubled by 'things that go bump in the night' occasionally. Old Tuck reckons he nearly came out of bed the night before last. Mrs. Tuck, sleeping in the same room, didn't hear anything, neither did I. So I think that must have been just another of the old boy's exaggerations. Personally I think our own planes are nearly as big a menace as the fly bombs. They seem to have a competition on over at Northolt as to who can come nearest to the roof tops."

Rough living inevitably took its toll:

"The camp has been troubled by a rather nasty form of stomach complaint, 'enteretis' [sic] I think is the official designation. I felt pretty bad myself for a couple of days but it doesn't last long, thank goodness, and I'm feeling quite fit now. Anything could be the cause of it I suppose."

"… One of the boys in my section taken away with enteritis has written me from England. I didn't get it bad enough! The complaint seems to be passing."

With the Paras

On 12th August 60th HAA was relieved at Caen and transferred to 1 Corps in support of 6th Airborne Division. They moved up to the Pegasus Bridge area: the strategically critical crossings over the River Orne and the Caen Canal which 6th Airborne had taken in spectacular style on D-Day. 206 Battery camped north-west of Bénouville.

"I'm afraid this will be rather late reaching you again, unfortunately we have been moving about again with but little respite for attention to personal affairs.

I feel very guilty about these periodical lapses, but things get very difficult at these times, and it is generally as much as we can do to get some sleep. However, we are once more settled in and hope things will be normal from tomorrow.

"… the weather has been damned trying. In addition we have all the wasps God (or the devil) made and the mosquitoes are undisputed masters of the air. I never thought there could be so many. People pass you in the mornings with bulging faces and lips… I swear they must be able to dig right through the blankets, because although I am careful not to take any to bed with me, I awake with various parts of my anatomy aching. I generally put a towel over my face and drop off to sleep in a sublime state of suffocation.

It tries ones temper exceedingly. A recent thunderstorm swept through the dugout which I had not the material to make watertight, just when I was getting into bed. The weather is so damned erratic now. I think this nomad life wears exceeding thin with everybody after a few weeks. The trouble is, when you move you can't take the dugout with you. My last one was a corker, but I lived in it three days before relinquishing it. Then nothing can really keep the dust out of your kit and bedding. However, we are luckier than the infantry, who must spend their time in a slit trench without even our meagre comforts."

Operation *Dragoon*, the Allied landings in southern France, started on 15th August. German forces retreating north were harried by resistance groups and replied with savage reprisals.

The radar sections withdrew for maintenance and training on 13th August while the regiment's guns were busy with ground shoots. Eric stayed with the battery. On 15th and 16th August 60th HAA worked with two field regiments, a light artillery regiment and a Belgian field battery to practise an Uncle Target ('drop everything') ground shoot at targets in the Franceville-Plage area at the mouth of the Orne. With about 100 guns firing at once the poor souls on the receiving end may not have understood that it was 'just' a practice.

"The last week has been a very busy one for us. We have been doing some field artillery work and I have set my own job aside to work on corrections for gun data. It's pretty hectic going, you have to get out about six different calculations in less than 3 minutes, but on the whole it's interesting and a change from my usual routine. I have only this to concentrate on, instead of chasing fifteen men around and in that sense it's as good as a rest. Sammy Beckerman has the lads in tow in the interim. He complains occasionally that I don't give him the chance to show any initiative – and so the last time he did so he found himself holding the entire baby."

"… the fact that I couldn't identify the firing handle after all those years on Radar proved to be only a minor hold-up on No. 4 gun"

The light regiment, 53rd Airlanding, became 60th's best buddies – the two worked closely together for the rest of the battle. A representative of 60th went to 53rd on 18th August to improve co-ordination.

On the same day Marshall von Kluge committed suicide: the enemy's defences were cracking as the *Wehrmacht* ran out of men, weapons and ammunition.

> *"We can't help but derive some cynical satisfaction from the abject appearance of the 'Supermen' who pass us lorrypacked on the road home. One wonders: what the hell were we ever afraid of? Dejection isn't the word. Resilience, if there ever was any, is vanished. Most of them look as though they don't care if they live. And the English suckers throw them the odd packet of cigarettes with the inhuman cry of 'Wheel them in...'"*

The Chase

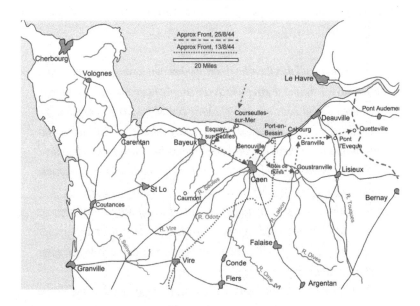

Map 6: Bénouville to Quetteville

Static morphed into mobile as artillery scrambled to keep the enemy retreat in range, typically moving up a day behind the infantry. 60th HAA's other two batteries moved up to Hérouville and Granville on 17th August; two days later they advanced again to Troarn while 206 Battery moved to Bois de Bures on the road east from Caen. Canadian paratroops clearing the wood on their way to the Seine found mines and booby traps left by the retreating Germans[xli] – which must have been at the front of the gunners' minds as they moved in. Also on 19th, a division of the American XV Corps crossed the Seine at Mantes Gassicourt (now Mantes-la-Jolie), about 100 miles upstream.

American and Canadian troops closed the Falaise Pocket on 20th August. The remaining German forces in Normandy were encircled and finally surrendered on 22nd.

60th HAA crossed the River Dives to positions near Goustranville on 21st August. 22nd saw them move up to Branville, then Beaumont-en-Auge, Glanville and Lavalee (west of Pont l'Evêque) on 23rd.

> *"I am afraid that there has been another non writing interval (about three days, I think) during which we simply have not had the time to pen even a field postcard… It of course can be no secret to say that we are advancing very rapidly, which has entailed a lot of hard work and the minimum of sleep – in fact I don't remember when I ever felt so tired for such a period. In addition the weather has chipped in with a couple of 'dirty days' so altogether we are feeling rather sorry for ourselves.*
>
> *This is being written about 6 a.m. I'm off duty in an hour or two and I've promised myself a peach of a sleep to make up for everything. I did the same the night before and was awakened after about an hour and told we were moving.*
>
> *When I wake up I will write a really long one darling, at the moment I just can't keep my eyes open. The censoring officer nearby*

is just about falling asleep over the mail and I must get him to run through this before we all finally pass out!

The French are giving us a great welcome. They even come and dig for us which of course is more appreciated than anything else! As somebody said yesterday when they were running around to oblige 'Give 'em the whole ruddy... so and so, we won't object!'"

He got his rest.

"We are still in a 'state of flux' but have managed to get that much needed sleep in the meantime and feel much better for it."

53rd Airlanding ferried a 60th HAA observer across the River Touques[xlii] on 24th, to direct fire on targets beyond their reach; 60th's 3.7s had over double the range of 53rd's 75mm pack howitzers but at more than ten times the weight. Next day the whole regiment crossed the river to take up positions near Quetteville and Saint-Benoît-d'Hébertot. As they did so Patton's 3rd Army was crossing the Seine at Elbeuf and Louviers, while Leclerc's[37] French 2nd Armoured Division entered Paris. General von Choloditz surrendered the city that afternoon.

The battle for Normandy was over.

In 12 weeks it had cost the lives of about 20,000 French civilians, plus another 15,000 killed in the previous months' bombing. Some 240,000 German and 226,000 Allied servicemen died; 200,000 *Wehrmacht* troops were taken prisoner. Hundreds of thousands were wounded, many maimed for life. Tens, perhaps hundreds, of thousands were made homeless as the steamroller of combat rolled

---

[37] Comte Philippe de Hautecloque took the *nom de guerre* 'Leclerc' to avoid putting his family in danger.

over their towns, villages and farms. The toll in property and livestock was incalculable. Brutality at times approached that on the Russian front, reflecting the desperation of heavily-armed men. Equally there were moments during the breakout when German commanders, not knowing where their own forces were or what the enemy was doing, must have empathised with their French opponents' dilemma in 1940.

Wind-Down

6th Airborne Division withdrew from the line for a much-needed rest. Their commander, Major-General Richard Gale, issued the following Order of the Day on 26th August.

SPECIAL ORDER OF THE DAY

1. *On the 6th June we came to Normandy. We seized the bridges, the Le Plein – Le Mesnil high ground and the Ranville areas.*
2. *What we seized we held.*
3. *For two months we sat on the defensive while General Montgomery's great plan unfolded itself.*
4. *On the 17th Aug we started a grim pursuit. Since then we have advanced 40 miles. This is an average of 7,000 yds a day as the crow flies, as the troops have had to march it has been half as far again.*
5. *We have fought and beaten the enemy at CABOURG, GOUSTRANVILLE, DOZULE, BRANVILLE, ANNEBAULY, PONT L'EVEQUE, and BEUZEVILLE.*
6. *In this fighting we have lost many good friends. We have, all of us, at times been tired out and weary.*
7. *We have fought side by side with our gallant allies, the Belgians and the Dutch. The Green and the Red Berets have fought as one.*

150 and 191 Field Regiments and 60 Heavy Anti Aircraft Regiment have supported us splendidly, effectively and loyally.

8. *I congratulate you on your great achievements: on your stamina, on your skill and on your grand grim determination.*

9. *The motto of the 6th British Airborne Division is "GO TO IT". You have gone to it and right splendidly you have done it.*

Figure 14: A Daily Sketch clipping pasted into the battery newspaper the following month

The praise was much appreciated:

> *"Incidentally did I tell you that the Regiment was cited specially in an order of the day, it said that we supported an offensive 'splendidly, effectively and loyally.' I'll tell you the whole yarn when I come home!"*
>
> He added, *"(Written in a starry-eyed moment: we nearly bodged the whole affair.)"*

60th HAA returned to its brigade. The regiment had shot down five aircraft during the campaign plus one shared and one damaged. It had fired 2,450 rounds at ground targets since landing; a foretaste of the next couple of months. There would be little call for anti-aircraft defence until they got to Nijmegen. Casualties were remarkably light: one killed and one wounded by an enemy shell, two injured in accidents.

> *"I am with the Radar section near a sort of 'rest camp' where we are doing precisely that plus maintenance and a spot of training, and to tell the truth I find it very welcome. I have had a recurrence of stomach trouble which greatly to my relief is disappearing rapidly, and I have felt tired and 'slow'. The last week or two with the Battery was pretty energetic and I'll let you have details of that later – after the due (official) lapse of time. We all have that 'approach of the end of the war feeling' and it's nice to look forward to all that you want to do when the time arrives."*

The 'end of term' sentiment had been building for some time. In Britain, newspaper space not dominated by war news focussed on how to reanimate the peacetime economy afterward. Fully half the country's 46-million population was working in the Services, Civil Defence or war production. Civilian export sales and product development were banned even as US exports blossomed. Aspirations to a fairer, property-owning society with a financial safety-net were balanced by the need to tackle the awesome war debt.

> *"I do hope this damned business is finished here before October. There are good signs that it may do so. The vaunted 'European fortress' seems to be well and truly cracking."*
>
> *"… With the fighting here so obviously drawing to a close I find it difficult to work up much 'continued attention' in respect of the job. It's different when you are getting ready for it and the big risks lie ahead. I find myself thinking more than ever about what I want to be getting on with at home, about the garden and the garage and the car etc. what sort of tours we can do – I warn you that I want our future holidays to be 'mobile' ones! I think plenty of travelling and seeing new places would be good education for the children too."*
>
> *"… Well, I hope we can look forward to the end of the war here at any time now. It's certainly worth an extra effort. Fancy the blackout disappearing in one glorious sweep!"*

On 6th July Herbert Morrison (Home Secretary) told Parliament that there would be no easing of blackout restrictions in the short term. Rules were relaxed in September to allow 'dim out' (moonlight equivalent) except when there was an alert in force. The blackout finally lifted on 30th April 1945.

The *Daily Telegraph* reported on 26th August:

> *"Mr Clifton Woodrum, chairman of the House of Representatives committee on post-war military policies, told the committee in Washington today that… October would see the end of the war against Germany.*
>
> *Mr Roosevelt… said he was about the only person who had not predicted the date of the end of the war."*

Roosevelt was right to be cautious: there were still months of grief and hard slog to go.

The respite didn't last long. Eric wrote at the end of August:

> *"I also begin to feel very much in need of a week's break from the routine. We have been more or less in an uproar of preparation or active service since that leave in January, and sometimes you could consign tents, the open-air life and army cooking to hell everlasting, with an intensity which varies according to how you are feeling...*
>
> *We had a short period (two or three days) at a rest camp. It fell rather flat with me because I wasn't feeling so hot, but I did manage a swim on a fine day, and I went to the pictures. But the annoying thing is you can't spend more than a short time out because there is absolutely no food to be had outside. Although this place is an official 'rest centre' there is not a sign of a canteen, and of course it presents the usual depressing spectacle of innumerable soldiers hoofing it back two or three miles in search of a tea or supper at their base. When you think of the restaurants 'de luxe' in London you wonder why just a little thought can't be expended on places like these. 'NAAFI' has the same effect on us as the word 'culture' is reputed to have on Goering."*

British and American forces were by then across the Seine at Vernon and Mantes. The Canadians liberated Rouen – what was left of it – after a stiff fight on 30th August. On 1st September they had the satisfaction of taking Dieppe, where so many had died in 1942, without a fight. Mercifully the news got back in time to forestall massive preliminary bombing.

The noise of battle faded north incredibly fast. Brussels fell on 3rd September, and Antwerp on 4th.

> *"I shall be very glad to return to the old country (says he like a lifelong exile). A more dismal prospect than a sort of glorified field*

exercise during the winter I have yet to imagine. The consolation is that Germany appears to be on her last legs. What do you think of the news of Brussels and Antwerp after Paris? Some going!"

"... There is a widespread feeling that the war is fast drawing to an end. Somehow there does not seem even a possibility of catching up with the front line, and everybody expects the end to come very soon. It is almost bewildering after the earlier stages of hold-ups and small advances, to be rampaging through France like this."

The Germans still held Le Havre, Boulogne, Calais and the approaches to Antwerp. Field Marshall Von Rundstedt was re-appointed Commander-in-Chief West on 5th September.

Elsewhere, the Finns agreed a cease fire with Russia on 2nd September, after which the Germans began to withdraw their troops into Norway. Under the terms of the armistice the Finns had to eject or intern German forces at the same time as demobilising their own. Some – mostly half-hearted – fighting ensued before the Germans finished their withdrawal at the end of November.

FROM SEINE
TO RHINE

Tour de (Northern) France

Despite talk of switching 60th to field artillery, the radar sections rejoined the regiment to defend Rouen and the nearby Seine crossings. 206 Battery went to Pont de l'Arche.

"Oh, I forgot to mention the different address – or rather our reverting to the old one. The section is once more part of the Regiment – it was planned at one time to separate us (Radar) as it was thought the Regt would no longer be in an AA role. Now they think different, apparently. Any letter you addressed to '60 Radar' should reach me alright."

All Allied supplies had to be brought by road from Normandy creating such a bottleneck that 8th British Corps was grounded to free its transport for other formations. Roads were gridlocked around the Seine bridges – a tempting target for the *Luftwaffe*.

"I've managed to get a wash between the showers after an all night manning session. Plus some shooting! – it surprised us more than it did them. With no harm resulting for either side."

The port of Dieppe gradually restarted from 7th September but logistics were a nightmare until Antwerp finally came on stream at the end of the year. Also on 7th, Eric wrote:

> *"I am afraid these letters are getting a bit interspaced but things have been more than unsettled again. We have moved a considerable distance, settled in, and expect to move again very soon, so I must make hay."*

After almost a week in one place it was time to pack again.

The Le Havre garrison surrendered on 12th September, by which time the Canadians had largely cleared the coastal area and V1 launch sites as far as Bruges – still excepting Boulogne, Cap Gris Nez, Calais and Dunkirk.

> *"One great satisfaction – the Troop some time ago were able to inspect a fly bomb site, which had been well and truly bombed by the RAF and subsequently captured. It was nice for the Londoners."*

The V1 assault continued, albeit at lower intensity, despite Herbert Morrison's claim that the Battle of London was over when the French sites were overrun. Simple, prefabricated ramps and a longer-range missile allowed the Germans to launch from camouflaged sites in the Netherlands. There was also an air-launched variant, and the V2 attacks were just about to begin. Both weapons kept coming until March 1945.

The regiment was released from the defence of Rouen on 9th September, moving to Harlettes near St Omer on 10th. Now in support of 1st Canadian Army, it advanced to the Grigny area ('206' at Mont-des-Boucards) for the siege of Boulogne.

> *"Rather an interval between this and my last letter I'm afraid. We have moved twice; the first move was quite a distance and we*

seem more than ever out of touch with civilisation. No mail yet (now about 14 days overdue) no newspapers or extra rations (beer etc!) that we look forward to so much, worst of all no fresh food or bread. In fact it's incredible just how much you can feel like a collection of shipwrecked mariners or forgotten men in the midst of normal country surroundings.

... I suppose the difficulties of the GPO [General Post Office] *are doubled and trebled now that the army is scattered all over France, and we know from experience that it doesn't take much to upset the superb organisation of NAAFI. We only hope they don't rook us out of our overdue whisky ration."*

Thanks to the enemy's headlong retreat the gunners now travelled through scenery that hadn't been fought over.

"The country through which we have passed is really beautiful. Some of it is like the Mendip countryside, except that it is generally much higher and very thickly wooded. The 'woods' are really forests, they stretch unbroken for miles, with the roads running right through them. The trees are chiefly pine, though there is a general variety. The country cottages are 'Timbered' and very attractive – a striped effect in black and white"

They enjoyed a week or so of domesticity while forces concentrated for the attack.

"We are not doing too badly for 'extras' these days, however. We gather mushrooms in the mornings (great competition), get milk from a farm, and swipe a few potatoes, which all helps the biscuits go down. We are still keeping busy, and 'they' find plenty for us to shoot at. I have recently had my first lengthy session on a gun.

These mornings now are really lovely, I think. Our present location is very picturesque (very different from the flat, dusty Caen area.) France is really very beautiful when you see a lot of it."

By the end of the week some 330 British and Canadian guns were ready to fire on German positions – not counting bombers and the coastal batteries near Dover. About 8,000 civilians evacuated the city between 11th and 13th September.

17th September saw the start of Operation *Market Garden* – Arnhem or 'A Bridge Too Far.' In nine days of heavy fighting the

Map 7: Normandy to Beaulieu

Allied armies pushed forward a remarkable 60 miles against an enemy now organised and fighting back. However, their inability to relieve the paras of 1st Airborne Division at Arnhem soured the moment. The withdrawal was already under way when Eric wrote: *"At the moment the fighting is still very critical. I hope we manage to relieve the Airborne people alright. They are grand chaps, we have made very close contact with them."*

If the operation had held its objectives the Allies could have entered Germany north of the Siegfried Line rather than having to batter their way through it five months later. Historians also argue that diversion of resources to *Market Garden* prevented the clearance of the Scheldt and opening of Antwerp port when it could have been done relatively easily. Oh well. Might-have-beens are fun but futile.

Market Garden left the Allies in control of a narrow salient – threatened by German forces on each side – as far as Nijmegen. This would soon be very relevant to 60th HAA.

Operation *Wellhit*, the siege of Boulogne, kicked off in the meantime with a massive air raid and artillery barrage. Lieutenant-Colonel Roger Rowley commanding the Stormont, Dundas and Glengarry Highlanders commented: *"An unusual feature of* [sic] *was the assignment of two heavy AA regiments to fire low airburst concentrations over known flak positions during the course of the bombing effort."*[xliii] 60th HAA were interested in Mont Lambert, a strongly-fortified hill commanding the countryside east of the town.

> *"I have not been at my usual job for some time now and I get a great kick out of working at something different. I am rather surprised at the kick I do get out of calculations and figures. And I went on the guns some time ago and loaded and fired for about an hour and a half."*
>
> *"… I have lost an old bug bear – indecision, and I feel that four years of running (or being part of) an army section has helped me*

considerably in this respect. Thus I glean the crumbs from adversity!
But there are worse things than the Army when it comes to knocking
off a few odd fads and fancies. It's nice to know with certainty that
you can face up to anything and probably give more than you take."

The hours of sustained, rapid fire were more than the guns could take: they were unusable by the end of the day. Its job done, and in need of repairs, the regiment was on the road again as soon as Mont Lambert fell on 18th September. Next stop: Calais.

Boulogne fell on 22nd September but didn't reopen until 12th October. Calais and Cap Gris Nez had to be taken first because their coastal batteries commanded both ports.

The regiment approached over flat countryside, under a smoke screen sustained for five days to shield Allied movement from the German guns.[xliv]

RAF 'softening up' raids began on 20th September. On 23rd Eric wrote:

> *"The guns are firing continuously all around and it makes for*
> *rather disappointing writing. There is also a half starved cat making*
> *dead set at me, and much as I sympathise with it, it has chosen the*
> *wrong time to get acquainted, as it will presently learn to its cost.*
>
> *Trying to get a bit of privacy is just hopeless. I've been so pestered*
> *this morning that I have betaken myself to an old barn to drop a line*
> *to you. And now it's the cat."*

The infantry assault started on 25th in weather too poor for most bombers to find their targets.

> *"I hope you are not getting the weather quite so bad as we are*
> *here. It has been simply dreadful. Yesterday we were nearly blown*
> *out and flooded. However, we have built a nice, comparatively dry*

Command Post and I have made cocoa with milk tonight to relieve the tedium of our spell of duty. 'All's quiet' as far as we are concerned."

The regiment was again slugging it out with German artillery – 168 Battery lost a gun in the exchange. The Calais garrison however lacked the persistence and skill of the best German troops and the attack made rapid progress despite largely intact defences.

A truce on 29th–30th September allowed 20,000 civilians to evacuate. Many of the German drivers bringing them out asked to be taken prisoner rather than go back; the city surrendered soon after. As at Boulogne the port was too badly wrecked for immediate use.

British coastal artillery gave fire support, damaging all four guns of *Batterie Grosser Kurfürst* at Cap Gris Nez which fell on 29th September. Dover was now free of enemy shellfire for the first time in four years; fifty shells had landed there as late as 26th. The King and Queen visited "Hellfire Corner" on 18th October to view the damage.

Figure 15: Cross-Channel gun emplacement at Cap Gris Nez, 1st October 1944. (IWM B 10465)

Speculators could now sell property they'd bought in Ramsgate, Broadstairs and Margate at immense profit.[xlv] Some things never change.

There was enough left of the guns to impress Eric when he saw them:

> "... we can say now that we took part in the assault on Boulogne and Calais, seeing England in the distance at the same time, and watched the final surrender of each port. We inspected the great cross-Channel guns at close quarters also. Each was housed in a fortress as large as a cathedral."

Eric was resigned to winter away but felt the prospect of release tantalisingly close.

> "The present weather heralds the dismal prospect of winter in the field. I can't say that we are altogether happy at the prospect. But we shan't grumble overmuch if it is the last. Christmas out here too! I'm afraid that's what it will mean. My fifth in the service. Cobham, Scotland, Hertford, Leicester. May the next one be in England... for a certainty."
>
> "... I can recall that morning quite vividly, when you saw me down to the train and we thought that the destination – Gravesend – was an unconscionable distance! I don't think I entered on any project with quite as much trepidation!
>
> ... Well this does look like being the very last anniversary of all."

Under plans published in September, age and length of service put Eric in the 25th release group. Better yet, demobilisation was to start after the defeat of Germany, with new conscripts replacing the early releases.

> *"The 'demobbing' plans look pretty good at first inspection. As far as I can judge I will be among the first 100,000 to be released... And no Far East nonsense, either. Thank God! I'm going to hobble away and leave that to all the younger men! I bequeath all my text books and gunnery charts to the rising generation."*

The newspapers at home had been dominated by war news since Dunkirk but now made space to look forward to the post-war world. Squaddies on active service found their thoughts drifting the same way in any spare moment.

> *"I am getting on for being able to type as fast as I can write. That's one little accomplishment I'm saving for Civvy Street. These plans for After the War, I think up about two or three every day! Well, I'm in the 'A' category, so I should be released with the majority of the 'early ones'."*
>
> *"... I am very interested in the army's plan to 'Brush up for Civvy Street' whereby the interim between the 'cease fire' and the demobilisation will be devoted in part to compulsory study. I thought it would be a good idea to take the NUJ's course on journalism and also do a spot of lecturing. They will require NCOs for this and I fancy the idea far more than guard duties and similar nightmares."*

There were moments when the job seemed almost done.

> *"I think the end is in sight now all right. Yes, it would be marvellous if the new arrival coincided with Hitler's downfall. How I hope so!!"*

At other times the light from the end of the tunnel just threw the daily grind into harsher relief.

"This open air life gets very tedious. It's the time you waste in doing the jobs extra to living 'rough' that are so annoying. Cleaning up mud, patching tents, mucking about with bedding and cooking utensils – it's all such a waste of effort when you could be concentrating on one job. But there will 'come a day' and oh may it be soon!

I love hearing about the progress of Hugh. He seems to lead his mother a bit of a dance sometimes, but on the whole he appears to be very good. I would give worlds for a peek at him"

"… I sometimes wonder what we shall think of these days and situations in the years to come, perhaps we shall be amused, which is certainly more than I can be at the time of writing. Hugh's arrival at Arbourfield when we were on those exercises prevented me from having more than a mere glance at him, and now out here I can't expect any definite news for quite a time. I am sure neither of us even faintly imagined such occurrences when we were married. Well it will be something to talk about in our peaceful old age – unless I am roped in for the Home Guard in a future crisis.

I have already had quite enough experience of war to last me a lifetime, in fact I don't think I shall go as far as to even discuss it in future years. If I show any tendency to – just bat me over the head with something hard."

Between pre-invasion exercises and lock-down Eric and Jennie hadn't seen each other in months. Mobile living, with moods dominated by the weather and trivial comforts, was the only world the gunners knew.

"Letter writing has been a bit upset by a couple of moves but I'm hoping to write regularly, and expect they won't be too long in arriving… the dried milk and cocoa are very fortifying in the small hours and you have the consolation of knowing you can brew a drink whenever you feel like one.

> *What a difference the weather makes to living as we are living here! A really wet day makes life as black as hell, and a fine one prompts one to sing and dance – well almost!"*

The *Daily Herald* reported in outrage on 18th September that Purchase Tax was being levied on parcels sent home by Overseas Forces.

> *"I have been able to acquire a book for the children (in Flemish) with some very nice illustrations, it's a sort of bound 'comic' – but vastly superior to our brand of children's paper. I am going to put it in a parcel I am making up gradually.*

Map 8: Beaulieu to Turnhout

It's terribly difficult to get hold of things now as we are not near any towns but I am doing my best."

"… One feels rather frustrated about buying stuff over here. Len and I fancied some handbags, but they cost anything from £10, and pretty ordinary leather at that; it really did seem exorbitant – and there is always the risk of losing it en route. The thing that I fancy most is the glassware which is reasonable, but here again it is so difficult to send."

As September ended 60th HAA withdrew to Boursin then crossed the border to Diksmuide in Belgium, bypassing Dunkirk which was still in enemy hands. Orders weren't long in coming and were no surprise: the rest of the brigade was already in the Antwerp area and the regiment was to join them there for anti-aircraft defence.

Water, Water Everywhere…

They'd barely arrived before they had to turn round. 49th (West Riding) Infantry – the 'Polar Bears'[38] – and 1st Polish Armoured Divisions were advancing north from Antwerp toward Tilburg to secure the left flank of the Nijmegen salient. They needed help.

On 25th September Hitler ordered von Rundstedt to drive the Allies out of the 'island' between the Lower Rhine and Waal rivers (from Arnhem back to Nijmegen) and hold the river and canal lines along which the advance had stalled. This would prevent the Allies using Antwerp port and buy time to prepare a counter-attack.

---

[38] The nickname came from their service in Iceland from 1940 to 1942. 60th HAA had already met them during Exercise *Spartan* in 1943. Originally raised as a Territorial division they were by now hard-bitten veterans. Their notoriety earned a personal attack by the German propagandist Lord Haw Haw who called them 'The Polar Bear Butchers' in a radio broadcast.

The landscape of northern Belgium and the Netherlands features a LOT of water: not for nothing are they the 'Low Countries.' Numerous rivers and canals cross the countryside, each forming a natural defence. The defenders blew dykes to flood the fields and expose any movement on the raised roadways. After a retreat they would methodically shell each of the few possible gun sites. Adding an unusually wet autumn into the mix made it a very unpleasant environment with hard fighting for every mile.

On 4th October, 60th HAA were supporting an advance from the small town of Merxplas.

> *"We are… firing at brief intervals all through the day and night so that every hour or half hour one is awakened by shouts and slamming of breeches and a salvo right over the tent.*
>
> *When you are so near it's like somebody leaning over and giving you a sound smack on the kisser at brief intervals… 'E' Troop are also alongside us with equally noisy guns and a noisy loudspeaker system. When Len is performing it just grates. Also there are fellow sergeants who lunge over me cursing when the 'Take Post' is ordered (also with a great amount of bawling) so on the whole I prefer to be out on the job at night."*

On the 5th the gunners followed the advance up to the village of Baarle-Nassau, crossing the Dutch border to support the 49th Division's attack on Poppel. They lost a jeep to a land mine, luckily without casualties.

A strong German counter-attack halted the advance; it failed but marked the start of two weeks' bitter, static fighting along the Antwerp-Turnhout Canal, in which neither side was able to gain much.

The gunners serenaded the Polar Bears and 1st Polish Armoured Division with continuous ground fire from 7th to 19th October. 'Bubbles' Barker of the Polar Bears gave some idea of the intensity:

"Some 600 or so [Germans] *tried to infiltrate around* [the Lincolns] *through the woods by day and night and they fought them off. We 'stonked' the Boche with everything we had and two counter attacks were put in to relieve troops who had been surrounded."xlvi*

Eric kept up a steady flow of letters despite the workload.

"The Troop has been issued with Field Service Cards and have made use of them, but I prefer to take a chance on the letter getting through. You would probably wonder what on earth was the matter if you received a FSC at this stage."

FSCs were buff, standard-form postcards that could be used for a quick line home. Eric was worried that they could also be confused with every family's nightmare – a casualty note. With their second child due any day he deeply felt the intrusion of censorship:

"… at a time like this I loathe *my correspondence being read by a rather flippant band of officers who are otherwise very decent…"*

Jennie had already addressed postcards to inform family and friends – including Eric – of the imminent child's birth: *"Seems funny sending a bloke a P.C. to let him know he's a father again."* He in the meantime was absorbed in the job.

"It's a good thing we can get acclimatised to this sort of thing which we undoubtedly do. The men were never healthier, and are in pretty good shape all round. They really love 'Having a bash' and the work that has been found for them to do since they arrived here is very much to their taste. If they can keep their guns firing they are happy.

It's the little thing that makes them annoyed. They are quick to resent any suspicion of neglect, and non-arrival of the little luxuries from NAAFI makes them more mad than an all-night digging in."

"… Life is hectic and pretty arduous, but satisfying inasmuch as we are doing some useful work. We are thought very highly of by the big-wigs concerned."

The regiment's war diary recorded *"Satisfaction expressed by both Divs as to results obt'd."*[xlvii]

Jennie and the rest of the family kept up a steady supply of parcels containing small luxuries like cocoa and cigarettes, and most importantly news.

"The papers are arriving regularly and again are most welcome. In fact how welcome it is difficult to describe: one gets the lousie feeling over here and a paper is like the sail on the horizon. We can generally hear the news on the Radio, but it is a poor substitute for Press comment, I think. I can never visualise the Radio superseding the newspaper for that reason."

After a while the strain began to tell.

"I'm afraid I can't date this at the moment as I haven't the faintest idea of what it is, nor even of the day. All the last few days and nights we have been on the move and life has been very unsettled and chaotic."

On 15th October the RAF tried to destroy the Sorpe dam, which the 1943 'Dam Busters' raid had failed to demolish. This time they used five-ton Tallboy bombs. The dam survived again, though an unexploded Tallboy was found when the lake was drained for repairs in 1958. RAF technicians defused it. Carefully.

Winter Campaigning

Figure 16: Canadian fun with a 9-ton gun in mud.
(Lt Ken Bell / Canada. Dept. of National Defence / Library and Archives
Canada / PA-151554 / MIKAN 3211345)

By early October it was clear to all that the war was not going to end quickly. The *Daily Express* reported on 5th:

> *"It looks as though we are in for a winter campaign, and we might as well face it… If you ask what stopped us there are probably three main answers:*

1. *The lack of nearby ports.*
2. *The renewed passionate resistance of the Germans once they fell back on their own soil.*
3. *The weather.*

Another point is that in Normandy we fought close to our supply dumps and kept the Germans dancing round our perimeter at the end of long lines of supply. Now the position is exactly reversed."

Even through the fog of post-war comment it looks like a fair assessment. In the cold and the mud of the Belgium/Netherlands border the prospect met with weary resignation:

> *"I'm sorry if the request for books for the winter produced a despondency, darling, but of course even if the war finished tomorrow the odds are that we should be here over the winter. The only difference is that the starting of leave would then be a certainty. I have a feeling that it won't start until things over here are practically finished. All the ports must be absolutely choc-a-bloc with supplies for the front. Much as we want to see home again, we don't want this business dragged out. It would be lovely to come home and say 'Well the fighting's over at any rate'. Your account of the flying bombs makes me want to concentrate all the more on it. Even a rest from the front doesn't seem 'quite the thing' when there's still plenty to do."*
>
> *"… I really can't judge how soon it will end. We're getting along all right. My view is that this is the last and toughest phase, it's not the fast job it was in parts of France. It's Caen all over again but it may suddenly crack in just the same way. Let's hope so."*

The nights were drawing in and the weather getting colder. On 19th October the cartoonist Giles reported from Holland in the *Daily Express*:

> *"I doubt if the average soldier's comments would get past even the most broad-minded censor, but one and all agree that:*
> *a)   It is cold.*
> *b)   It is wet.*

c)   *There may be worse places.*
d)   *But not many."*

He still observed that squaddies would find a joke in the bleakest situations. Eric himself, now semi-permanently detached from radar, was close to a sense-of-humour failure.

> *"We are getting the real super autumn mornings now – not to mention evenings – and oh boy is it cold. Especially when we have a night move and run up telephone lines and pack up equipment with an icy air in our fingers. These night flits are too numerous by far. I am well ensconced in my new job, I haven't seen my boys or Sammy for about six weeks now. They are back at Regt Base feeling, I think, rather out of things!*

> *... We are all OK, rather tired, of course, but life is pretty tolerable except that it's so damned cold mornings and evenings and the night falls so fast that there's nothing much else to do bar go to bed if you can't manage heat or fire. The idea of sitting down to a fire under electric light seems fabulous. Undoubtedly the summer is the ideal campaigning season! This is where some premises taken over as canteens would be much appreciated. However, sometimes we are not even fortunate enough to harbour near a house."*

The cold at least suggested alternative entertainment.

> *"No wonder they are so fond of skating up here. It looks as though the ice will form at any moment. I often wonder what sort of a figure I should cut at that nowadays. The favourite months are January and February."*

Rommel shot himself on 14th October. The pounding of Germany continued as RAF Bomber Command and the US Eighth Air Force flew over 3,000 sorties dropping 9,000 tons of bombs on Duisburg in less than 48 hours. The RAF had enough aircraft left over for 240 to attack Brunswick at the same time, and more than 300 to be employed on other tasks.

Eric wrote:

> "...*I have got this trick of just ignoring the things I do deeply resent (including the war, separation from you, living like a gypsy and so ad infinitum) down to a fine art – the danger is that you come to accept them if you are not careful. But if you dwell on them at any length you become so badly 'rattled' that you cease to live the life either moderately cheerfully or efficiently...*
>
> *On the whole it is easier to put up with all this out here as we are really doing something to finish the war..."*

The sense of a job to do was mutual. This from Jennie crossed in the post.

> "*Of course it stands to reason that the Germans will make the best possible defence of their own land. So there is probably still plenty of hard fighting ahead. Still I have a feeling that the 'crack up' will come suddenly when it does come – & may it be soon."*

The postcard announcing their second son's birth took five days to reach Eric and was followed next day by a fuller account of her confinement. He immediately replied.

> "*Rather funny how I broached the news to Len about two hours ago. I was so excited that I rushed up and said that Geoffrey Alan had arrived, and he took it to be a new man posted to us!"*

Another milestone a few days later passed in a blur of action.

"I had an 'all duty' day yesterday so I couldn't write as I wished to on the day of our wedding anniversary. But you can guess I was thinking of you quite a lot and wishing I was there in person. Curious that I have only spent two of these anniversaries at home and five in the Army."

Glittering Antwerp, Playground of the… Knackered Gunner

In Britain we think of the V weapons as purely for our benefit, but Brussels and Antwerp were just as heavily battered. Antwerp in particular was hit from early October 1944 until March 1945 and suffered worse than any other city; 106 V1s and 107 V2s killed 3,752 civilians and 731 Allied soldiers there. Some 3,600 properties were destroyed.

Figure 17: Antwerp Leysstraat from a pre-war postcard

The attack was expected and many of the available AA guns were sited to protect the two cities from the V1 threat. Nothing could be done about a V2 in flight. Mixed regiments were brought over from the UK to strengthen the defences as the campaign progressed.

Eric was in the area as the assault developed but mentioned it only once.

> *"I saw 'Cover Girl' last night starring Rita Hayworth and returned to the Little Room with a story – of how our hero entered a room and stood bewildered as a V2 descended in the vicinity. 'Now that's amazing' said Sammy Beckerman, as the laughter… subsided. 'I was in that same cinema'… suddenly there was a terrible c-r-a-s-h; BOOM went a V2 within the vicinity.*
>
> *'I propose we change the subject' spake a blanketed voice."*

On 28th October a V1 killed 71 people in Antwerp and destroyed forty homes. The urban posting still had compensations for gunners who'd spent four months under canvas. Writing on 25th October:

> *"Living here seems absolutely wonderful. We are near a city which contains cinemas and canteens and the billets are situated in a fort which has beds and electric light and a camp kitchen. It's the first time I have had a roof over my head since Brackley."*

The novelty faded within a week:

> *"One can get out often too, but it is surprising how that palls. I went out with Len a couple of times and did a tour of the town, and if ever you want to be disillusioned about a country at war, a city like this is just the place for it. I'm sure the men occupying their time in the dance bands and cabarets and running cafes would amount to the strength of a battalion. Beer is about 1/- a glass on an average and anything from*

5/- for a stiffer drink. They are quite frankly out to skin the army and get the utmost from every soldier – and I'm afraid in most cases they get it. It's a stiff price for liberation! But thank God there are some good hostels and soldiers' restaurants organised as well. All very disillusioning though – but a city is never representative of a country.

At first, the atmosphere is quite dazzling and presents a scene of great gaiety – the bands are superlatively good and they have a flair for gaudy decoration and mirrors and bizarre lighting. After you've sampled it for an hour it looks as cheap as dirt. It strikes me as about the most futile way of frittering away one's time and money that was ever devised, unless one has a mind like a vacuum or is interested in the attentions of a hostess (Brrr!). These last are a pretty sordid collection – from all over Europe, I should say, speaking German quite as fluently as American slang, and not remotely interested in drawing distinctions, national or ideological.

The 'gaiety' has the same ring of sincerity as a religious meeting that forever rattles a money box under your nose during the fervent rendering of psalms

One thing I must say I do appreciate; they have organised a big hotel as a hostel for sergeants and warrant officers, where you can buy a drink at a reasonable price or a three course meal, and write in a sumptuous apartment that boasts a bar and a string orchestra. There are also baths and beds for a 24 hour leave, library etc. It is under the management of the NAAFI & a feather in their caps."

Jennie replied:

"By all reports London is all organised to skin the 'doughboys' and colonial troops just about the same way as you complain. As you say you can't judge the people by the cities. There always seems to be an artificial air of luxury and gaiety about them – which is merely depressing, somehow the simple pleasures of life seem much more satisfying and complete.

231

I can just imagine your reaction to the hostesses. As you remarked – Brrr! I should think even the men who are interested must find them a pretty poor substitute."

Natives – Friendly?

The gunners formed varying impressions of the country they moved through and the people they met.

France

"The locals scrounge unendingly for cigarettes. We are generally sympathetic at the start but too much of it is a damned nuisance."

"… The French are busy celebrating their liberation – with a vengeance! It really is good to see – makes you realise just how unbearable conditions must have been in the country. The sight of British troops is still a spectacle for them in the countryside through which we have passed – it's funny to see them crowd to the windows and then fly out and besiege the lorries. The requests for cigarettes is overwhelming – and good Lord, they are received like gold. The boys give them away, too, just about exhaust their supplies."

As time passed the pestering began to get on their nerves.

"I have strolled out once or twice, but frankly I do not care much for the people, the villages, or the drinks. The people, especially the children, cadge endlessly, it really does get exasperating to be asked for a cigarette about fifty times during a stroll down a main street. The men are not much as specimens, but I suppose all the worth while people are either in the Maquis or are prisoners of

war. The occupation of their country seems to have left them with no sense of pride.

Of course one gets different impressions of them. One village can be charming, obliging and generally attractive. Other places you just can't be bothered with.

The drinks are certainly nothing to rave about. 'Calvados' is distilled cider. The cider itself is about the best long drink – very meaty. Of course the Germans grabbed all the beer. They also removed the Benedictine. We are left with Calvados, vin rouge, and one or two rather inferior drinks. So the cafe is no temptation.

The French are very pessimistic about their stocks of Champagne – they think it will be years before France is able to export any of good quality. The same, incidentally was said of our whisky by one in the know! We are apparently very 'down on the stock' – consuming much more than should be released. Well, as long as I can drink an occasional beer I shan't worry."

"… The 'scrounging' has lessened considerably – for one thing we are wise to it and insist on a little bartering. We manage to get milk and sometimes new potatoes and mushrooms, which all helps out the menu. I have some peaches ripening – swopped for a packet of 'doofers'."

"… [The gunners] are most generous with their rations too. The French were quick to realise this and undoubtedly played on it. Of course they soon tumbled to the fact that all their cigs were being cadged from them and nothing proffered in return, in fact anything they bought they well and truly paid through the nose for, so they suddenly stopped it, just like that! I must really tell you sometime of the bargaining that ensued, and of the surprise of the natives when they found they weren't getting things for nothing any more."

Belgium

"Beyond saying that we are 'somewhere in Belgium' I must, of course, not relate any details. But the people are charming, the country clean and orderly and in every respect attractive – for instance they have pubs! When we are lucky enough to be able to visit them. The beer is dark and sweet and altogether a 'drop of good.' There have been no regrets about moving out of France. The children here are the most delightful of all. They attend and leave school in solemn little orderly parties, most are fair, girls have their hair in plaits and are fresh complexioned and slightly 'goggle eyed' they come up and shake hands very grandly, saying 'Thank you for liberating us' in English! The boys respond 'Oh that's alright, any time, you know!' and remarks to that effect – but they are delighted at the warmth of the welcome. A convoy journey is quite unforgettable, we are showered with apples, pears, tomatoes and hot soup and coffee. We harbour near little farms and villages where they flock out to speak to us, all very neat, with clogs and little aprons and 'Dutch' caps, all very friendly and charming. I simply had to give my 'guns' on my arm away to two of them as a souvenir – that is all they ask for, no scrounging, no 'cigarettes for Papa' – thank God.

They made us come along to a victory dance and although we had only a few hours for sleep, some of us went along. The music provided by a sort of 'fair' organ, operated by turning a large wheel. Most were waltzes, very fast which licked us completely – you would have loved to have seen young and old gyrating round dizzyingly, the old men with cigars in their mouths, partnering little girls of six of seven. The fellows were no end taken up with them.

To our astonishment they had a record of the Lambeth Walk and knew just how to dance it, so of course, that was our cue. Then out of courtesy, they played it over and over again! Then they asked us to sing 'The washing on the Siegfried Line' – told us how they could be

*shot for singing it under the Germans and the dance ended with the
boys performing 'Knees up Mother Brown' and then a combined
rendering of 'Tipperary.' We thought it was well worth the lack of
sleep."*

*"... I like these fellows very much. They are enamoured of the
British and most of them speak the language. Two of them invited
me to supper the other night and we had a very long conversation,
chiefly political. Some of it is worth while recording, but I must leave
that for later, I'm afraid."*

"... The Flemish are entirely different, we haven't had one *request
for free cigarettes although we know they are very scarce, and such
generous treatment that everybody is deeply touched. There is no doubt
that they have a very warm regard for the English. In some cases they
lined the streets to wave to the vanguards even when the towns were
being shelled. One man I was speaking to was very amusing on this
subject. His wife had been ill but insisted on getting up to see the
English when they arrived. Then she went out and gave them 'the
refreshment'. Soon after the shells began to drop and her husband
begged her 'Now my dear, you have seen the English – now come
down to the cellar!'*

*What is most refreshing is their cleanliness, and the lovely
individual modern design of their houses, this place must be the
talented architect's paradise. The interiors are generally tiled in a
tasteful colourful design, and my word! do they shine – quite in your
family tradition! Who on earth ever spread that awful lie about the
Belgians being dirty? Nowhere is there the least vestige of it –
absolutely the opposite."*

*"... I am intrigued with the Flemish tongue – it is so similar to
English, and there is no difficulty about the pronunciation. I think it
is the language I could really take to (I haven't any real inclination
to acquire French). I find the character and sturdiness of Flemish very
attractive, as attractive as the people. You would like them too I feel*

sure. *Another thing we are going to do darling, visit Belgium! I should love to come back here."*

The Netherlands

"The people here are so overwhelmingly friendly as to be a bit of a nuisance, they swarm around and are not backward in coming forward or coming into our private sanctums, and always the request to buy cigarettes! It really gets very monotonous.

The town we passed through yesterday was having a sort of 'liberation celebration' – band pounding in the streets and more people than I ever saw at the coronation time. Everyone was wearing orange – either as a cap or a scarf, belt, or dress. The Dutch flag was flying everywhere, of course, similar to the French, but a horizontal red white and blue. They are a cheery and very friendly crowd, very easy to get on with."

"… The Dutch have a grand sense of humour. For people with so little to laugh about they laugh a lot. One old man was digging up the stump of a tree for firewood – a miserable bit with long roots. 'Much trouble for little wood' he said and when we agreed he elaborated 'Too much bloody trouble.'

Harry Kitch had a group of about 20 kids around him another time teaching him some Dutch. He just couldn't get one word right, and one of the kids repeating it with great gusto spat right in his eye! They all howled for minutes on end!

… The natives are absolutely unanimous – they like the English best! The kids just flock to them, and soon know everybody's names. Which reminds me of how a visiting Colonel was stopped by one of them who wanted to know if he knew where Tim Donovan was! – The said T.D. being one of our gunners who had promised to let him have some cigarettes."

Our Gallant Allies

A remarkable feature of the 1944 European campaign was the integration of disparate Allied forces. There were of course tensions and scratchiness at all levels: the disputes between Eisenhower's commanders are well described elsewhere and don't need repeating. That shouldn't obscure the fact that it *worked*. For example 60th HAA supported Polish armour, British and American infantry within the First Canadian Army.

> *"The Canadians say 'Let's get this Goddam business over and get back to a decent country and we don't mean yours'. They have very dim views of spending any more time in Britain."*
>
> *"… I like the Canadians too. I've never met a bunch yet who looked sour or dispirited and God knows they have cause to. Sometimes during a shoot they are on the same wavelength as us and the informality is highly diverting. 'Report when ready, report when ready' (to fire) then 'Say, give us just one minute, just one minute'. 'That is OK by us, that is OK by us' and so on. I was having a meal on the bonnet of a Jeep once when a Canadian major jumped in, said 'Sorry to disturb yer feed feller' and was gone – and very nearly with my plate."*

The Americans viewed the British and Canadians as somewhat risk-averse – understandable when the badly mauled 59th Division had already been disbanded to provide replacements and the 50th was to follow suit. On the other hand the US approach seemed simply wasteful of life to the British. Major General 'Bubbles' Barker of the Polar Bears wrote: *"I fear the Yanks do it with undue casualties. They simply don't know how to use their artillery. I can switch my guns onto any point in a moment."* Eric, from his perspective, was no more flattering.

"The Americans are very disappointing – not much individuality, no wisecracks, and all of a muchness and unto themselves, talking little and usually looking lost and dispirited. They are rather 'rubber stamped' with none of the toughness, high spirits, or individuality of the British or Canadians. Our blokes don't seem to bother with them – except to remark rather cattily upon how quickly they get down if a shell comes anywhere near."

In fairness he was probably describing the men of 104th ('Timberwolves') Infantry Division, who were in the middle of their first combat experience.

Equipment and Clothing

Supply problems forced the regiment to improvise unofficial (and decidedly non-uniform) solutions:

"I have added to my stock of winter clothing – a warm jacket worn by the airborne people, a Balaclava, and one or two other odds and ends…"

"… It's one of our quiet days which in the ordinary way would have enabled us to get our washing done, but of course it has rained uninterruptedly. I have concentrated on the darning and sewing accumulations… looked over my equipment and sorted out some winter underwear to match the climate. We were supposed to hand them all in before we left England and I'm very glad I didn't. Likewise the extra blanket (three is the official quota) which I stowed away in the equipment. God knows when we shall receive an official issue.

It's the same with the tents which is a most peculiar situation. We had no official issue whatsoever and the men began to devise 'bivvies' out of the tarpaulin carried to wrap stores. They nowhere met the demand so the remainder were 'found' and cover enough for all the personnel provided. It was generally expected that this would be a makeshift until the real thing arrived, but up to now absolutely nothing in the way of official cover has turned up. It does make you wonder how they expected us to survive. Or perhaps they didn't!"

Troubles with Transport

The PBI (poor bloody infantry) had to go everywhere first, take the heaviest casualties and endure the roughest of living. They must have envied the gunners riding to battle in lorries. The joys of mechanisation palled though when the wretched things didn't work.

"I had an adventure on one trip that was the reverse of pleasant while it lasted; my lorry broke down and when it had been restarted we were unable, in the dark, to locate the rest of the convoy. The state of the lorry grew worse and worse, finally the carburettor caught fire. We managed to put out the flames mercifully (we were carrying ammo) and I had then to set out on foot to try and locate the Unit. I did manage to locate them eventually (that is a story in itself) and took out a breakdown truck to bring mine in. When we were in harbour (at a farm) we found ourselves a lovely barn of hay to sleep in. We shared it with some Polish gunners already settled in there. We were all so tired that we just drew overcoats and hay over ourselves and settled down in all our clothes. I was high up near the roof and was just dozing off when I became aware of all the things I had put in my pockets during the day pressing on my back very painfully! – even in my scouting days I never had such a collection! There were spanners and washers, cigarette boxes, ration tins – all crammed into every pocket. I hated the idea of getting up to empty them, besides it would have meant disturbing men all round me, so I rolled carefully

first to one side, then the other, drew them out gently, slid them into my boots!

That, I thought, was causing the minimum of noise and movement. But I hadn't reckoned with the eerie sound it must have made, especially the boot part of it. First a couple of Poles awoke and conversed in rather startled accents, then a British voice, equally apprehensive said suddenly sharply 'What-is-it – a-bloody-rat-up-there?' I don't think a remark has ever struck me as being so wildly funny. I lay and simply burst with laughter for about ten minutes, then decided to suspend operations. In the morning, of course, I had forgotten, and tried to pull on my boots at Reveille, to the great amusement of the Poles. I wonder if they put two and two together?"

"… On this occasion we were as filthy a couple of specimens as ever were. I had taken a couple of tumbles during a winching operation – hauling a trailer out of a veritable bog by means of a steel chain operated by the driver of the towing truck. Kilner had doubled up in mirth at our appearance, and asked me from the sanctuary of his Jeep if it was for my complexion. I've never seen mud like this – where vehicles go in up to their axles and stick fast. Along comes a GTV [Gun Towing Vehicle] to pull it out and slap! Into another trough it goes, and then up comes another to the rescue – with the same results, until they resemble a lot of elephants writhing in a quicksand and roaring in agony. It brings one to the point of boiling rage – and then to laughter, you can't help it. One of the vehicles was being pulled out inch by inch, everybody holding their breath and praying, when suddenly with a terrific crack the towing hook came off, pulled clean off. For some reason everybody who until then had been on edge and swearing copiously exploded with laughter. 'All the fun of the fair', 'Last shot rings the bell', 'Hand the gentleman that flower vase'. Everybody rolled in mirth at something approaching calamity and the driver removed his cap and bowed. This at a spot where it was pretty unhealthy to linger!"

"… Movement is a nightmare. Every step you take is a slither and a boot full of wet slime, vehicles are bogged and have to pull each other around, trailers (and men) disappear into ditches, and altogether it's about the most exhausting and maddening existence imaginable. In appearance we resemble sewer-rats – and our language just about matches it.

Do you remember how the cats used to try and get off the mark on that polished lino when they were scared – going hell for leather and getting nowhere? That's just what happens to our trucks every hundred yards or so – a sudden halt and a frenzied threshing of wheels and then she settles down and heels over like a torpedoed ship. And then it's dismount and a haul on a filthy winch cable And so ad infinitum.

When an officer comes up in the middle of all this and reminds you that the column is behind schedule or holding up another crowd – well honestly. I would take them and well meaning M Police by the scruff of the neck and shake them until their teeth rattle. I have to be content with either ignoring them or saying as offensively as possible 'I know…!'"

Turn Again, Gunners

October gales hampered Cherbourg and badly damaged the Mulberry harbour at Arromanches. Eisenhower stressed the criticality of Antwerp in a letter to Montgomery on 9th: *"… I must repeat, we are now squarely up against the situation which we have anticipated for months; our intake into Continent will not support our battle. All operations will come to a standstill unless Antwerp is producing by middle of November."*[xlviii]

9th October also saw the start of the Moscow Conference between Churchill, Stalin and US Ambassador Harriman. Churchill was frustrated in his aims to bring Russia into the war against Japan and involve the exiled Polish Government in discussions about the future of their country. There was, however, agreement about the post-war balance of power in the Balkans.

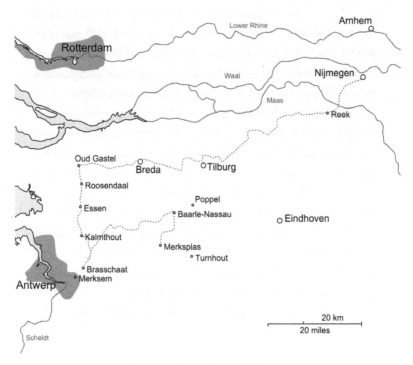

Map 9: Merksplas to Nijmegen

On 16th October Montgomery issued new orders giving absolute priority to securing the Scheldt and sea access to Antwerp. The right wing of the 1st Canadian army swung west toward the city, sealing off the isthmus leading to South Beveland and Walcheren Island. 60th HAA and the Polar Bears accordingly doubled back to the area around Brasschaat on Antwerp's eastern outskirts. The gunners arrived first, on 20th October, so grabbed their rifles and went looking for enemy patrols reported in the area. Their luck held: they didn't find any.

"I am afraid this letter will reach you after another lapse of time... things have been most difficult again, a lot of moves plus

242

reorganisation and it has left all of us a bit flummoxed as regards mail and an address."

The battery, briefly, reunited with its radar section.

"There is not much news I can tell you about at the moment. I am back with Sammy and the boys and we are on a new job. The weather is foul and the ground cover unbelievably muddy and tonight especially we all feel overworked and tired."

The Germans knew as well as Eisenhower and Montgomery that holding the Antwerp approaches was a game-changer for either side. The defenders were seasoned troops, well dug in and as well equipped and reinforced as the depleted German Army could manage. Already, on 13th October, the Canadian 5th Infantry Brigade's Black Watch had been virtually wiped out in an unsuccessful attack. Continuous, heavy fighting succeeded in clearing the south bank of the Scheldt by 3rd November. Operations starting on 24th October took the South Beveland peninsula on the north bank. Finally, combined land and amphibious assaults between 31st October and 8th November captured the remaining German forces on Walcheren Island. After three weeks of minesweeping and repair the port was usable on 28th November.

60th HAA moved a few miles north to Kalmthout on 22nd October. Two days later one of 206 Battery's gun tractors was damaged by enemy shelling, again without injury. Eric was still with the radar section but didn't know for how long. On 25th things slackened enough for him to dash off a letter.

"My letter writing has deteriorated very rapidly these last few days, I'm afraid, but we are now 'resting' in billets and things should be normal for a few days at least. The interim was very crowded and

hectic; it was my first work with the section for quite a long time. The commitment came to a rather premature end, and now they are back and awaiting another job. I don't know yet whether I shall remain with them or revert to my old job with field artillery, but I hope to stay here at least for a short time and do some work on the equipment. I don't much mind either way."

We can only guess what had the team so busy in the *Luftwaffe's* absence. It may have been a stop-gap part of Antwerp's V1 defence but without the latest radar and predictors they couldn't have done much against fast, low-flying targets. It is more likely that they were locating enemy mortars for counter-battery fire. The six-barrelled *Nebelwerfer* was among the most effective, and feared, of German weapons. The Canadians used AA radars operationally to spot them in the battle of the Scheldt,[xlix] so the timing is about right.

New formations rotating into the line reminded Eric that he was now a veteran.

"… The unit we were working with was a good one but comparatively late arrivals and a bit unused to everything. It's remarkable how 'experienced' one feels at this stage – even a bit 'superior' in dealing with majors and troop commanders who haven't had much experience in the line. Seeing them dither always makes me amused at my old fears of being in the same state…"

The newcomers were probably the Timberwolves (see above).

As the Poles attacked Breda and the Polar Bears tackled Esschen on 26th–27th October, 206 Battery grabbed a quick rest at Fort Merksem on the outskirts of Antwerp.

"I have been meaning to write all the evening and thank God the room has settled down now, all busy writing letters and silence

temporarily reigns supreme. Sammy and Corporal Jimmy Green have desisted from practising a tango they saw danced in a cafe last night – thought it would be a good item for Christmas. You must certainly meet Jimmy after the war. His hobby is theatricals and he is a 'balletomane.' The trouble is this is such a confined space for rehearsals.

We have a nice little room for the NCOs of the section, the only trouble is it was taken by assault and most of the glass in the windows and doors is missing, besides there are various bullet holes to cause draughts. We had the 'Sanitary' people round today checking up on accommodation and overcrowding! They instantly condemned the room, saying it was too small for all of us, and were worried about us not having sufficient air! Thereupon we laughed rudely and uproariously and declared we were getting more and more ventilation each night on account of the bombs and what-nots (albeit in the distance) shaking out what glass remained and asked them to call again. But they remained unconvinced, and declared there were many flats in the town empty and there was no reason for overcrowding. We instantly saw their point of view then and pointed out various buildings we would not be averse to taking over. But it really is ridiculous. When you are in the field you are expected to provide what cover you can devise and nobody bothers to come along and find out how you are faring. When you are settled in something like civilised quarters they begin to worry."

Jennie replied: *"I should like to see Sammy and Jimmy practising their tango. And it is nice to hear that you have a ballet enthusiast in your midst. I wonder if he will convert you."* Eric saw 'For Whom the Bell Tolls' in Antwerp and wrote a lengthy commentary (see 'Threads').

I have opened your parcel and am delighted at the contents… I opened the tin of jam tonight and we sampled it for tea. The woollies will be most welcome too, the days grow appreciably colder. I hope you can spare the orange juice. The Ostermilk [tinned, dried milk] *is also very welcome, likewise the cocoa.*

The urban interlude gave Eric and Jennie the chance to keep up with their sons' progress and plan Geoffrey's christening. The five to seven days' lag in postal delivery must have been deeply frustrating.

> *"He sounds an engaging little chap. It will be nice when he is a few months older and we can see what sort of a younger brother Hugh has got. It would be exciting to have a picture of him and still more exciting to come home and see him."*
>
> *"... Hugh is at a very interesting stage now and I do wish you were here to see more of his knowing little ways. Geoffrey does not show many signs of being like Hugh. But I think he is very attractive... I think you will feel very proud of both of them when it is your good fortune to see them again."*

The regiment moved up to Esschen on 28th October. While covering the Polar Bears and Poles at Roosendaal on 29th it suffered premature detonations, traced to fuzes which triggered if fired in heavy rain. They were hastily withdrawn.

Roosendaal fell after a day's heavy fighting. 'Bubbles' Barker described it as *"... not much of a place, bombed by the US A.F. early in the year. My chaps resting before finishing off the party in the Maas estuary. We have crossed 20 miles in 10 days and had to fight for every inch of it."*[1]

The gunners moved up to the village of Oud Gastel north of the town. Now within range of the Maas they shelled enemy positions on the river and troops crossing it. A third of the guns were nearing the end of their lives after months of continuous use. For Eric, still with the radar section near Antwerp, the novelty of depot life began to pall.

"I'm afraid I'm feeling infernally dull just at present. This business of marking time in a large camp doesn't suit me at all. It's all right for the first day or so but then life gets so dreadfully monotonous and seems to rob me of about half my energy. In the field I seem to be able to accomplish a lot besides my official duties. Here it's all petty routine for damn-all, and it is hampering and damned irritating. This is one aspect of soldiering I never get even remotely reconciled to."

Be careful what you wish for.

The opening of Antwerp promised an end to the armies' chronic supply problem. Strategic focus switched back to the Rhine and Germany beyond. Montgomery issued new orders on 2nd November for First Canadian Army to finish pushing the enemy north of the Lower Maas then take over the Nijmegen front from the sea to the Reichswald forest, releasing the divisions who had been fending off the Germans since *Market Garden* for a new offensive. Lucky them.

This made no immediate difference to 60th who spent the night of 2nd November supporting the Polar Bears and Timberwolves in an attack toward the Maas. The 49th especially thanked the gunners for the accuracy and efficiency of the artillery support they received during the three-day attack. Surfacing the next day, Eric wrote:

"My complaints about there being no active service for our unit were a bit premature as no sooner was the letter written than we were whisked off directly and again find ourselves operational.

Of course, there being no end to one's grumbling, I could complain now that the weather is cold and we are in a very bleak stretch of country. However, electricity on tap does make a difference, there is always somewhere warm to be at nights and we can always brew ourselves a drink."

"… Some farm people have fixed up a room for three of us, Sammy, myself and a staff sergeant. It rather reminds me of that room

*we had at Minehead. Strange to be sleeping in a bedroom again –
don't half spoil you!"*

*"… I would like particularly to be home now. Sometimes one feels
that the prospect of doing so in a reasonable time is pretty faint, but one
never knows. The progress here has really been not at all bad. I hope
for the sake of the people here that the Germans are cleared out of
Holland soon. If the threat to flood Northern Holland is put into effect
it will affect about 7 million people and will have terrible consequences.*

*It's good to know that Belgium has suffered very little from the
war and that it is now entirely cleared of Germans."*

Nijmegen

The reorientation of the front caught up with the regiment on 6th
November: the gunners ceased fire and harboured briefly in a
brickworks east of Roosendaal while their commander, Lieutenant-
Colonel Turner, surveyed new positions at Nijmegen.

Lieutenant-General Sir John Crocker commanding 1st (British)
Corps wrote: *"I know the formations you have supported, Polish, American
and British, have all been most appreciative of the help and co-operation
received from your regiments. All have done splendidly but perhaps I may
mention particularly 60 HAA REGT which joined us earlier than the
remainder and which has been specially brought to my notice for its enterprising
and valuable work."[li]* His son, a tank officer, had been killed in action
a couple of weeks earlier.

Next day the 60th moved up, overnighting at Reek near Grave,
to relieve 107th HAA who had been busy in both ground and anti-
aircraft roles at Nijmegen since late September. This would be their
cold, wet, muddy, miserable home until February 1945.

Their arrival coincided with reduced *Luftwaffe* activity in
preparation – though no-one knew it – for the German Ardennes

('Battle of the Bulge') offensive which started on 16th December. The AA mission included tackling V1s on their way to Antwerp as well as the new German jet fighters. Both were tricky calls: the regiment was still using the No 1 predictor which was ill-suited to fast targets and snap engagements.

As well as their friends the 49th they now supported the 50th (Northumbrian) Infantry Division: battle-scarred veterans of Dunkirk, North Africa, Sicily, Normandy and Arnhem. This was the 50th's swansong: it would shortly be the second infantry division broken up to replace losses elsewhere.

On 12th November in northern Norway the RAF finally sank the *Tirpitz*, to the Navy's relief. At Nijmegen the same day saw the start of four days' artillery duelling in support of the Northumbrians. Eric found time to dash off two letters, though not in the best of moods.

"I sometimes can't help feeling a bit amused (it's a pretty grim joke) that there is not a thing that I do from day to day that I would not have recoiled from with horror a few years ago – in fact when I realised I was in for this I said 'Well I'll have a go, but I know I'll never reconcile myself to any of it – it'll be a damn bad business'. I don't know if the balance sheet will be to my credit at the end – I suppose I must take a chance on it... if this is education it's a pretty primitive and expensive one!

... I have one idea that I write far too much in the 'soldiering mood' – which is as typical of the real 'me' as Boris Karloff.

... I might add that neither in the actuality or in retrospect do my experiences of war give me any cause for fear or worry. Enemy action or the continuous racket of our own artillery has never caused me to lose a moment's sleep, put me off my stroke or dream a single disturbing dream. I think I know why this is – it's not of the first importance. It's not what I really worry about. In fact it's a palliative,

it's something that I can do and it gives me a surface satisfaction to do it as well as I can. It's nothing compared with that lurking discontent about duties at home unavoidably neglected, my separation from you and the children all this time, and of course, the job…

Apart from performing my duties to my own satisfaction I have not one shred of ambition left; thank God I have shaken off that frame of mind in which I sought promotion or a commission… Until I can be back with you and we can carry on afresh and seek our own relaxation I'll crawl around in mud and do my damndest – at any rate it's real effort – Len said the other day 'If Jennie and Jimmy [Len's wife] *could see us now, I wonder what they would say' – a thought that always gives him especial pleasure…"*

By 13th November the general grimness was at least relieved by a dry dugout – a joy to be cherished – and army ablutions.

"The interim has been awful. We have dodged all over the place, in the worst weather, mud up to our eyes and (speaking personally) in the worst of tempers.

… We are bogged – absolutely bogged – in a place where there's so much water that we might as well become marines and sail ourselves about.

However at the time of writing there is at least one redeeming feature – we have taken over some well built dug outs complete with stoves. Len and I are sharing one, and tonight we've ignored all orders to emerge and consult authority – we're here to stop for this evening anyway. Sammy and Vic Brushett are the unlikely men on duty.

… Well, I suppose we shall complain and grumble when we get home again, but there will be precious little excuse for it.

Barring a slight cold I don't feel too bad. I should welcome a really good hard winter out here – plenty of frost and hard ground – one can manage to keep warm then. It would put an end to dripping slimy clothes and sopping boots.

Thank God the army still does us well for showers and clean changes of clothes – the mobile showers follow up all the time and it is one of the grandest bits of the organisation – makes you feel a bit human occasionally."

Jennie never read them.

ENDINGS

Goodbye '44

J ennie died suddenly on 14th November 1944. It came as a bolt
from the blue three weeks after the birth of their second son.
Eric transferred immediately to 49th Reinforcement Holding
Unit – a temporary posting for reinforcements, training, leave,
rest camps and personnel in transit – on compassionate leave. On
20th November the county council temporarily took his newborn
and infant sons into care. By 27th he was back home writing cheques
to clear outstanding debts, pay for Jennie's funeral and administer
the estate. By 9th December he had arranged for his sons' lodging
at an orphanage: the Babies' Hotel and Nursery Training College
near Guildford. He was negotiating with Jennie's family over the
removal of their property and her effects from the house, which he
rented to a Flight Lieutenant Whitely from 1st January 1945.
Simultaneously he was trying to sort out payment of Guardian's
Allowance with the Army Paymaster – a bureaucratic maze which
took until March to clear. By 7th January he was back with his
regiment in Nijmegen.

We can only imagine the grief, disorientation and manic activity
behind this bare story – and remember it was repeated with
variations many, many times over the six years of war.

He may have been too busy to notice the Home Guard standing
down on 3rd December. Seven thousand of them, representing the
whole country, paraded for the last time in front of the King, Queen
and princesses. They were formed in May 1940 as Local Defence

Volunteers; expected to face German shock troops with local knowledge, improvised weapons and not much else. Their equipment, training and contribution developed steadily during the war but, in perhaps the clearest sign yet that the whole dreadful business was drawing to a close, they were no longer needed. The Nazi Party had in the meantime created a German equivalent, the *Volkssturm*, the previous October.

Public attention in Britain was turning to the post-war world. Building pre-fabricated housing for demobilised servicemen, setting up new airlines and buying land for a civil airport at Heath Row featured prominently in the news.

On 1st January the Soviet Union installed a puppet government in 'liberated' Poland. Next day Allied bombers flattened the centre of Nuremberg.

Eric missed an almost equally miserable time at Nijmegen. Once again in morale-sapping, static, defensive positions the weather and the Germans conspired to make life difficult. Repeated

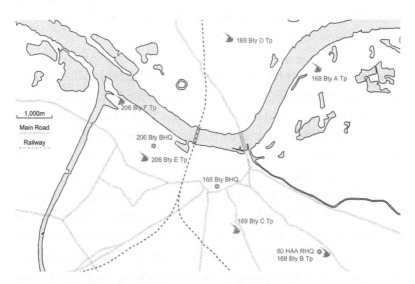

Map 10: 60th HAA dispositions at Nijmegen in January 1945

attempts to dislodge the Allies from the bridgehead kept the regiment busy with daily ground shoots and occasional anti-aircraft fire while ceaseless rain made conditions almost unbearable.

169 Battery was shelled on the 16th and 19th November. They lost one killed and one wounded, two vehicles destroyed and a gun damaged. The enemy clearly had their range so they moved to new positions.

In the dark and the rain, water and waterlogged road look much alike. One of 206 Battery's jeeps drove into Nijmegen Reservoir drowning all three aboard. Eric wrote of an earlier incident:

"Poor old Sam! He was endeavouring to march in with a lorry towing a generator the other night and never turned up. He was subsequently found – the whole outfit had run into a dyke. He is a bit on the worrying side and the episode caused him to have a minor 'nerve storm' – when he was finally pulled out and reached us he went straight to bed and lay there well into the following day, and neither threats nor coercion could move him. When he said 'Bugger the breakfast' and the same about dinner I was really alarmed, but he staggered up and got some tea."

On 25th November flooding forced two troops and 168 Battery HQ to evacuate their positions. They moved to the brickworks, where the still-rising water cut them off next day. One troop and the BHQ had to be further evacuated by barge on 14th and 15th December. For nearly four weeks all their supplies were ferried in by DUKW (amphibious truck).

In Athens on 3rd December police and British troops violently dispersed a demonstration against the disarmament of independent guerrilla groups. 28 demonstrators were killed and 148 injured. This triggered 37 days of full-scale fighting between British troops and anti-Nazi resistance groups; an embarrassing and unedifying

*Figure 18: Bombing and 'Market Garden' left Nijmegen in a poor state
(Source: US Army Signal Corps via Wikimedia Commons)*

spectacle. It left a legacy of fragmented, resentful politics and has been described as 'the first battle of the Cold War.'

December in Nijmegen continued the cold and wet theme – wetter still after the Germans blew the riverbanks on the 2nd. Static didn't mean quiet: the 'island' between Nijmegen and Arnhem was constantly disputed between the Polar Bears and enemy forces. Trenches filled with water as quickly as they were dug. Patrols had to use canoes or wade through freezing water. Each side routinely shelled the other.

German paratroops made a determined attempt to dislodge the Polar Bears on 4th December. The resulting bitter battle lasted ten days. 'F' Troop (Eric's) silenced a troublesome machine gun near Arnhem in the counter attack.

The regiment lost 23 men transferred to infantry, and its commanding officer, who was promoted.

As local fighting petered out on 16th December the Germans launched their Ardennes offensive. The attack achieved complete surprise and brought a renewed air assault. Nijmegen wasn't directly threatened but fighter-bombers attacked the Maas and Waal bridges at low level on 17th and 18th, after which bad weather grounded both sides for several days.

On 21st December the threat of airborne attack forced the gunners to set up anti-paratroop defences with doubled guards. The assault didn't materialise but enemy low-level sweeps resumed on 24th to keep them on their toes.

More positively, the floods subsided far enough to supply the stranded troops by lorry instead of DUKW. 206 Battery HQ achieved the holy grail of a dry billet by moving into a school. And *nothing* was going to get in the way of their Christmas celebration – enlivened by cinemas, Entertainments National Service Association (ENSA) parties and a film crew. Lieutenant Christopherson, an officer of the troop, sent Eric an account of the party.

> *"Xmas Day and back in the Plotting Room. I thought you might like to know how we were getting on and how we spent the day of the year.*
>
> *It began with Sergeants and Officers taking a piping hot cup of tea round to the delighted Gunners, who proceeded to spend an energetic morning hitting the old hay and beating their heads on the blankets. In justice to the exceptions, I must add that the cooks – noble fellows, with a group of selected men, translated themselves to the factory where we were to have dinner; and the names of Craftsman Shaun and Gunner Crothers, pillars of the church, no doubt in 'Civvie Street,' earned good marks by accompanying those ~~bastards~~*

gallant officers, Adams and Christopherson to 9 o'clock communion.

By 1.30 pm the blokes were congregating, & a hubbub of pleasant anticipation disturbed the grateful atmosphere of the odours of the Xmas dinner. We had a couple of Xmas trees, holly & paper decorations – home made – I bought the paper, Smith the batman & Mr Holloway & the Spotters manufactured the paper chains.

They sat at small tables, four at a table & the usual inefficiency of Sergeants & Officers was thrown into greater relief than ever as they acted as waiters. In their defence, though a Puritan wouldn't admit it as such, I must say that they had drunk deeply that morning, & to keep nothing back from you, the previous evening too.

Sgt Joyce was particularly funny; he greeted every spoonful of food, be it pork or turkey, be it Xmas pud or peaches, with a profuse 'Thank you' delivered in that moving voice, charged with deep emotion, of which he is so capable. Hodge was wildly funny: & Albert Smith with a bowler pulled down over his ears did a dancing version of 'Any Old Iron' which I shall remember for a long time. It was filmed by some Army Photographic Service men who were present. They also took Kendall and Crudge singing – and Beckerman! (God! with a too wide, fixed smile like a tailor's dummy!) issuing cigars to the men.

After the meal, which was a credit to Greenaway, Hobbs did some conjuring tricks which I missed, because I was helping to dress the panto players, but which I hear was an eye opener.

The panto was an uproarious success. I was a bit anxious beforehand because we'd never rehearsed in dress, & most of them had been tight as lords half an hour before. It was a version of 'Cinderella' aimed at a Troop audience. I got the idea one night when Bale was having his leg pulled about the size of his feet & I thought that an inverted Cinderella where an enormous rubber knee boot replaced the glass slipper might make an amusing theme. It developed greatly from there, thanks largely to the co-operation of the actors who made lots of suggestions which I seized on at once &

incorporated. But apart from the twists of the plot, the wise cracks and the song – yes! we had a song – the actual acting was surprisingly good. Joyce, as Prince Charming, did a skit of Cap. Newton giving an Orders Group which brought the house down; 'Cinder-Bale' was equally good; & Hodge as 'Fairy Fly wheel'(!) dressed like Groucho, & Hooker & Mr. Holloway as the Ugly Sisters all shone with meteoric brilliance. I wish you'd been here to see it; and to help with it too!

Well that's all for Xmas. The 'Shower' is not revived yet – & there is a great need for it now that we are stuck in one spot. – I have made another Wind Machine!!! – The best yet, I claim. It consists in your Wheel of Fortune, slightly added to, and a single table; and there is only one operation! The old wind graph is scrapped altogether. How is it done? – I'll tell you when you come back.

Oh, by the way; we have been forestalled! I got an anthology for Xmas from home called the 'Knapsack,' collected by Herbert Read, which seems to be inspired by a similar idea to ours about the possibility of a popular enjoyment of the robust poets. Here's a quote from the Blurb:

'This is a fighting man's book and it contains, besides high thinking heroism and relaxation, sorrow and laughter'.

I hope you are keeping well and I trust that you are succeeding in settling all the problems you were recalled for in so cruel a fashion. It has been a sad Xmas for you; may the future be kind to you.

My very best wishes for 1945; looking forward to seeing you again."

In the closing days of December the mud gave way to a bitter freeze. A new commanding officer, Lieutenant-Colonel Lyons, joined from 25th Light Anti-Aircraft regiment. On 30th an air observation post (light reconnaissance aircraft) spotted an enemy parade and called in the regiment's guns to disperse it.

On the same day 1st Polish Armoured Division made the first of several costly attacks on Kapelsche Veer, a tiny hamlet about fifty miles

Figure 19: The 1944 Christmas Party

downstream of Nijmegen. It was strongly garrisoned by German paratroops, who held out against all comers until the end of January.

Happy New Year.

The Final Shove

As 1945 began the Ardennes offensive still absorbed Allied attention. Nonetheless its momentum was faltering: gritty American resistance at Bastogne, and Patton's and Montgomery's extraordinary work to close off the German flanks blunted the ground assault.

The *Luftwaffe* secretly amassed some 800 fighters by pulling squadrons from other fronts and mobilising those in training. On New Year's Day it unleashed Operation *Bodenplatte*: wide-ranging, low-level attacks across the North West European theatre in a desperate attempt to regain the initiative. Artillery and fighter defences were surprised but alert. The four-day air battle destroyed many Allied aircraft and installations, mostly on the ground and quickly replaced: human casualties were relatively light. On the other hand the *Luftwaffe* lost nearly half the aircraft involved and over 200 irreplaceable pilots killed, wounded or captured. German aircrew went into action with murderously little training – RAF pilots on the ground were heard to shout "Weave, you fools, weave!" as they approached.[lii] The survivors could never be dismissed or ignored but it was the *Lufwaffe's* last hurrah as a fighting force.

On 8th January the German propagandist "Mary of Arnhem" broadcast a convincing but fake BBC piece praising Montgomery's efforts in the Ardennes at American expense. It plausibly followed a self-centred Montgomery press release and temporarily soured relations between the armies.

At Nijmegen on 13th January, artillery fought off a renewed attack on the bridges by German *Biber* ('Beaver') one-man midget submarines. Lt Colonel D V G Brock led the defenders who were immediately christened *HMS Brockforce*.[liii] None of the submarines survived.

Five days later the German 6th Parachute Division attacked Zetten near Arnhem. Two days of vicious fighting left the Polar Bears back in control of the village having taken 340 prisoners and inflicted an estimated 300 casualties on the enemy for 220 of their own.[liv]

In breaks from daily ground shoots and intermittent anti-aircraft work 60th HAA replaced 17 worn-out gun barrels: heavy, cold labour. Early in the month the frost was so hard they were firing guns at night to prevent them freezing. A late Christmas present arrived in the form of updated predictors – the No. 10 at last. Predictor No 10 was the British name for the American Bell AAA Computer purchased from late 1943. It allowed AA guns to engage faster, higher-flying targets and made fully-automatic engagements possible when used with the American SCR 584 (UK designation Radar No 3 Mk V) and powered gun mounts. British regiments in NW Europe didn't receive many until the end of 1944, and the V1 defences of Antwerp and Brussels had priority.

From 27th to 31st January the Canadians mounted a final, successful assault on Kapelsche Veer, helped by two GL Mk 3 radars which located and kept track of enemy mortars.[lv]

Despite his generally acerbic view of officerdom Eric was on cordial terms with those of his troop, especially Newton and Christopherson. Captain Newton, by then a logistics planner at 39 Movement Control, wrote to him on 3rd February.

> *"… it is not much of a job but it is not so bad for me as it is connected with shipping of which I know a little and in which I am extremely interested… I was bitterly sorry at leaving the Troop of whom believe me I was very fond and very proud – they were (are – sorry) a splendid lot and always gave me the most magnificent support, I was hoping to have finished this war with them but still, there it is."*

Eric wrote back with troop gossip and Newton replied:

> *"… I am sorry not to have been present to witness Gardner's prowess with the pick and 15 core cable – I feel I would have enjoyed his comments as much as he would have enjoyed mine. I miss the companionship of the Troop more than anything – they are a grand lot of lads – which brings me to your commission. If you are still really keen – don't sit and wait or nothing will happen. Keep on at the*

O.C. via Mr Foulds until something does happen… I had to send
in my recommendation to the O.C. and I did my best for you… This
life is very chairborne and a racket – neither of which I very much
like and I shall probably speak out of turn before long!"

It was time to move again. The front line ran almost due south from Nijmegen along the western edge of the *Reichswald* forest: pretty well where it had been since *Market Garden* in September. Behind the forest the Germans had prepared fortifications in depth (the northern end of the Siegfried Line). Soft ground, rivers, flooding and forest made it difficult to exploit Allied superiority in numbers. Still, to end the war they had to fight their way into Germany.

Operation *Veritable* kicked off on 8th February after a massive build-up of troops and equipment. It started with the most intense British artillery bombardment yet seen: nearly 800 pre-selected targets shelled to a meticulous timetable. 60th HAA fired more than 3,800 rounds over nineteen hours, again suffering premature detonations in heavy rain. They were on call for concentrations and counter-battery fire until the battle moved beyond range, then reverted to their anti-aircraft role.

Interestingly, they were ordered *not* to shoot at passing V1s during the build-up: Allied forces were so densely packed into the assembly area that a downed missile was almost bound to hit something important.

At the Yalta summit of 4th to 11th February Churchill, Roosevelt and Stalin agreed post-war spheres of influence in Europe and the four occupation zones in Germany. Stalin dominated the conference, keeping the territory Russia had annexed in eastern Poland and recognition of Soviet interests in China. He agreed in principle to join the war with Japan once Germany was dealt with.

13th February saw Marshal Koniev's army just 70 miles from Dresden, an architectural landmark and communications centre. In

Britain a long procession of aircraft headed east as RAF and USAAF bombers began a two-day attack to help the Soviets by paralysing transport[lvi]. The resulting firestorm killed some 25,000 people and remains controversial today. In the ranking of horror it trails Warsaw (1939; 40,000 deaths), Hamburg (1943; 45,000 deaths) and Tokyo (1945; 100,000 deaths). Polish aircrew were almost mutinous before the raid, having just discovered the loss of eastern Poland under the terms of the Yalta agreement, but their government-in-exile urged acceptance.

Veritable, which Eisenhower later described as *"a bitter slugging match,"*[lvii] cleared the *Reichswald* by 22nd February. It continued as Operation *Blockbuster* until 11th March when British and Canadian forces linked with an American attack from the south. The Allies now held the west bank of the Rhine and, thanks to the US capture of an intact bridge at Remagen, a foothold on the other side. After a pause to build up forces, a set-piece assault starting on 23rd March crossed the Lower Rhine in several places.

There was – relative – quiet on the 'island' between Nijmegen and Arnhem. The Polar Bears had a series of short, sharp fights for individual farms and hamlets and the Royal Scots Fusiliers raided across the Lower Rhine with smokescreen and artillery support. The spring thaw gruesomely revealed German and British bodies until then covered by snow.

On 9th March Hitler sacked Gerd von Rundstedt, one of his ablest commanders, for the third and final time. The ailing, exhausted field marshal removed his family to the safest place he could find in Germany and was eventually taken prisoner on 1st May.

The Allies now occupied parts of Germany, raising the question of behaviour toward a civilian population seeing them as conquerors not liberators. Fear of spies, saboteurs and Nazis evading prison led to a strict 'no fraternisation' rule. This was easier said than done in the face of desperate need. The following extract is from a long despatch by Rex North in the *Sunday Pictorial* of 11th March.

"*I can assure you it is not easy to deal with a defeated people who, instead of being sullen and revengeful, are anxious only to co-operate.*

... I have seen khaki-clad colonels stand helpless and embarrassed before Germans.

For they had found out a staggering truth: that it is easy enough to kill Germans but much more difficult to know what to do with them when they refuse to fight you any more.

... Sooner or later someone will have to give them both chocolate and soap, as there is no other way of teaching these people that there is a better way of living than they knew under the Nazis.

YOU AT HOME SHOULD UNDERSTAND THIS NOW, SO THAT WHEN YOUR SONS AND BROTHERS COME HOME TO A BRITAIN JOYOUS IN VICTORY, YOU WON'T START AN ARGUMENT WHEN THEY SAY: 'I GAVE MY CHOCOLATE RATION TO SOME GERMAN KID.'"

British householders were encouraged to reduce their gas and electricity consumption. A hard winter had left the country short of the coal needed to produce both.

In further signs of the approaching end the fire-watchers were disbanded, a short stretch of Brighton Beach re-opened to the public, and it was announced that General Pile, commander of anti-aircraft forces, would take up a new post in charge of the government housing programme on 16th April.

V1 and V2 attacks finally ceased at the end of March as the Allies overran the last launch sites. The final month killed nearly 800 people.

The pace picked up on 2nd April when Operation *Destroyer*, to seize control of the 'island,' started under a huge artillery barrage. Once again 60th HAA were busily throwing high-explosive over the Polar Bears' heads. The operation went well and was complete by 5th. After further preparation and the customary barrage Operation

Quick Anger took the Polar Bears across the river east of Arnhem and into the town during the night of 12th. Four days' fighting cleared the defenders (including some Dutch SS) from Arnhem and the surrounding heights. Six months after *Market Garden* the Brits were back and the road to northern Holland was open.

The Allies entered a ruined town. Dutch support for *Market Garden* had infuriated the occupiers who evicted the population, looted anything valuable, destroyed many of the buildings and fortified others. Allied bombing and shelling over the winter and the occasional short-falling V2 had scarcely improved the scenery. Finally a German freight ban caused widespread starvation over the *'Hongerwinter.'*

Figure 20: A Sherman Crab flail tank in front of burning buildings in Arnhem, 14 April 1945. (IWM BU 3515)

The 5th Canadian (Armoured) Division and the Polar Bears continued toward the Ijsselmeer, leaving the 60th guarding the Nijmegen bridges as the sound of battle faded north. On 3rd May the regiment moved a few miles east to Emmerich, a Rhine crossing captured early in April. The move saved them from transferring to infantry with the rest of the brigade. Captain Newton popped in for a chat as they were packing.

> *"... I have no real job as yet but was told by the Moguls in Brussels to get out and 'cover the area' and was supplied with a 15 cwt in which to cover it; what they omitted to tell me, and admitted that it was because they didn't know, was what the area was! So I do fairly well as you can imagine; I covered the Nijmegen area last Thursday* [3rd May] *on the off chance of its being one of the places I was intended to visit, and found all at the Power House fit and well; on arrival there I was immediately confronted with the Brigadier's car and on enquiry... found that he had arrived to give the Tp a farewell pep talk as the Regt was moving into Germany the next day... Apparently the Regt has been selected to become part of the Air Defence of Germany (?) and is leaving 74 Bde in favour of 101 Bde. The rest of 74 is I gather being turned into infantry units. The Tp received the news with very mixed feelings but as I pointed out at least they will be kept more or less together.*
>
> *I smiled happily when I saw Sgt Lake just hitching his little piece of nonsense on the back of LI and I thought he looked a little embarrassed and shamefaced! Anyway it was quite sad to see the CP* [Command Post] *all demolished and what was left of my armchair in the middle of the ruin... needless to say they were a tractor short with the result that the PF was being left behind. Actually they are not moving far but are defending a Bailey bridge over the river at a very badly knocked about town about an hour's run away.*
>
> *Capt Foulds was on a recce when I arrived so I only just saw him when he returned; Messrs Christopherson and Knight were*

however in very good form. I did not see Sellers at all as he was with Capt Foulds but I understand that he – this time in company with Sgt Harris – had set fire to himself again; this time he was setting fire to all the cordite from a separated round for the benefit of some newcomers; I believe that they were very impressed. Well, well! And after all I told them about doing stupid things too.

… Altogether I had a very pleasant day and it was more than pleasant seeing all the old faces especially as I had all the old familiar cracks made at my expense and needless to say no respect! A bit of luck my going when I did – one day later and I should have had it."

All German forces in the Netherlands surrendered on 5th May. Newton was caught up in the celebration:

"… there was a big time in the old town when the news about Holland came through; after a short but sharp session in the Mess yours truly was then entertained until 0345 a.m. by some civilians and ended up being kissed by everyone, male and female! Almost disgusting but I was compensated by the fact that they literally could not move their eyes the next morning whereas I could only not move my head."

The war in Europe ended on 7th May. 60th HAA had the honour of firing a victory salvo at the GHQ celebration that day, and the press printed a history of the regiment.

Captain Newton wrote:

"I had a long letter from Sgt Joyce the other day; the firing of the victory salute involved a move at 0330 hours in pouring rain but earned the whole regt 3 days leave in Brussels. The whole regt are apparently now non operational but with all equipt back in Belgium which I should imagine means that something is in store for them!"

*Figure 21: 3.7-inch guns of 60th HAA Regiment fire a victory salvo,
6th May 1945. (IWM BU 5319)*

President Roosevelt died on 12th April, just weeks before victory.
Hitler committed suicide on 30th April.

The War's Over – What Do We Do Now?

General demobilisation began on 18th June. Each man, irrespective
of rank, received the same free issue of civilian clothing: suit (or
sports jacket and flannel trousers), raincoat, hat, shirt, two collars,
tie, shoes, studs and cuff-links.

British food rations reduced from 3,000 to 2,850 calories per

Map 11: Nijmegen to Tilburg, Emmerich and Stekene

person per day to provide for famine relief in liberated countries. The ration for German civilians was set at 1,400 calories per day.

Two surrendered U-Boats, U-776 and U-1023, were put on public display at various British ports. The Dogger Bank fishing grounds re-opened on 21st May.

Winston Churchill's National Government resigned on 23rd May. RAB Butler, interim Minister of Labour, had to deny newspaper rumours that demobilisation would accelerate if the

Conservatives won the election. The intention was to release 750,000 men and women under Class A (age and length of service), and 75,000 under Class B (special trade or skill) by the end of the year.

The General Election on 26th July was a Labour landslide and Clement Attlee became Prime Minister. Captain Newton commented:

> *"I try and have an open mind on the subject, but I can't help feeling that it won't work out quite as promised; there are far too many people who are either too stupid or too lazy to earn a living who will expect the Govt to produce the wherewithal out of yours and my pockets; I can't help feeling too, that the trade unions are going to prove very awkward before long. However I shall be very interested to hear what your ideas are."*

Eric, a lifelong socialist, probably disagreed.

Both Churchill and Atlee represented the UK at the Potsdam Conference between 17th July and 2nd August. The conference set post-war German borders; divided Vietnam along the 17th parallel; and recognised the Lublin Government of Poland instead of the London government-in-exile – cementing Soviet control of eastern and central Europe.

Separately the US, UK and China issued Japan an ultimatum to surrender or face 'prompt and utter destruction.' The Imperial Government ignored it until atomic bombs were dropped on Hiroshima and Nagasaki, on 6th and 9th August respectively. Also on 9th, the Soviet Union invaded Japanese-occupied Manchuria. Emperor Hirohito announced the surrender of the Japanese Empire on 15th August.

Eric's Travels

On 15th May Eric finally got his chance at promotion, moving to 148 Pre Officer Cadet Training Unit at Wrotham Hill in Kent. The regime there was largely a repeat of the fitness and infantry training he did before active service, which must have been galling for someone just back from the field. Captain Newton stayed in contact.

"I shall be interested to hear your reactions to OCTU [Officer Cadet Training Unit] and whether the 1945 version differs much from the 1940."

The reality of officer training did nothing to settle Eric's ambivalence about a commission. Newton wrote on 27th May:

"You ask my advice as to whether to carry on with it; well my advice to you is to do exactly what you feel most like doing without considering the army or the OCTU concerned. If you have no violent feeling either way I would stay; if the authorities don't know or don't bother about release groups that is their affair and you need have no compunction about that; I think the Bty Capt is quite right that they can't hold you even if you are commissioned on the day of your release and in any case they won't send you abroad with a release group as low as that, in addition the fact that you are commissioned may have some bearing on your war gratuity…"

In the end he didn't finish the course. On 26th July Newton wrote:

"I was so sorry to hear about the OCTU although really I don't know that you are any worse off except possibly financially when you come out. If you don't regard the time spent at OCTU as wasted and you have now a congenial job where you can keep an eye on the boys – why should you worry? That is going to be the chief job – keeping yourself occupied…"

By then Eric was attached to Depot, signalling his return to Britain and the chance of at least part-time contact with his sons.

Despite Eric's low discharge group he stayed in uniform until 1946. He transferred to a holding unit in January and was finally released on 25th March. He was pulled back for further training during the Korean War, and dusted off his uniform again for the Suez Crisis in 1956. In the event he wasn't needed for either and his liability for recall ceased at the age of 45 in 1957.

The Regiment's Travails

The regiment, now part of 75th AA Brigade, moved to Stekene near Antwerp on 19th May. From 24th they were busy preparing guns for a Supreme Headquarters Allied Expeditionary Force (SHAEF) exhibition in Antwerp. Newton wrote on 27th:

> *"Stubbington has also been relieved of his arduous duties and is now a learner on the No.10 – much to his annoyance and I should imagine Sgt Lake's! I would very much like to have got down and seen them again but they are west of Antwerp and I am afraid are too far away for me.*
>
> *I myself am fairly well occupied and quite occasionally even busy (no rude comments please). However I must admit that I don't take it really seriously but really as a method of passing the time till the day arrives. There is still plenty to drink in the mess with the result that I am still hoping one day to get to bed before midnight and still hoping not to have to drink 5 cups of tea at breakfast. However it can't last much longer and I imagine that very shortly the cupboard will be bare. That will be the day!"*

On 31st May the regiment deployed to Luneberg Heath, where the surrender was signed, under 21st Army Group. Five days later they moved to a Nieuport practice camp which had been set up in

January to train crews in the Radar No 3 Mk V/Predictor No 10 combination. Captain Newton visited on 8th July, just before their return, and later wrote:

> *"I got there about tea time, and found them just going out for the last time before returning to Stekene, so I am afraid I did not see many of the boys. They appeared to have had quite a good time – the weather had been good and they had done quite a lot of bathing. Sgt Lake seemed a little upset by the fact that it is now his turn to be in charge of an instrument which continually goes out of action and I gathered that the Radar personnel are not stinting in their comments... Kitch seemed a little restless but I tried to convince him that compared with most of the army he had very little to complain about...*

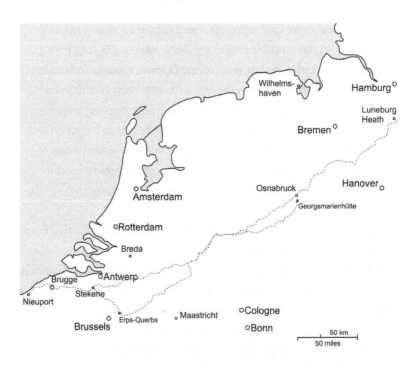

Map 12: The Regiment's travels from Stekene

I had a very good party in Ostend that evening with the officers from which I returned regrettably not strictly sober. As a result of which I had a thick head when I got up at 6 a.m. to see them off; anyway it was a most inspiring sight to see 9 tractors per troop steam past pulling the most exciting selection of instruments – I gather they carry a spare No.10.

I had not much difficulty in persuading Capts Barham and Foulds to stay behind for the morning, so we had a bite and lunch before I started on my return journey."

Major Reeve, the battery commander, was injured in a car accident on 23rd July and hospitalised for several months. Newton commented:

"Scandal; the OC, returning from a more than usually alcoholic party one night, turned his jeep over, and is now in England with a broken jaw and a cracked skull; Capt Barham's theory is that the elephant he was following turned off without putting out his trunk, but as he was apparently found in bed the next morning with his head in a waste paper basket, I don't see that he was in a position to say. However I believe it has all been explained to the satisfaction of the authorities. I believe he had just been accepted for retention in the army as a regular – possibly this was intended as a warning."

Captain Barham took over, succeeded by Kilner when Barham was released at the end of September.

On 1st September the unit moved to Erps Querbs near Brussels, then to occupation duties at Georgs-Marien Hütte south of Osnabrück on 29th. The army's main concern was to provide food, shelter and a functioning administration in the face of wrecked infrastructure and approaching winter. Christopherson wrote on 27th October:

"Haven't had time to appreciate conditions in Germany at the present moment yet; they seem docile. They're a thorough race – their house fittings (we've requisitioned a house for BHQ) are strength itself – when they lower the barriers at level crossings to stop road traffic while the train goes by, the crank operates a bell simultaneously as a warning! Today I told the headmaster of the school we are taking over that a certain room had to be cleared by tomorrow before the Troop arrived; after first saying how difficult it was at a weekend and on Sunday morning to get labour, he realised it was a 'must' and next thing we know was that dozens of German school children were all carrying piles of books, instruments, boxes etc out of the building.

The language difficulty is a great barrier, after the comparative fluency we'd attained in French. Of the two Germans we've interviewed so far one is pro British and the other pro Hitler – still maintains that the German is the best soldier in the world and that Hitler was deceived by the men financing him.

I gather that more trouble is to be expected from the discontent of the DPs [Displaced Persons] – Poles and Yugoslavs chiefly – at not getting back to their countries, than from the Germans; though lack of food and fuel this coming winter might bring trouble from Jerry too."

The following extracts from the regiment's orders paint a similar picture:

"Although the German is down and out at the moment and appears docile, this may not always be so. Some of them hate us intensely, and the sight of foreign tps [troops] controlling and holding them down increases this hatred. Some time they will try and hit back guerrilla fashion, the lack of food, fuel, homes and many of the necessities of life this winter may quite easily start things off.

The moral is, do not take the Hun for granted and regard them just as you would the civilians at home."

> "*… In this Bde* [Brigade] *Area, DPs have been conc*[entrated] *at registered camps and settlements under arrangements of 104. Mil Gov Det. DPs who were resident in the area before the war and those who are usefully employed have been permitted to remain at their normal residences and all DPs should be in possession of a Certificate of Residence issued by 104 Mil Gov Det.*
>
> *DPs are categorically forbidden to change their official place of residence without first obtaining the permission of 104 Mil Gov Det.*"

Apart from police duties the gunners were kept busy with cleaning, painting, courses on everything from boot repair to wireless, and sport – they dominated the 75th AA Brigade sports day in September.

On 4th November they returned to Georgs-Marien Hütte. The guns and equipment were prepared for storage, and progressive demobilisation reduced the regiment from its original strength of 900 men to about 700 by the end of the year.

Of the people we have come to know:

Sergeant Lake was mentioned in despatches.

Sergeant Len Nash ran a furniture business after the war.

Lieutenant Christopherson was promoted to Captain. In a bizarre twist his daughter was a contemporary at the *Daily Mail* of Eric's second wife.

Captain Barham, who had been with the regiment at Dunkirk and mentioned in despatches, was promoted to Acting Major.

Captain Kilner was mentioned in despatches and promoted to Acting Major.

Captain Newton was demobilised on V-J Day (15th August 1945) and returned to the remains of his house in Essex; it was demolished by a V1 while he was in Normandy.

By the end of the year Eric had lost contact with the regiment, and our interest fades.

THREADS

A simple narrative misses topics running through the correspondence, sometimes for months. This chapter lifts a few themes out of the background for a clearer view.

The Second World War was pivotal in more ways than the participants knew. Some realised it meant an inevitable sunset on an empire which had called in every possible favour, run up crippling debts, and most importantly defaulted on its side of the imperial deal. We could not defend our dominions.

At home old assumptions about our 'natural' rank and place in the world crumbled. If the First World War put women into factories the Second put them into uniform, bringing a seismic shift in the sexes' balance of influence. The influx of black GIs from 1942 challenged Britain to live up to its self-image of tolerance and fairness. Anti-Semitism was seen before as a bit tacky but not beyond the pale: Hitler showed us where that road leads. The Soviet Union's military sacrifices earned our admiration and its political system looked – from a distance – like hope for a better world. The 1945 election brought in Labour's first majority government on a landslide.

At mud level Eric's sardonically watched his old paper's antics and tried to launch a succession of local newssheets, while pay and promotion were a running sore. Jennie continued her full-time work and ran their house through blitz, blackout, queues and shortages. Throughout they kept up a lively commentary on contemporary books, films and music; punctuated by a sadder one on the gaps appearing in their circle.

This is the view from beneath as reality tilts.

Russia and America

While their leaders forged a special relationship (inevitably more special on this side) British and American voters were sceptical of each others' motives. In striking counterpoint a July 1942 survey asked Americans who they thought was trying hardest to win the war: 37% said the United States, 30% Russia, 14% China, 13% 'don't know,' and just 6% Britain.[lviii] In June 1943 50% of UK respondents to a similar question named Russia, 43% Britain and 3% the US.[lix]

Americans saw three and a half million men garrisoning the class-ridden British Isles while their politicians excused a litany of defeat abroad. They perceived a nation trying to preserve its privilege and fading, obsolete empire with everyone else's blood and treasure.

Across the Atlantic the view was rather different. Two years into a brutal, existential conflict the country saw a supposed ally sitting on the sidelines, profiting handsomely from Britain's distress until pitchforked into the war by the Japanese attack. A little grim amusement was unbecoming but understandable.

> *"Yes, the Japs and the Yanks really seem to have got to grips. America seems to have developed ARP hysteria in a more acute form than we had it at the beginning of the war – instead of profiting by our mistakes. The Japs can certainly hand it out – let us hope the Americans can take it. I am surprised to hear the amount of criticism I do of the Americans. I don't think there is much love lost between us really."*

> *"… The Japs seem to be putting the Yanks (not to mention ourselves) in a spot. Personally, I think the American navy has spent too much time contracting for Hollywood and hanging around Marlene Dietrich for its own fighting good. Tragedy apart, doesn't it make you smile to see the great talking shop face to face with the end of a real gun?*

And they certainly won't be able to pose as saviours of humanity any more. They'll have to save their own skins, and quickly."

A *Daily Mirror* feature titled 'Anglo-American Friendship Depends on Education'[lx] concluded that:

"... there can be no lasting Anglo-American understanding while United States education is mainly confined to history, geography and the social system of an area between the Atlantic and Pacific Oceans.

And there can be no such understanding while our own children are given an education which regards anything not between John O'Groats and Land's End as beyond the boundaries of human knowledge."

The Soviet Union, on the other hand, had the benefit of the doubt. Michael Foot argued in a 1940 article that Russia's greatest fear had to be single-handed conflict with a major power – specifically Germany – and it was thus in her interest to support Britain.[lxi] Stalin however seemed content to let the European powers strangle each other until *Barbarossa* took the matter out of his hands.

"The Russians seem to be putting up a devil of a scrap against the Hun. It would have been a lot easier for them if they had started in '39. Have you noticed the spate of Russian music on the radio? Everything bar the old 'International'. I see a legion of French fascists is about to depart for the Eastern front. Nice people!"

"... One good effect of this war will be to create an indestructible pro Russian feeling which I am sure will remain despite all efforts to obliterate it from 'up top'."

Soviet propaganda strenuously encouraged the sentiment. Jennie was enthused by a local meeting to write:

"One of the things Andrew Rothstein[39] told us (in order to illustrate the thirst for knowledge and culture in Russia) was that it is quite a common thing for the great national newspapers to devote as much as a quarter of their space to articles about poets, philosophers, artists etc – especially in commemoration of anniversaries, centenaries and so on. I expect you can guess what would be the effect on any newspaper in this country which started trying that (even assuming it could ever get the idea past the Board of Directors)… But there are still plenty of people who are pleased to regard the Russians as unintelligent barbarians, and think we are rather lowering our dignity in associating ourselves with them, even in the fight against Hitler and his gang."

By early 1943 the Germans were suffering their second Russian winter, trapped in a conflict they could neither win nor escape. The terrible human cost of the Eastern Front was becoming clear.

"The Russians are still doing well, aren't they? I read a very good article by Walter Graebner[40] on the Russian war effort which was a bit of a shock – he said quite bluntly that she is only maintaining her colossal effort by depriving the civilian population of more than their necessities – the civilian gets less than the 'irreducible minimum' of food, and he thinks that the situation will be pretty serious by the Spring. So it certainly behoves us to do all we can by them, if we want to keep Russia on her feet. I think too many people take the Russian victories at their face value without bothering to examine the effort involved."

---

[39] A Russian-British journalist, lifelong Communist and Soviet spy. At the time he was press officer to the Soviet mission in Britain.

[40] American author and journalist who edited 'Their Finest Hour: First-hand Narratives of the War in England' in 1941

We didn't know the half of it.

Ironically, in 1945 US Secretary of State Cordell Hull vehemently denied press gossip that he was anti-Russian.[lxii] It is difficult to imagine such a statement a couple of years later.

Beveridge Report

Britain standing alone in 1940-41 was clear what it was fighting *against*. There was more debate about what we were fighting *for*, prompted by a growing realisation that the *status quo ante* wasn't the best of possible worlds either. Lord Horder wrote in a *Sunday Times* editorial on 20th April 1941:

> *"'When the fighting finishes we will start to build a new world.'
> So wrote a colleague of mine recently. 'But why not start now?' was
> my reply."*

As Russia entered the war in June 1941, Arthur Greenwood MP announced an Inter-Departmental Committee on Social Insurance and Allied Services. It was headed by Sir William Beveridge, a noted economist and expert on unemployment insurance. The committee reported back to Parliament in November 1942. After some dickering about cost, its recommendations were published the following month.

The report urged social security 'by co-operation between the State and the individual' to defeat the five 'giants' on the road to reconstruction: Want, Disease, Ignorance, Squalor and Idleness. It was widely welcomed and became the intellectual template for the welfare state. Jennie's reaction was typical:

> *"Did you hear Beveridge on the subject of his report after the
> nine o'clock news last night? I got home just in time for it. It all sounds*

*very good. The only thing is will it get a government which will
seriously attempt to put it into practice?"*

The government used a February 1943 debate on the report to
announce that it would not be implemented immediately.

> *"The Beveridge Report now is just what I expected to happen.
> I knew the Government would hedge at the awful step of providing
> a little social security for the people they praise so continuously. What
> a gang to hitch one's wagon to! Makes you wonder what spine or
> conscience the Labour men in the Cabinet possess now, The Herald
> is doing a fine job reporting the full debates. I would like to read any
> Standard opinion on the subject, Michael Foot should be able to
> spread himself to great effect.*
>
> *What puzzles me is the complete lack of interest in it among the
> men. You wouldn't think it was anything to do with them at all,
> when asked about it they admit that it does affect them, but firmly
> believe that nothing will be done anyway, so they are cynical but not
> in the least angry.*
>
> *They listened to the war news tonight and then when the
> announcer began to speak about the debate somebody started to play
> the piano and that was that. Never was there a truer saying than that
> one about people getting the government they deserve. Makes you
> wonder if things will ever be right when governments so blatantly get
> away with it."*

Churchill warned the nation in a broadcast on 21st March not to
enter commitments we didn't know how to pay for, but reiterated
his belief in the principle.

> *"Here is a real opportunity for what I once called 'bringing the
> magic of averages to the rescue of the millions,' therefore, you must*

rank me and my colleagues as strong partisans of national compulsory insurance for all classes, for all purposes, from the cradle to the grave.

Every preparation, including, if necessary, preliminary legislative preparation, will be made with the utmost energy, and the necessary negotiations to deal with existing worthy interests are being actively pursued so that when the moment comes everything will be ready."

Beveridge was elected MP for Berwick-on-Tweed in 1944 after the death in Normandy of George Charles Grey. He campaigned on a new plan *"…to make impossible any return to the mass unemployment which marked the interval between the two wars."*[lxiii] He held the seat only briefly, losing it to Labour in the 1945 election. By way of consolation the Atlee government quickly implemented his plan.

Why Are We Fighting?

Politicians and film-makers have invoked the spirit of Dunkirk and the Blitz ever since: a picture of people selflessly and cheerfully enduring impossible odds. It would be churlish to deny the courage and grit of British civilians but naive to assume the image was the whole. It would take heroic self-deception *not* to be frightened and dispirited in face of the bombs, blackout, rationing and continual bad news of the early war years. You would need an unlimited stock of illegal substances to dodge the later war-weariness.

Perhaps the nadir was early 1942. Pearl Harbour had pitched the US into the war, but while both allies suffered defeat after defeat in the Pacific it was unclear how or when the Japanese could be stopped. The Russian winter offensive made inconclusive gains while the never-ending see-saw of fortune in North Africa seemed no nearer resolution. Meanwhile the U-Boats enjoyed their second 'happy time' off the undefended east coast of America.

A government reshuffle in February prompted this from Jennie:

> *"Let's hope the new Cabinet will get on and get something started. I think everybody is 'fed up' with hanging about, with nothing happening. Apart from everything else – a war is such a bloody bore – isn't it? I can't think why we go on putting up with it. The longer it goes on the more I'm convinced it was damn silly to start it in the first place."*

Eric's frustration boiled over as February slid into March with no obvious progress.

> *"There doesn't seem to be any signs of a great spring offensive on either side yet. Ridiculous to think that we have been at war for 2½ years and don't seem to have got properly started yet. I think it is going to be a case of 'the first forty years are the hardest'."*

Later, with El Alamein still in the future, the gunners were treated to a glimpse of life under occupation.

> *"We had a most interesting lecture the other day. A Polish journalist told us of his experiences in occupied Poland, and was very frank about Britain. Said that all the British soldier needed to turn him into a first class fighting man was two weeks of slavery ('We've had two years of it!' – from the back.) I agree with him that actual experience of Nazi methods would make all the difference, but all the same a campaign to relieve boredom or a cause worth fighting for would probably have the same effect."*

By mid-1944 the war had decisively tilted against the Axis. Allied armies were ashore in Normandy and slogging their way up the Italian mainland, a series of sledgehammer offensives took the

Russians to the Polish border, and the American island-hopping campaign steadily pushed the Japanese back across the Pacific. Parliament and press were beginning to debate how the country would adapt to the post-war world. Sometimes, though, the light at the end of the tunnel just illuminates the privations and heartache within it.

"I suppose we (as a country) blundered into this awful mess, and we (as individuals) did not do all that we might have done to prevent it and therefore we have to take our share of the blame. I suppose in the end war was inevitable, and therefore the only thing to do is to get on with the fighting and get it over, so that we can settle down to leading more or less reasonable and useful lives again.

… I hope to God that our generation will have the courage and the sense to ensure that this is the last war. The idea of our children having to face up to what we have had to face appals me. If any good comes out of war, I hope it will be that the world will be a better place for our children to live in."

In September the doomed Warsaw rising was drifting to its bloody conclusion. The Polish Home Army loyal to the government-in-exile was systematically crushed and 150,000 – 200,000 civilians were killed as the Soviet Army watched from the east bank of the Vistula. It was inevitable in the *realpolitik* of the time that the Allies would recognise Stalin's puppet Committee of National Liberation over the protests of the exiled Polish leaders.

"I see there's been another row over some indiscretions of the Polish Cabinet. The latest of many, I suppose. I'm afraid I've precious little sympathy with them. Their anti Russian attitude was largely responsible for the outbreak of the war in my opinion."

Women Gunners

John Steinbeck, already a famous novelist, came to Britain in 1943 as a correspondent for the *New York Herald Tribune* and incidentally working also for the OSS – predecessor of the CIA. He illustrated this foreign war which would cost so many American lives with a series of verbal miniatures – bomber crews between missions, Dover shelled from Cap Gris Nez, a minesweeper's work.

One sketch depicts a mixed AA battery on the South Coast, an idea as alien to his US readers as to the Germans across the Channel. He describes an alarm, the precision and professionalism of the women's response, and their insistence on being treated as soldiers. He praises their endurance and courage in the face of constant alerts and frequent air attack.[lxiv] He saw the maturity of a seismic shift in attitude over the two previous years.

In 1941 General Pile's AA Command finally began to receive useful quantities of the guns, instruments, radars and searchlights it needed. This raised the issue of how to crew them. Pile records that he was short of 1,114 officers and 17,965 other ranks.[lxv] Ever the innovator, he revisited an idea he had first explored in 1938: to use women far beyond the clerical, catering and cleaning roles they had so far filled.

He overcame practical and organisational obstacles, and prejudice verging on horror, by August 1941 when the first 'mixed' (overwhelmingly female) battery went operational in Richmond Park. Ultimately 74,000 out of 210,000 Auxiliary Territorial Service (ATS) women including, Winston Churchill's youngest daughter, were employed on AA Command's gun and searchlight sites. A mixture of volunteers and conscripts they did not physically work the guns but they did everything else up to and including the order to fire. Unfortunately, in Pile's words, *"… the same political issue prevented them from firing back at any bomber which engaged them with its machine-guns."*[lxvi]

"The girls lived like men, fought their [search]lights like men, and, alas, some of them died like men."[lxvii] 717 ATS lost their lives during the war,[lxviii] including 24 killed at Great Yarmouth when their seafront billet was bombed in a 'Hit and Run' raid in May 1943.[lxix]

Much of the initial fear concerned 'discipline' or 'morals,' meaning sex. In the event Steinbeck observed that male and female members of a battery socialised as a group but instinctively avoided 'walking out' with each other.

At first Eric was among the many gunners who treated the idea with suspicion.

"What do you think of all this bilge about the ATS girls? Dammit, one would think they'd been through hell fire lately just because they'd manned during an alarm. They've got some silly b- on in 'In Town Tonight' talking about 'how she done it' – this is about the tenth broadcast on the subject. The AA seems just about ready for a tour of the music halls. Still, I suppose the wireless must say something about the army, even if it's nothing more inspiring than a tea party on a gun site. ('The girls all had hot drinks afterwards' etc) Gertcher! Personally I've far more respect for the nurses and ambulance drivers in an air raid, just as I think our job is a picnic compared to that of the firemen in a blitz."

"… There is no end of turmoil in 206 over the rumour that this is to be a mixed battery; the rank and file seem to be horrified. There's no doubt that girls seem to be very much resented as Ack Ack personnel."

The women's keenness, enthusiasm and sheer competence silenced the naysayers. The furore died down and they became an unremarked feature of wartime life. Two years later, serving at Lowestoft, Eric wrote:

"We had good first hand experience of the 'gentle sex' in action, and it was extremely impressive. The girls didn't bat an eyelid and put up a very fine show. The majority of them are Scotch, and all were wildly enthusiastic."

Some of the resistance came from ATS leaders themselves. Major-General Jean Knox was reported to say that women were meant to give life and could not be trained to kill, even in total war.[lxx]

Their separate command and disciplinary arrangements caused some friction: ATS gunners identified with their battery and didn't appreciate their superiors' view that they were ATS first and gunners second. Jennie observed merrily:

"I see that the ATS are going to have a 'Gestapo' to keep them in order generally and see that they don't overdo the make-up! Imagine being on the carpet for a too liberal application of lipstick. What a war!"

She saw the long-term implication as well.

"I also wonder how many of the wives who (many for the first time) have found economic freedom during the war, will be content to go back and be dependent upon their husbands' earnings. Many, I know will be only too glad to do so – just as there are still plenty of Russian women who feel that 'woman's place is in the home'. But will there be a majority who would rather stay in industry or the professions? Or perhaps the state of the country will make it necessary for the woman to continue to help in production and perhaps then we shall have to adopt something akin to the Russian system! I feel that the average man of this country will be more difficult to convert to that state of affairs than the average woman – what do you think?"

Race

The influx of over 100,000 US troops made black faces a common sight on British streets for the first time. Reactions varied – both to the troops and the attitude of their white colleagues.

In September 1942 the *Sunday Pictorial* reported angrily that a vicar's wife near Weston-super-Mare had tried to impose a six-point code on the village women.[lxxi] It bears quoting.

1. *"If a local woman keeps a shop and a coloured soldier enters, she must serve him, but she must do it as quickly as possible and indicate that she does not desire him to come there again.*
2. *If she is in a cinema and notices a coloured soldier next to her, she moves to another seat immediately.*
3. *If she is walking on the pavement and a coloured soldier is coming towards her, she crosses to the other pavement.*
4. *If she is in a shop and a coloured soldier enters, she leaves as soon as she has made her purchase or before that if she is in a queue.*
5. *White women, of course, must have no social relationship with coloured troops.*
6. *On no account must coloured troops be invited into the homes of white women."*

The parishioners overwhelmingly rejected her advice and the paper made its own views clear.

> *"Any coloured soldier who reads this may rest assured that there is no colour bar in this country and that he is as welcome as any other Allied soldier.*
>
> *He will find that the vast majority of people here have nothing but repugnance for the narrow-minded, uninformed prejudices expressed by the vicar's wife.*
>
> *There is – and will be – no persecution of coloured people in Britain."*

Later in the month Hannen Swaffer's column in the *Herald* reported more discriminatory remarks:[lxxii]

> *"We are grateful to the people of Britain who have welcomed us to their homes,' writes a group of American coloured soldiers, 'and also for being made welcome in your public bars and dance-halls. We are fighting for freedom.'*
>
> *But the Bishop of Salisbury, quoted in the 'Warminster Parish Magazine,' insists that the sharp distinction drawn between white and black across the Atlantic is justified by experience.*
>
> *'On no account should young women make acquaintance and take walks with soldiers of African blood,' he writes."*

Swaffer evidently felt the two statements needed no further comment.

In June 1944 Eric echoed the widely-held view that US forces had brought their attitudes with them:

> *"I was interested the other day in an article about the prejudice of the people of this country in regard to colonial troops. The writer claimed that this had been fostered by the Americans themselves. This certainly bears out our experiences. I was really shocked at the violence of their feelings in regard to n***os. When discussing them one American bitterly complained that the British were 'spoiling them.' Isn't it funny that a fight for 'freedom' includes such paradoxes in the ranks of its champions?"*

General Eisenhower found time from the pressures of the Normandy campaign to review the death sentence passed on Leroy Henry, a black corporal from St Louis, for raping a white woman in Combe Down near Bath. Local residents believed his version of the event and raised a petition in his favour, which swelled to over 30,000 signatures. The allegation turned out to be malicious – there was consensual sex followed by a dispute about the price. Eisenhower quashed both sentence and conviction.[lxxiii]

The Sunday Pictorial

Paper rationing was introduced soon after the outbreak of war and not fully lifted until December 1956. At first newspapers were limited to 60% of their pre-war newsprint which dwindled over time to 25%. Papers not only shrank in weight, but production caps based on pre-war circulation made them difficult to find. Editorial teams also had to cope with the call-up of key staff and learned the hard way to disperse their precious stocks across multiple stores as an air raid precaution. Still the presses rolled, though standards slipped a little.

> *"If I had any tears left I would shed them copiously over the procession of filthy layouts and bad artwork pouring out at this period. Some of the Government's own brand would call forth the worst convulsions."*

Eric's early postings in Kent allowed him to drop into the *Sunday Pictorial* for a chat with his old mates on the way to or from a home leave, or on a flying trip when there wasn't time to get home.

> *"Freddy Grist has dropped his In and Around column, and started a weekly letter to a pal in the forces, the first one to me apparently! By bad luck I didn't see the Pic this week."*

He contrasted the rigid routine of army life unfavourably with the freewheeling anarchy of a newsroom.

*"Are newspaper men superficial? Or does this whole business
of shooting quids into the air and sleeping rough and God knows
what take the cake for inanity? It doesn't say so in the Drill Book, so
I suppose not.*

*I am still unmilitary enough to consider Cudlipp a far more
useful man to society than all the brass hats in Aldershot."*

Like its half-sister *Daily Mirror*, the 'Pic' felt that war was no reason
to ease up on the government's performance. Like the *Mirror*, it
sometimes felt the backlash.

*"As you probably know – I never can quite remember whether I
told you – Frank Charman*[41] *is at Cardington training, so he says,
to be a Pilot-Observer. Percy Bosher* [a staff photographer] *is
leaving us in January for the Artillery. And today the boss is just
preparing to listen to an attack on himself in Parliament!*

*You probably saw the box in the Pictorial last Sunday about
Quentin Hogg asking Mr Bevin if he was aware that the Editor of
the Sunday Pictorial is 27 or thereabouts and that he has not been
called up under the Armed Forces Act. Then Hogg is going to make
a pig of himself and ask 'What about it?'*

*Cudlipp took me out for a drink last Saturday when he knew
what was happening and it was suggested by Bernard Gray that the
villain of the piece might possibly be Margesson, the Chief Whip of
the House, who has been attacked mercilessly by Cudlipp for some
weeks now."*[lxxiv]

---

[41] Frank Charman was the *Sunday Pictorial's* chief photographer and had a notably
'creative' approach to his art. Cudlipp wrote a glowing but double-edged obituary
after his death in 1985.

In fact Cudlipp had already asked to be taken off the reserved list, and applied to the army. He went on to edit *Union Jack*, a British forces' paper inspired by the American *Stars and Stripes*. Over time he gathered a rare array of talent including William Connor (the incomparable columnist 'Cassandra'), Peter Wilson (sports writer) and Hammond Innes, the novelist. Eric picked up second-hand news of them in the constant churn of army postings.

> *"I was amused at a remarkable coincidence yesterday. One of our sergeants transferred to us from an infantry unit, and he happened to hear by chance where I worked, and asked me if I know Peter Wilson! Apparently Peter was in his platoon when he first joined the army, and his account of Peter as a soldier was most amusing. He described him as a 'great fat slug' and said 'You should have seen him when we finished with him – he was jumping around like a greyhound!' Of course his remarks about Peter getting a commission were unprintable."*
>
> Jennie replied: *"Peter might even manage to get into work in the morning after the army has done with him."*

Stuart ('Sam') Campbell replaced Cudlipp at the 'Pic' for the rest of the war.

> *"They have appointed Sam as acting editor – with most visible results. He's off hand, 'superior.' With a 'can't spare a minute' kind of attitude, also obviously jittery and shows signs of cracking under the strain. He's also well hated by everyone in general."*

Eric's opinion of the new regime didn't mellow much with time.

> *"Sam wrote a perfectly disgusting article on Sunday. I won't weary you with the gist of it if you didn't see it but it's so bad and*

insulting that even the 'Mirror' leader protested about it today, chiefly to dissociate itself from it. Well I'm beginning to be ashamed to be associated with the paper. I wonder what on earth Cudlipp thinks about things."

"… Sam reminds me of an expression of Charlie Watson's. If he gets any lower his bottom will touch the pavement!"

His colleagues still at the paper suffered the occupational hazards of the trade as well as the privations and dangers of wartime London.

"It was rather a shock to read of Freddy Grist's death in the Sunday Pic yesterday. I don't know if you read it. The last operation just about finished him and he caught a cold which developed into pneumonia. I suppose one couldn't expect a fellow of his habits to live long, but I think it's a dreadful tragedy all the same, he was such a hell of a nice chap underneath all that fooling and if he'd gone a little steadier he could have done some brilliant work."

Others had more specific dangers to contend with. Bernard Gray covered the outbreak of war from Germany, the Battle of France embedded with the British Expeditionary Force, and flew to Norway with a bomber crew. His reminiscences were published after he was lost with the submarine he was riding in search of a scoop.

"I saw the Pictorial this weekend, they have an article on his book just published – 'War Reporter.' They report it as the work of a 'typical working man, whose life was centred around his wife, family and pint of beer'. Oh yeah! The last gets a bit nearer the truth."

D-Day and its aftermath brought new opportunities for journalists who didn't mind the sound of gunfire or the inconvenience of ducking now and then.

"Do you remember me mentioning meeting Rex North the last time I was home on long leave? He is covering the invasion for the Pic and sent a very good story from the Cruiser Belfast which was well presented. He was formerly in the artillery and was invalided out. Funny how his job has taken him into the thick of it"

Rex stirred up controversy with a despatch claiming that most French people preferred four years of relative peace and order under the Germans to the mayhem of the landings. He repeated a false rumour that Germans had trained their French girlfriends as stay-behind snipers.

Jennie continued sending papers while Eric was on active service in France, Belgium and the Netherlands. With the European war clearly in its last throes the Press began to debate the shape of the post-war world. At the same time the V1 assault was a reminder that counting chickens was still unwise.

"The journalists seem to be very preoccupied with the return of the personnel to their jobs after the war and some sort of refresher for them. Personally I think a fresh outlook and the pleasure gained in the recommencing will more than compensate for the 'out of touch' period. The Pic staff struck me as being a trifle jaded when I saw them last. I hate to visualise the effect of the flying bombs upon Sam Campbell. I think he must be running the paper from Maidenhead."

Wall Newspapers

Boredom, vile weather and primitive living conditions in Eric's Clyde postings – with the seeming inanity of army methods – left the troops' spirits as damp as the mud they waded through to their posts. He decided to do something about it.

> *"I am also starting a 'News of the Week;' board which will present items of special interest to the men, clippings from our press and from the Soviet War News (good opportunity) also, I hope, a few contributions from the men themselves. It will take the place of a weekly magazine.*
>
> *The Mayor is coming down next week and I think I am booked for an interview with him. So that may get me somewhere."*
>
> *"… I did manage to get a Mirror containing the famous cartoon[42], by the way, also a 'Pic' of Sunday. Like you I thought P.W.'s[43] article pretty lousy and about as senseless a commentary on guns as could be. The cuttings you have sent are going to be invaluable for my 'news board' and clippings from the 'Standard' particularly welcome. I am wondering if it is going to be subjected to censorship!"*

The project had to be abandoned along with over 300 books he had collected for the battery library when the regiment moved south for mobile training. In September 1942, now settled at Twydall, he revived the news board under the title 'Blaze Away.'

> *"The wall newspaper is progressing rather slowly – chiefly owing to pressure of work – but the stuff is accumulating and it should be ready by Sunday.*
>
> *I daresay you remember me speaking of Johnnie Milaw; he is a real find – has written glorious gossip column, including 'me and my eiderdown'. I'll let you know more of the details when we get things 'sorted out.'"*

---

[42] The Zec cartoon, 'The price of petrol has been increased by one penny. Official.' See 'Song of the Clyde.'

[43] Probably Peter Wilson, sports writer and 'Man They can't Gag.' He and William Connor (Cassandra) were the only two Hugh Cudlipp brought with him when he 'defected' from the *Mirror* to the *Sunday Pictorial*.

It was again interrupted by postings and lay fallow until the battery arrived in Normandy. Now something was really needed. The gunners' view of the critical battle raging around them was limited to an occasional aircraft alarm or 'Twenty rounds on this map reference as soon as you like, please.'

"...we are starting the Troop paper tomorrow. Calling it the 'Daily Shower' using an Army term which has often been applied to the Battery, needless to say it is the reverse of flattering in implication."

"... I'm afraid the Battery newspaper was again put off at the critical moment. The trouble is I haven't now a colleague who could muck in and keep it going when I'm busy – and our branch of the unit entails [sic] the bulk of the work during a move and when in action. I wish some of the officers would wake up and do a bit more – they are really hopeless when it comes to anything like that – quite nice chaps but initiative is certainly not their strong point... Their handling of news for the men is just as bad, nobody bothers to call a parade and read the latest from the front, which does come in fairly regularly. It's the expressed wish of the authorities that this should be done. The same applies to the newspaper: any or all of them could run it if they made the effort."

"... And – we have now actually PRODUCED our Battery newspaper. Reception of first issue – decidedly favourable. Central panel (WAR NEWS) is changed every morning on receipt of radio news bulletins, features inserted as devised or dreamed. Will post you a selection of those which are replaced."

"... We are amusing ourselves in one way or another, in evening saunters, reading and in producing copy, mostly very libellous, for the wall newspaper."

"... The 'Daily Shower' has made a real hit. The third edition is now almost ready (we 'change up' on features once a week) and contains articles and letters by Capt Newton and all the officers and plenty from the men. I am running a series entitled 'When I get back *to Civvy Street'(!) about what we want to do after the war, and the best article or letter on this subject wins 20 cigs. I am sending you shortly a sketch of the layout and some articles. The most amazing contributions are the poems. Three of the officers and three ORs have written some and they are quite good and very amusing. There is a general suggestion that the items are collated and saved for a future perusal. So I think I will start a scrap book, with a miniature layout of each issue. I find writing, illustrating, layout etc, on any subject comes very easily (far more than in the old days) which makes me more than impatient to make another start...*

It would amuse you to see how the paper is produced. We haven't a vestige of glue. We use flour paste. Most of my work has to be done during the intervals in my duty hours. One of these periods starts at 4 a.m. and the Editorial staff foregather at this unearthly hour in a damp dugout surrounded by all the paraphernalia of gunnery and begin to plot the new edition, with a borrowed typewriter and a mug of stewed tea. Capt Newton was horrified at this early start, says 'Good God' (or something worse!) 'old man – you're surely not bursting into print at this hour – in heaven's name stop that bloody typewriter!' Having to sleep on the spot he gets the thin end of it. And then Arthur Lake (my sten friend!) comes in at 6.30 (he is the News Editor, knowing shorthand) and turns on the short wave which crackles and emits a burst of horrible swing, which causes the sleeper to awake again and say no wonder his hair is going grey!

I'm glad we decided to do it, because we were in a pretty parlous state as regards amusing ourselves. A gag like this brightens life considerably."

"... The Daily Shower (in its third edition) is still going strong and an established favourite. I am enclosing an 'ode' written by Mr Adams and Mr Christopherson[44] *– and it says much for our broad*

---

[44] See Figure 22.

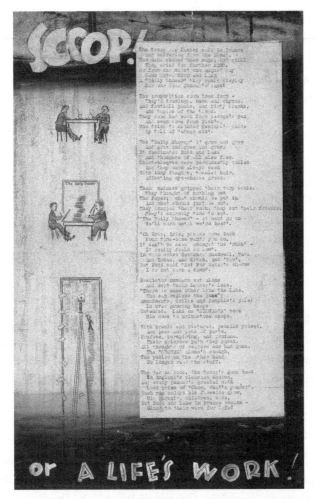

Figure 22: 'Ode' to the editors of the 'Shower'

mindedness that we've decided to print it I think! They have already written one other in similar style Not bad eh? I thought you would be amused at the grisly fate forecast for us."

Mobile life again proved too much for the *Shower* as the pace of movement and action accelerated. It closed after the fourth issue.

"I have been forced to say goodbye to the Daily Shower for the time being. Still there are hopes that it will carry on. It was an experiment that went very well but involved rather too much work, including the typing and the presentation. The night I left it was blown down in a storm and the glass shattered which was regarded by all as an omen!"

Popular Culture

Eric and Jennie shared a voracious appetite for books, film, drama and music. He never quite gelled with her love of ballet, nor she with his predatory instinct for chess.

Some of his acquisitions were well received on the gun site.

"The book of Rudyard Kipling poems has proved very popular in the barrack room and we had some grand fun last night while different fellows took it into their heads to recite. Jimmy Ticehurst's rendering of 'Gunga Din' ended in his forcible removal but he continued from memory outside in the dark! He's the Sussex lad with the ear-splitting voice."

Others less so.

"I am very interested in Richard the Third, also in the small Shakespearian dictionary at the back. Elizabethan English is strikingly similar to West Country dialect, isn't it? One feels a need of some 'meaty' literature in these circumstances, this particular need being noticeable in more than one fellow here. There are too few of them, of course, which is a pity as the majority get very bored by reeling off one thriller after another and boredom leads to rows and horseplay with sometimes regrettable results. I noticed two cases of murder or manslaughter in the (Sunday!) papers lately, committed by Army men in Army surroundings, both of which could be traced

to boredom or to somebody getting ragged and posturing with a rifle.
The majority of blokes here are pretty intelligent but it is amazing
how rows are caused by silly arguments, and one can imagine the
results of such tiffs among, say, a group of miners or navvies.

I wonder why the average Englishman's reaction to anything
that makes him think is to shout it down as 'highbrow'? Then he
gets into a bleak environment like this and finds himself barred from
his usual mental stimulants and mentally high and dry. So instead
of doing anything about it he proceeds to go all primitive and accuse
his neighbour of being a silly bugger. The aforesaid S B being only
too anxious to make something of it, the result is a perpetual din!"

Their letters include lively discussion of the books they have read –
supported by a book club subscription at 5s 5d – about £11 at 2013
prices – a year. For example:

"That Gilbert & Sullivan book, 'Discord and Harmony' is by
Cosmo Hamilton and it is very good indeed. There are some amusing
bits in it, such as the description of an awful row on the eve of the
production of 'Pinafore' when Sullivan broke his baton in half and
refused to go on. There is a good description of them 'Sullivan had
uncommonly tender corns and Gilbert uncommonly large feet!'"

Inevitably their interest drifted into politics.

"Have you heard about the book 'Your M.P.' which has caused
such a stir? It's the same series as 'Guilty Men' and written by Tom
Wintringham under a nom de plume. Old Beverley Baxter, who is
picked out for mention, has 'been licking his wounds in public ever
since' asking Parliament to stop the sale of paper to the publishers etc.
It is a record of the speeches and votes of about 300 Government
M.P.s and Wintringham condemns them out of their own mouths.

I've only borrowed a copy at the moment but it's certainly worth buying."

The book, published in 1944 under the pseudonym 'Gracchus,' is an eviscerating study of the speeches, actions and voting records of some Tory MPs in the pre-war and early war period. It argues that *"The policies of* [the Baldwin and Chamberlain] *governments gave aid and comfort to our enemies, and left us, in 1940, without allies capable of effective resistance to them."* The book treats Baxter, a noted appeaser, relatively lightly.

In the same vein Cassandra's book 'The English at War' circulated enthusiastically around the battery. Its central argument, that British military and civilian commitment is let down by poor leadership, somehow resonated with the gunners.

> *"I read Cass's book straight away and enjoyed it immensely. I am a great admirer of Connor's work, as I believe him to be utterly sincere and certainly a very forceful yet authorort… (hell) AUTHORITATIVE (got it) writer. I particularly liked the section devoted to the fighting men. I think I could add an appendix but then, what soldier could not?"*

For Whom the Bell Tolls chimed well.

> *"Hemingway's book is proving extremely popular and I must really announce a closing date or it will be here indefinitely. Did you read that it is being filmed with Gary Cooper? Hope they don't cast Wallace Beery as Pedro! Or Dorothy Lamour as Maria!"*

In fact Eric caught up with the film a couple of years later – in Antwerp.

> *"I saw 'For Whom the Bell Tolls' last night. Never thought I would get the chance to see that over here, and in sumptuous surroundings. It is a remarkably good effort and captured the spirit of the book very well.*

Of course, both the political sidelights and the romance is toned down considerably and the dialogue, while taken almost completely from the book, is out of sequence, and has 'simplified' phrases inserted to make the plot clearer – a good example is – 'This is a war with Germany and Italy on one side and Russia on the other and with Spain in the middle,' etc – which clashes horribly with the inspired Hemingway dialogue. Gary Cooper is far too reticent and stiff to be a good Jordan and puts in too many 'yeps' and 'sures'. The rest are perfect. I had a few small doubts about Ingrid Bergman, but she is very lovely and acted beautifully. Pablo and Pilar are damned good. Pilar is huge (not fat) fierce and in every way the real thing. The final fight for the Bridge was a bit Deadwood Dick in places, but the flight and the parting was grand and very affecting, on the whole a very good effort. My opinion is: you want to read the book first – those who didn't found the plot slightly incomprehensible – and a film could never be made to do the book full justice. But everybody says it's the best film they have ever seen."

Gone with the Wind also transferred from print to screen during the war.

"Am enjoying GWTW no end. It certainly is a marvellous story. Thoroughly debunks 'Uncle Tom's Cabin' – probably to the other extreme – the 'N*****' dialogue is lovely isn't it? Of course the author never admits that slavery was wrong in the first place and the luckless Southerners brought all that trouble on their heads by their adoption of slave labour. Also the conditions of plantation life was somewhat idealised. Still it's nice to read something of the other side!"

Eric and Jennie managed to see the film together during a brief leave. On the occasional trip out from a gun site he was happy with lighter fare.

"I went to the pictures in the evening. Didn't think I would enjoy the film, it was 'Tall, Dark and Handsome' (Caesar Romero) but it

proved to be very good, a gangster film with a difference and some of the best dialogue I've heard for a long time. One jewel: tough man to his moll 'Give me the bracelet or I'll smack you from under that permanent!!' Story in brief was of a gangster too soft hearted to bump his rival's gunmen off, secreting them in a vault beneath his rooms.

The fun started when they got out, running around the town as 'dead men' and scaring their comrades into fits. Eventually the 'Big Shot' himself has to feign death to escape and his rival pays the funeral expenses. One of the 'dead men' looking on says 'Was my funeral as good as that?' and his wife retorts 'I did the best I could on the two bits you left me!'"

"… I went down tonight to see 'Yankee Doodle Dandy' which is the life story of one Jimmy Cohan, a song and dance man, and quite factual, I believe. Cagney is ever so good in the part. Among the tunes written by Cohan was 'Over There' which, of course is very spectacular when presented in the film. It's funny how patriotism seems to run riot over there. We should consider a British film like this one in rather bad taste. I've never seen so much flag-wagging since Miss Howe celebrated Empire Day at Providence Road! – but at the same time it is done well. Cagney as Cohan tells the President his life story, which runs through the film as a commentary. At the end Mr R presents him with the Congressional Medal, which of course, knocks him for six emotionally. He dances down the last few steps of the White House to the subdued strains of 'I'm a Yankee Doodle Dandy' and finds the Troops (1942) marching by singing his last war song 'Over There'. Of course he has to join in and march along singing it with them and weeping rather copiously, old, bemused and be-medalled! Just like the ending of a 'Saturday Evening Post' story."

---

[45] Morton was a journalist working at the time for the *Daily Herald*. He was also a pioneering travel writer with a prodigious output including the '*In Search of…*' series of UK guides. He continued publishing until shortly before his death in 1979.

They kept up a running commentary on H V Morton's[45] travel books, matching his writing to Eric's experience of Britain's windswept fields. The books brought a nostalgic reminder of lost peace and, perhaps, hope for its future recovery.

> *"I think plenty of travelling and seeing new places would be a good education for the children too. HVM (H V Morton) has a lot of sound ideas about the way to spend a life. Well let's hope we can soon put it into practice."*

The Fate of Friends

The population of the UK in 1939 approached 48 million, of whom nearly six million served with the armed forces. 384,000 service men and women lost their lives over the next six years, along with 67,000 civilians[46]. Though not comparable with the horrors in the Soviet Union, the occupied countries, and eventually the Axis powers themselves the numbers give a telling picture of a country where almost every household experienced loss.

The following extracts need no further comment.

25th March 1941 (Eric)
> *"I felt a bit ashamed of my little troubles when I heard that one of the boys has lost best part of his family in the blitz in the East End, and he didn't know till he went home this week end."*

9th November 1941 (Eric)
> *"I was very sorry to hear about Harold being so unwell. I think that Dennis' death upset him a great deal, and he appeared to be in*

---

[46] Casualty figures vary widely between sources. I picked Wikipedia as being somewhere in the middle of the range and good enough for illustration.

*a state of frustration as regards not being able to join the RAF himself.
I do hope he will grow out of it – it's pretty certain he will, I think.
I must write to him soon."*

7th May 1943 (Eric's sister 'Ba')

*"I met Mrs Gilbert today and they have had news at last of their son
who was missing. He is prisoner of war in Malaya, she seemed very bucked.*

*You will be sorry to hear that Peter Groom is missing from a
bombing raid. He was stationed at Malta. You know who I mean,
don't you, they lived in St Stephen's Road."*

24th June 1942 (Jennie)

*"I hear from Ma that Muff's Ray arrived home last Thursday
for three weeks leave – don't know yet whether they are going to get
married but I shouldn't be a bit surprised."*

24th September 1942 (Eric)

*"Am very anxious to know whether Kay and Reg have heard
any news of Bruce: my word it will be tough if he has disappeared.
But maybe he has been found by this time. I'd give a lot to know if
it was Bruce I saw in the High St. on Tuesday."*

26th November 1942 (Jennie)

*"Peter Stoddart has arrived home safe and sound and doesn't
look much worse for his adventures."*

26th January 1943 (Jennie)

*"Renee thinks Jack has gone abroad. He had embarkation leave
at Xmas and another short leave since. He went back to rejoin his
unit to go abroad and as Renee has not heard from him for several
days she concludes he has gone. She seemed considerably depressed."*

14th February 1943 (Jennie)

"Irene had not heard from Jack. Of course it is usually several weeks before you hear anything when they go abroad. Funny to think of old Jack turfed off abroad somewhere. Did you hear about his brother (the one who was in New Zealand) coming over here to train and being killed in a flying accident. This was some time before Christmas I think. I forget whether I told you before."

22nd February 1943 (Eric's mother)

"Dennis is going through very rough training. He had to scale a 80ft cliff with live ammunition all round him. He said he was pretty scared and was saying 'Hail Marys' right to the top."

21st May 1943 (Jennie)

"Did I tell you that Jack Jay was sent out to Africa? Apparently they arrived just about as the campaign was finishing. Lulu told me Renee hears from him quite regularly about every four or five days. I must try and get in touch with Renee again when I come back."

Shortage and Rationing

The period from September 1939 to April 1940 saw little land fighting except in Poland, and was dubbed the 'Phoney War.' At sea there was no such thing. German U-boats and commerce raiders immediately went on the offensive. Britain introduced a convoy system for merchant shipping and rationing to control demand. Butter, for example, was limited to a quarter pound per person per week at the end of 1939. The ration reduced to two ounces (57g) butter plus four ounces of margarine and two of lard nine months later.[lxv] Newspapers published recipes claimed to make powdered eggs less disgusting and people were encouraged to 'dig for victory,' turning their gardens over to vegetables. Just about any way of producing food off-ration was worth trying. Jennie's Aunt Ede, also a teacher, wrote from Bristol:

> *"Maybe you did not know that with the help of my form (boys and girls) I am breeding and rearing rabbits for fur and the table at school. We started just after Easter with one buck and three does and increased until we reached 85 early in September. Now we have killed off a fair number for meat. My youngsters (aged 12/13) love looking after them and we combine the practical feeding, cleaning etc with theory lessons in biology and botany. Quite a useful spot of wartime effort. Incidentally a fair number of the children have started rabbit keeping at home on the knowledge and experience gained at school."*

Meat was rationed by price: 1s 2d (about 6p) per person per week. The amount people could buy thus depended on availability and quality. Bread, vegetables, coffee, fruit, fish and beer were not rationed; nor were meals eaten out, though popular resentment at well-off people flagrantly bypassing the restrictions led to a 5s cap on the price of restaurant meals from 1942. Supply and demand were moderated by price – for example, by the end of March 1941 scarcity had driven the price of cod steak up to 1s 6d (three-quarters of a conscript's daily pay) per pound.[lxxvi] Conversely, in September 1943 there was not enough labour to lift the potato crop; the national press appealed for volunteers and civil servants were offered special leave to help.[lxxvii]

The civilian petrol ration was abolished in March 1942: from then on only essential users could keep their vehicles running. At the end of the year bus services outside London were stopped at 9 PM and no buses were allowed to run before 1 PM on Sundays.[lxxviii]

There was no food ration for pets. Very many, especially of the larger dog breeds, were either given to the forces as guards or destroyed. Some breeds had to be restocked almost from scratch after the war, contributing to later genetic issues.

Gunners learned to make tea on the hoof between alarms, drills and fatigues.

> *"By the way dear, do you think you could make me one or two little muslin tea bags just big enough to hold half a dessert spoonful of tea I'd like them for my drinking bowl!"*

Primitive gun site facilities didn't encourage lingering over ablutions. A handy side-effect was an oversupply of soap coupons.

> *"I think I shall be able to save you at least two cakes of soap per month – maybe three. We get one coupon per week, which is above our needs and I know it will be welcome."*
>
> *"… I am sending you 3 cakes of soap tonight which I hope will be useful. That's the best of being on a site where you can't wash much!!"*

Some restrictions eased as the Battle of the Atlantic swung the Allies' way. Children received more clothing coupons from late 1943; sausages returned to their pre-war meat content and the maximum price of green vegetables reduced in July 1944. At the same time a limited supply of silk stockings was available to women who could afford the eye-watering cost of three clothing coupons (a sixteenth of the annual allowance) and up to £3 15s (£150 today) per pair.[lxxix]

Victory did not end rationing, which actually grew stricter in some areas after the war. The last restrictions, on meat and bacon, were finally lifted in July 1954. Nearly fifteen years of shortages, queuing for essentials and reduced freedom nonetheless left the British population healthier overall than before or since. Full employment, price control, unavoidable exercise and just about enough of a designed, balanced diet cushioned pre-war poverty and avoided post-war excess.

School

Jennie was justifiably proud of lifting herself from an unpromising background to a responsible, respectable teaching job. Her Aunt Ede in Bristol was also a teacher and commiserated over the trials of running a school in wartime.

> *"We have just closed school 10.30 as the coal supply has run out and the temperature is too low for staying on. I remain until noon to help with free dinners."*

In the grim midwinter of 1941 Jennie did her best to introduce a bit of seasonal cheer.

> *"I did the classroom and it looks quite nice. Makes the kids feel a bit 'Christmassy' – though Heaven knows there is not much to make us feel that way this year. We shan't even be able to get a bit 'lit up'. I have so far only succeeded in getting a bottle of cooking sherry and one of ginger wine."*

The next month brought an initiative to ensure the kids were fed during the day. Being out of the home this was doubly attractive because the food was off-ration.

> *"We are starting 'school dinner' on Monday so I expect we shall have to do one day's dinner duty each. Also, of course, there will be one more lot of money to collect and keep accounts of – which all helps to take the teachers' time and ensure that the rising generation doesn't get properly educated.*
>
> *Anyway we are having a special NUT meeting on the subject of extraneous duties so perhaps something will get adjusted. I say PERHAPS."*

"… We started the dinners at school today with Agnes and Boss taking the first day. Apparently everything went off OK and the kids got a first class dinner at 4d and some of them got it free. Getting quite communistic aren't we? I take my turn on duty with the Boss's help tomorrow.

The chief snag as far as I am concerned is that they use so much gas in the kitchen for cooking that practically none comes through my radiators. So I suppose something will have to be done to adjust that next."

"… I was on dinner duty on Tuesday. The Boss was there also and Agnes stayed to help too. We got a very good dinner at 6d each (I think that's partly why the Boss stays every day – being very fond of his inner man). The kids also did very well at 4d per head and those who cannot afford that get it free. It is amusing to notice how all the kids on the dinner list turn up OK in all this bad weather. We have about 50 stay each day – which we hope to increase to 100 as the scheme progresses – which will be nearly half the school. The two women who do the cooking are very efficient and really clean. I think the kitchen at Cowley Church Room is really clean for the first time in my whole acquaintance with the place. So you can see we have been very lucky getting two really first class workers. It is really quite a pleasure to work with them because they really give of their best."

As the year spun by and the days lengthened sports day came round – with the inevitable wartime theme.

"We are having our school sports tomorrow. So of course the kids are all somewhat excited. My boys are having a 'Fire Watchers Race', donning gas masks, tin hats etc en route.

We are also having a 'Zoo Relay Race' in which some are seals – which makes me think of when you gave an imitation of a seal in progress to the Ealing cubs – remember?"

Summer holidays were no respite. In perhaps the world's most highly mobilised country most able-bodied adults were swallowed up in the war effort. Schools picked up child care.

"Tuesday I have to start my holiday duty. It will be pretty mouldy if the weather is bad, still my programme is pretty adaptable to indoor and outdoor activities. I think a couple of the staff have banked too much on fine weather and outdoor activities. Still we shall see.

I see the film version of the Jungle Book is around locally. Funny thing – I picked the Jungle Book as holiday literature for my little crowd, so if they can scrounge up enough cash I think we might go to the films one afternoon."

1943 brought a new colleague. Jennie was less than complimentary.

"Talk about people being hopeless at a job! I don't think I have ever struck anybody quite so bad as that woman who is taking the class next to me at school. I shouldn't have thought it possible for anybody to be so thoroughly incompetent and such a complete B.F. I think there will be a riot in there before long. When they ever get any work done I don't know. I can sympathise with you over your recruits. It really gets in your hair to have people like it around doesn't it?

Of course, from the point of view of the kids' education it is absolutely tragic that such people should be employed as teachers. But there you are – that is one of the results of the war! It makes me sick to see the kids I worked hard with last year being so mishandled – especially as on the whole they were quite a good lot."

"… Mr Green, the inspector, blew in at school on Thursday afternoon. He seemed quite pleased with my class generally and was quite sympathetic over the appalling noise going on in the next room. He said 'Good Heavens – is that the noise you have to put up with!' Still there seems to be nothing to do about it. It is Mrs G or nobody.

Personally I think 'nobody' would be preferable – but some of the others do not share that opinion."

"… It has just begun to rain and all the dinner kids are streaming into the next room where the ineffable Mrs G holds sway. If the rain doesn't cease soon I shall have to go in and do something about it. Anyway it will not be possible to do much writing. She has been getting in a lovely muddle this week with all the Savings. When the Boss complained about her to the inspector the other day he said 'In these days you have to be thankful for anything that walks on two legs.' But I wonder! I'm sure if she went on the stage as a caricature of the teaching profession people would say it was a terrible exaggeration."

Maternity leave from Easter was a blessed relief. As things panned out Jennie never went back.

Wireless Valve

Today we take radio for granted: we can listen in our car, on our mobile phone, through our TV or anything connected to the Internet. A table-top radio, if we want one, is incredibly reliable and cheap. It's instructive, as a tiny example of wartime shortages, to look at the saga of Jennie's kitchen wireless.

This was a substantial investment. A pre-war radio would cost anything upward of six pounds (about £240 in today's money); a utility wireless at the end of the war over double that. Very few people had television sets, which were in any case useless as there were no transmissions. Newsprint constraints made papers very thin (typically no more than four pages) and they sold out quickly, so the kitchen radio was often a family's main source of news and entertainment. Until it stopped working.

Jennie experienced that catastrophe in April 1941. At first it was tolerable: the set worked but not very well and cleaning contacts seemed to make a difference. By September it was clear that wouldn't be enough on its own.

> *"Mr Wilkins turned up on Thursday to see the wireless, he seems to have made it a little better but said he would like to test it with a KT63 if he can borrow one. There is an American make valve 6F6(G) – Mullard (or other American Brands) which is equivalent to KT63 and apparently easier to obtain – so perhaps we could get one."*

In March 1942 the valve finally went terminal.

> *"I went over to Shenley Avenue and found Mr. Wilkins' abode. His wife thinks he can come over on Friday evening and see to the wireless – for which I shall be very thankful – as I miss it quite a bit, although the programmes are chiefly 'pretty bloody' in these days."*

This was a priority shout – to Eric on the Clyde and Jennie's family in Bristol.

> *"Let me have the particulars of the valve darling as Pa thinks Mr Wallington will be able to get me one being well in at the Bristol Wireless Co."*
>
> *"… In the stress of the last few days I am sorry to say I overlooked that valve number. It is KT63 output valve (10/6 + 2/4d[47]). If you cannot get it in Bristol I have a good opportunity of collecting it on Wednesday or Friday in Gourock."*

---

[47] About 64p in all, equivalent to £28 today. A quick Internet search suggests they change hands now for about £25.

By the second half of April things were beginning to look hopeful.

> *"Wireless valve! The shop at Gourock have hopes of getting hold of the one we want. If so I shall get it in my case (I don't know what arrangements you made) but it can always be re-sold to Mr Wilkins if Mr Wallington purchases one as well for us."*

The concerted effort produced a fix, though it sounds improvised.

> *"How is the valve behaving? Let me know if the set goes at all 'squiffy'. Am still hoping to purchase the correct one, and also any spares I can find."*

It evidently held. Apart from a momentary panic in July 1942 when the extension speaker gave trouble that was the end of the matter.

Pay

As a conscript Eric started on around two shillings (10p) a day, or about £27 at 2013 prices per week. Despite a generous allowance from his employer it was a drastic cut from his civilian salary of eight guineas (£8.40) a week.

> *"I'm going to have your present ready this week end and only wish I had one former week's salary to spend on you – that's the lousiest part of it, when you want to spend some dough on somebody else; it doesn't matter a damn when you are with blokes who are in the same boat."*

Living on a gun site at least brought free food (of a sort) and uniform but meant he had to rely on neighbours' goodwill for the jobs and repairs he would normally have done at home. Jennie shouldered the entire burden of looking after the house as well as holding down a full-time job.

Things gradually improved as the army grudgingly released proficiency pay but the nirvana of trade pay (an extra 1s 3d a day) seemed to recede faster than he could pass the required tests. A scandalous 1941 decision removed radar operators' trade pay retrospectively because all they had to do was 'twiddle some knobs.'[lxxx]

> *"We are all very worried about the prospect of leave being cut down. What a life! Well, we seem to be getting right back where we started. First they remove the trade status, and now this. It makes you sick when you hear about how well wireless men are treated in the Navy and the RAF. Why didn't I try for the RAF?*
>
> *The reaction of the old hands is terrible to behold. When they had calmed down sufficiently they all began writing letters to their C.O.s begging to be removed from the GL. Since they have been in this racket they have lost all chance of promotion. If this goes on I predict a serious shortage of efficient OFCs* [Operators Fire Control] *and serve them right."*

Skilled men found themselves unexpectedly in debt and the supply of recruits dried up.

> *"The announcements on the radio about the need for men, prospects etc was received with hoots and similar cynical noises. What price trade pay? At present a man who drives an army lorry is in a higher grade."*

Part-time harvesting in September 1941 – at about three times his army rate – drove the point home. To add insult to injury, their duties kept increasing.

"Apparently we are to be trained to make our own tests and adjustments in future, which is normally carried out by radio officers and ordnance. Which would be fine if we were getting nominal trade pay. What blasted cheek!"

Official suggestions on top of accumulated resentment provoked near-mutiny.

"We had an amusing session last night. An officer called a 'muster' parade and announced an R.A. Benevolent scheme, reading from a pompous document which referred to the R.A. as a 'great comradeship' (roar upon roar of ironic laughter, in which the officer himself joined). The gist of it was that a penny a week kept one off the breadlines in the future, which provoked an amazing and refreshing storm. Practically the whole room got to its feet and pointed out that it was fighting for democracy and expected democracy to provide a solution to those troubles after the war. The scheme was condemned on principle! A little indication of what lies in store for any fat headed government that attempts to hedge on its obligations.

This spirit is now very manifest in the army. The first paralysing effect of army discipline has worn off and soldiers are once more becoming individuals."

Trade status finally materialised early in 1942.

"Only news here is that we are all being Trade Tested on Thursday – undergoing a severe inquisition so that a grudging army council can make sure that it is not throwing an extra 1/3 a week away on an unskilled man – after being bullied into making some sort of a cash grant. Such breathtaking generosity makes one all the keener, of course, to pass the wretched test. I have been entitled to draw Trade pay for over a year now. Niggardly swine!"

On making lance sergeant in 1943 his pay packet swelled to about £3.23 a week and active service brought a further increase to £3.94. By contrast the lowest-paid US private earned fifty dollars (about £20.00) per month plus overseas allowance.

Qualification

Eric could improve his lot by promotion, either through the army hierarchy or a recognised specialism. He repeatedly explored both in alternate fits of enthusiasm when avenues opened and despair when they closed again.

The most promising route to specialism was a Technical Instructor (TI) qualification. By September 1941, nearly a year after his call-up, he was confident enough in his skills to prick up his ears at the chance.

"I have been doing a lot of swotting in maths and wireless theory lately as there is a probability of vacancies for a technical instructors course. I should very much like a stab at it. I am glad to say that my 'trig' is now on a sound basis."

The opportunity looked real enough: production of the GL Mk 1 radar had ceased and Mk 2 supply was ramping up quickly: 230 had been delivered by September 1941 and the total would more than double by the end of the year. The Mk 1 was laboratory-standard equipment rushed into production so experienced operators like Eric needed both practical skill and underlying theory to keep the cantankerous kit on air. They were ideally-placed to bring on the hundreds of new crews needed for the better-developed Mk 2.

It wasn't to be; operational need won out. At the end of October he wrote:

"Prospect of the T.I.'s course is receding as we are supplying a demonstration team soon and no one can be spared. Too bad. Still there may be another chance."

Or then again perhaps... Just three days later:

"I had a bit of good news yesterday. The IFC (Brigade O.C., GL) visited the camp yesterday and I hear that I am going on an instructor's course. There were no vacancies on the one I applied for, but there is a place for me on the next."

November passed in a blur of hopeful activity.

"I'm glad I swotted it up (Trig) as it forms an important part of the T.I.'s course. I am working out a course of study for the above: it's rather a staggering total covering Mk1 and 2 sets, power-unit circuits and advanced wireless theory, besides gunnery and plotting. But it's all much easier when you've been some time at it. I've been on this for seven months now."

"... Latest development in my own 'private offensive': I'm seeing the Major tomorrow, and my old pal (?) the T.I. has turned up and has promised to recommend me to the Divisional IFC for a T.I.'s course. My name must be sprinkled in quite a few places now. Probably all pigeon-holed."

"... There is a very good chance of that TIs course coming off after all and I shall probably go with them. Which will suit me very well indeed. Anyway I shall swot and pester them until I do get it. And have had some very good reports passed on by Radio Officer."

All went quiet again for the rest of the year but February 1942 brought new encouragement.

>   "'The Course' – prospects of same have slightly improved. Was asked to address a letter last week to the O.C. stating qualifications etc. He will forward this to the appropriate quarter, adding a recommendation of his own…
>
>   Am doing as much swotting as possible and bought the best book for the purpose when on leave. It is the Outline of Wireless[48], costs 15/- but is well worth it."
>
>   "… We all had a much needed get together last night in the canteen and I took the opportunity of tackling the OC about 'that course'. He said they have not been stopped but there is a formidable waiting list. Hope springs eternal."

What goes up must come down – hope and expectation included.

>   "I'm afraid I was a bit 'knocked' at the discouraging reports re that course but have regained a philosophical attitude and I have decided not to worry unduly about the 'stalemate' – why the heck should I disturb myself, anyway."
>
>   "… Another thing that hasn't added to my cheerfulness is the Radio Officer's announcement – in response to another very earnest enquiry – that he thinks that T.I.'s courses are being discontinued! Wham! Candidly I wouldn't be surprise me in the least, but I'm still hoping."

What comes down sometimes bounces. In August, with over 1,100 GL Mk 2 sets available, the topic came up again.

>   "There seems to be a drive to enrol more wireless men, and there is a hint about new instructors, so I am working up my theory like

---

[48] Author: Ralph Stranger, Publisher: George Newnes (1932).

blazes, still 'oscillating' between that and the commission! Pathetically optimistic, that's me!"

The following month Eric was finally promoted to Paid Acting Lance Bombardier. Training new crews – without a TI's badge – was part of his day job. By the end of the year Mk 2 production was tailing off as the first vastly improved Mk 3 sets began to come through. That was a whole new game – which Eric was to excel at.

Promotion

Throughout his army career Eric's desire to get on contended with his sceptical view of class and authority. He was confident he could do the job – a confidence almost brash when he applied for a commission straight from gunner's rank.

> *"He was telling me that the officers at Left Troop have a very high opinion of their GL section (!) and have offered to give us any extra training that we desire. I told him that I thought it an excellent idea, and that a few of us ought to go in for gun and instrument training, plotting etc. My idea is that if I don't get my chance of an instructor's course I shall have a good go at a commission in the near future."*

In 1942 the Royal Army Ordnance Corps was expanding rapidly to cope with the logistics of the North African campaign and the return to mainland Europe. Gunner Nudd felt the opportunity was too good to miss.

> *"A notice appeared about a week ago to the effect that applications for certain commissioned ranks in Ordnance would be invited. Len*

Nash and I forthwith accepted the invitation, and I think our application will be recommended by the Major."

"… I don't set too much store by it, but at least the application doesn't do any harm. The trouble is that my 'background' might be a whole lot better – as it is really surprising how little one's Army efforts are taken into account. I don't think that advertising and Press work will be a good recommendation…

There is also, of course, that much lamented lack of School Cert or Matric but still! As I say, I will not place too many hopes on it. It would be just too darn foolish.

That being my avowed state of mind I am going to state here and now that this Army might be a lot more successful in its search for fresh material if it gave more attention to a man's individual efforts and less to 'background' – which doesn't necessarily make a man a better soldier. And that still goes whether I land it or not…

'Robbie' asked me if I was so sensitive about a 'scholastic' record – which admittedly I am at periods like this! – why I didn't consider taking the London University special Matric which he says is quite easy. It doesn't sound too bad an idea. Of course French is one of the five subjects, but apparently it consists of a fairly easy translation and so wouldn't need a terrific preparation. Other subjects are Algebra, English, Geometry and Electro Magnetism."

For a while the prospects looked encouraging, going on a 'sure thing.'

"The officers here seem to take our going to OCTU [Officer Cadet Training Unit] for granted…"

But no.

"My RAOC application has fallen through, lack of suitable qualifications the reason."

In September the tombola span again.

> "On Monday I was ushered into the presence of Kilner and asked if I'd ever considered a commission!
>
> I decided to be tactful and just say 'yes' and subsequently I was interviewed by the Adjutant who painted as black a picture as possible of the prospects of anyone getting through OCTU and the probability of being turfed out of OCTU! – and then asked me why I wanted a commission. I said I wanted a more active and responsible job etc, and he said he didn't think that a very good reason, officers get shoved into humdrum jobs and got into a rut – was there any other reason? I mentioned one's natural ambitions, and it transpired that wasn't a good reason. Then he asked me what branch I wanted to serve with, I said Artillery, and he said most probably it would be the infantry – one couldn't pick and choose!! Very helpful and invigorating, what? He wound up by saying I would stand a poor chance as a gunner! Kilner did up and say my promotion was 'coming along', thereupon he advised me to apply again in a couple of months! I have written at some length about this just to demonstrate the sort of person we have to contend with, I never felt more like telling a bloke to go to hell in my life. Do hope to meet some of them after the war. My God won't I tell them something."

In parallel, Eric was increasingly cynical about the ability of the officer class. General Pile coined the phrase, 'below and behind,' to describe the typical aiming error in practice shoots, ascribing it to gunners' tendency to lag behind their indicators.[lxxxi] Eric felt the problem was at least equally due to Gun Position Officers giving the 'Fire' order too late: *"Their job in action is simply to say the right thing at the right time – and even that is a formidable thing for most of them."*

> "There seems to be a general saying that in our army General Rommel would at best be Sergeant Rommel. I could go further and say

*that in the Reichwehr some of our officers would be lavatory orderlies.
It would at least indulge their craving for spit and polish! And they
could use some of their daily orders re blancoing as toilet paper."*

Long after the war he wrote:

*"And I shall never forget an occasion when I, fresh (or jaded)
was sent straight from a battle school (live ammunition, six men
killed[49]) to board a train en route for another fairly arduous course. It
was a matter of minutes, and I, a mere sergeant, committed the sin of
jumping for my life – into the snob coach! I was immediately
confronted by a lieutenant (one-pipper), the authentic model, pink-
cheeked, OCTU-fresh, immaculate, nineteenish – who asked 'Are
YOU travelling first-class?' How I longed for that bren-gun with
which I had been operating only twenty-four hours before!
Alternatively, his name and address, for future enquiries."*

Pile might not totally have disagreed. He compared the state of the
armed forces in 1942:

*"The Navy was professional. It was not awfully scientific. It
made many obvious mistakes, but, whenever there was a chance of
battle, its professional ability at once stood out...*

*The Air Force was highly scientific, but not yet professional. Its
laurels rested on the efforts of a few pilots. Its prestige, owing to the
Battle of Britain, was extremely high, but, because it was not
professional, it was led to seek after strange gods and to believe that
bombing was, of itself, a war-winner.*

The Army was not yet either professional or scientific."[lxxxii]

---

[49] Probably an exaggeration.

At that time the Army Council began to insist on officers having adequate fitness and mental agility as well as military experience. The clear-out of commissioned dead wood raised Eric's hopes of a more professional approach.

> *"Still it's a refreshing bit of news about the tests for all officers over 45 (pity about the age limit) I also have noted that to judge from what nearly every paper is saying the Army is completely 'found out' at last. Ring out the old and bring in the new – if there's still time!"*
>
> *"… I was very tickled at that cutting you sent me re Army discussions, copied from the Soviet. Coincided with another clipping about the new selection of officers idea, involving psycho-analysis and a complete disregard of education and 'birth' – copied from the German Army, which has used this system since 1933!! With all these new innovations inspired by the dictatorships, we seem well on the way towards making our Army more democratic."*

As things panned out he followed the conventional promotion route via Bombardier and Lance-Sergeant, achieving substantive Sergeant's rank at the beginning of 1944. It took a while.

> *"The Regt T.I has informed me that it is proposed to make me a sergeant in 'due course' – ha, ha! Remind me of the words of the Bedouin love song – 'when the sun grows cold and the stars are old' – nice to have the promotion handed to you with the discharge. 'Paddy' Knight, one of the officers is very amusing on the subject of the deferment. On 'Co-op' [air co-operation] the other night he was GPO [Gun Position Officer] and just back from leave. He phoned up to ask 'Is it, sergeant, bombardier or still gunner Nudd?'"*

Throughout his time in the army Eric balanced cordial relations with officers of his battery and deep distrust of the behaviours that went with the King's commission. He also had a persistent feeling that he could do better. On active service in late 1944 he wrote:

> *"It's remarkable how 'experienced' one feels at this stage – even a bit 'superior' in dealing with majors and troop commanders who haven't much experience in the line. Seeing them dither always makes me amused at my old fears of being in the same state and my reluctance to take a commission for that reason. I even fancy myself as Battery Commander – but needless to say do not even remotely seek it at this stage. Having nearly thirty men to look after is just comfortable. That comprises my own people plus signals and drivers etc."*
>
> *"… Apart from performing my duties to my own satisfaction I have not one shred of ambition left; thank God I have shaken off that frame of mind in which I sought promotion or a commission."*

This ambivalence may explain his failure to complete a pre-OCTU course in 1945.

CODA

In March 1946 Eric found himself with his demob suit and the army's thanks back on the Street: the Street of Adventure, Street of Disillusion or Street of Shame according to your perspective[50]. He returned to his job on the *Sunday Pictorial* closely followed by Hugh Cudlipp, now a Lieutenant-Colonel. Sam Campbell departed discreetly for *The People*.

Harry Procter, a terrifyingly talented investigative journalist, joined the 'Pic' a few years later and found, *"the most efficient newspaper-team the world has ever seen, or probably ever will see. And this*

Figure 23: A cartoonist's view of Hugh Cudlipp's career. ('Number Ten' was the pub favoured by Mirror *and* Sunday Pictorial *staff).*

---

[50] The first two are books by Philip Gibbs and Harry Procter; the third is *Private Eye*'s usual epithet. Fleet Street is still accepted shorthand for the British national press, wherever they have physically landed.

newspaper, with its mammoth circulation, was run, I was amazed to discover, by a small handful of hand-picked journalists.[lxxxiii]"

It wasn't all sweetness and light; Harry Guy Bartholomew (Cudlipp's boss) knew how to nurture a grudge and had never forgiven his defection from the *Mirror* before the war. He got his chance when Hugh missed a late-breaking story, gleefully firing him on Christmas Eve 1948. He was unemployed for a few hours before accepting Lord Beaverbrook's invitation to edit the *Sunday Express*.

The wheel of fortune turned again at the 'Pic.' Bartholomew was ousted in March 1952 and Hugh Cudlipp returned in triumph. He blew in like a whirlwind, changed everything around and then left to sort out Cecil King's interests in Australia. While he was there Sir Keith Murdoch confided *'I am worried about my son Rupert. He's at Oxford and he's developing the most alarming Left-wing views.'*[lxxxiv] Hugh was probably the wrong person to empathise – but the errant son's later return to Britain brought all the pain of a well-aimed boomerang.

Eric's life looked up when he met Marguerite Cope, a secretary on the *Daily Mail* foreign desk. She met with his sons' approval and he with her parents' despite the ready-made family; they married in 1950 and had a son the following year. Their reception for 35 guests at the Gayton Rooms in Harrow cost £43 6s 6d (about £1,300 today).

In December 1951 he was inveigled to join Sam Campbell on the rival *People* with no job title but an expanded role "... *in charge of all production, in the broadest sense, and I want you to initiate and develop new ideas to the paper generally and to play a big part in our future planning.*"[lxxxv] This was heady stuff as was a starting salary of £23 a week (£34,800 per year at 2013 prices). The staff at the 'Pic' gave him a typically double-edged send off.

"You are old, Mr. Nudd
And I note, with surprise,
That your legs, late at night, are so feeble.
Is it bold, Mr. Nudd
> *(Entre nous, is it wise?)*
To go leaving this job for the People?
At near-middle-age it is late for a change.
The young blood has long turned to water.
I suppose it's too late for your pals to arrange
A job here in a different quarter?
You could, for a start,
Work with Jack, on The Art,
Or maybe with George would be sporting?
It would still give a chance
For that Nuddible glance
Which directed at Janet, is courting.
But perhaps all is best.
You could do with a rest.
Retire him. Go sing for a pension!
After all, you perceive
Many here do believe
Poor old Eric has Nudding worth mention.
No regrets. No hard thoughts. We know
Nudd must go.
Good luck to the ~~shit~~ in Long Acre
And if anyone thinks
That the whole business stinks,
He's so right, oh so right
TROUBLE-MAKER"

The workload on *The People* was savage: combining design and
layout with production meant there was no let-up from Tuesday

Figure 24: Office horseplay
Hannen Swaffer, Fleet Street grandee is seated. Eric swings a
T-square at Jimmy Savile's head.

morning until the last edition went to press Saturday night. He developed innovative promotional materials and a bold, colourful style to match the paper's remorseless diet of exposure, confession and sensation. His talent for producing layouts that dropped naturally into type made him popular with compositors who had to bridge the gap between late copy and fixed print deadlines.

There was still time for a few side projects. He started a book on the Street with Arthur Wragg[51] and, presumably inspired by his Clydeside experience, began to write verse in the style of Robert Burns. One example referencing the Glencoe massacre[52] reveals an ambivalent attitude to his boss: respect, perhaps admiration, but never trust.

"'Twas in a Highland glen
  That I met McDonald man
So we gathered for a drappie an' a wrangle
  An' they spake still o' the foe
Wha' had trapped them at Glencoe... 'Oh –
  NEVER COME TAE BLAWS WI' A CAMPBELL!'
  When tae Odhams I returned
  Aye, this lesson had I learned
Ye cannae risk a goolie or a gamble
  Ye're as hapless as a fly
When ye meet yon piercing eye... so
  NEVER COME TAE BLAWS WI' A CAMPBELL!
  If ye doubt me, ask them a'
  Wha' has suffered in the fall
The highest an' the lowest aft a-ramble
  O' the times when there were dirks
Stickin' oot o' bleedin' shirts... aye –
  NEVER TURN YOUR BACK UPON A CAMPBELL!
  But – when a' is spake an' spared

---

[51] Wragg illustrated books, newspapers and record covers with disturbingly stark pen and ink drawings.

[52] Clan rivalry and national politics came into deadly alignment at Glencoe on 12th February 1692 when 120 men under the command of Captain Robert Campbell slaughtered 38 MacDonalds, who were their hosts at the time. Another 40 women and children died of exposure after their homes were burned.

There is only this yon laird
Whae has the final word without preamble
Make it short and make it plain
Or you're askin' to be slain
   AN' NEVER ARGUE BACK AGIN THE CAMPBELL!
   For his clan's five million plus
   An' he'll raise the Fiery Cuss
Tae a' wha dare tee dither or to amble
   Toast the chieftain o' the mass
circulation wi' the brass…
   YE CAN'T AFFORD TAE BE WITHOUT THE CAMPBELL!"

Figure 25: Never turn your back upon a Campbell!
Eric later designed the Barbara Castle's 1964 election flyer.

Figure 26: Barbara Castle's 1964 election flyer

In 1959 Campbell, whose own position was ambiguous until 1957, finally gave Eric a job title – Assistant Editor in charge of Production. The proviso was that he continued his other duties as well. They included looking after outside contributors such as star columnist Arthur ('Tony') Helliwell in New York. His letters are full of gossip about the meanness of his allowance, trying of get anything usable out of Elizabeth Taylor or sign up a restaurant owner with mob contacts, and the perils of drinking with a submarine crew ashore. There was however a constant unease beneath his cheerfulness.

> *"On the face of it I'm a lucky son-of-a-gun. More or less my own boss. Three thousand miles away from the rat race. Living in glamorous New York. What more do I want?*
>
> *I'm blessed if I know, except that my feeling of insecurity increases and there are times when I feel like packing up and having a crack elsewhere before it's too late. That, of course, maybe the plot behind all this. I wouldn't know. Forgive my gloom. I didn't intend to fall into this mood when I began writing – but it helps…*

Sam, I must say, couldn't be nicer. He writes often. His letters are full of praise. He almost fawns. And yet… and yet…!"[lxxxvi]

Eric was in the unenviable position of an agent runner: balancing personal loyalty against the company's needs. The confessional worked both ways: they privately discussed an opportunity for Eric to transfer to *The People*'s sister paper, the ailing *Daily Herald*. In the same letter Tony wrote:

> *"What puzzles me about the prospective move is that Sam should be ready to let you go. He must be crazy because there is no-one on the paper – including him – with your genius for make-up and display – and it will suffer sadly if you do go."*

Figure 27: Design for a 1962 promotional leaflet
Eric considered Letraset cheating. We can only imagine his reaction to desktop publishing.

A rescue party was trying to reanimate the paper under editor John Beaven. Eric decided to take the offer.

> *"It's a splendid move up the ladder for you Eric and a tremendous opportunity – although I can well appreciate that you have some worrying, nerve-straining months ahead. I was, of course, half prepared for your news by your previous letter, although I did not think that you were immediately destined for such an important job. But Nat's[53] appointment does surprise me. And I simply cannot understand Sam letting his two key men go. 'The People' I think must surely suffer, because, whatever my personal feelings about Nat and his 'non-professionalism' I have a high regard for his ability and intelligence and I would have thought that he had made himself practically indispensable to Sam. Incidentally I know John Bevan [sic] slightly. He's ex-Manchester Guardian isn't he? He and I covered our first 'warco' assignment – some Canadian Army manoeuvres in England – together...*
>
> *Of course I know nothing of the plans for the 'new' Herald – but I gather that the changes are to be pretty sweeping. I hope – for your sake – it clicks Eric. Success in this new venture could lead to really big things. But it will be a long and tough uphill struggle chum – and I DON'T envy you."*[lxxxvii]

Eric started at the *Herald* on 1st January 1961. Almost immediately Odhams Group, owner of the *Herald* and *The People*, was the subject of a bidding war between Thomson Newspapers and IPC, publisher of the *Mirror* and the *Sunday Pictorial*. IPC won and in April Hugh Cudlipp – again – came crashing through the ceiling as new chairman of the *Herald* and chairman-designate of Odhams. Sydney Jacobson replaced John Beaven as editor the following year.

---

[53] Nat Rothman was deputy editor of *The People* at the time.

Figure 28: Nudd awaits the opening of hostilities

IPC was mainly attracted by Odhams' stable of magazines. A saturated periodicals market, rising costs, and competition from television made rationalisation imperative; combining the two groups made it possible. *The People* was profitable and could be left to its own devices but the *Herald* was a problem child. Part of the deal was that IPC would keep it going for seven years and try to revive its flagging fortunes. Forced to support the Labour Party and the TUC at all costs, and with a mainly old, male and poor readership, the paper was beyond saving. Cudlipp grew to hate the *"bloated, listless boa constrictor suffering from fatty degeneration of the heart"*[lxxxviii] dumped in his lap.

Eric didn't feel too good about it either. The promised office and staff didn't materialise, the poisonous politics of a failing business would have worn anyone down, and he couldn't give the job his full attention: *The People* kept pulling him back for feature promotions.

The *Herald* gave up the ghost on 14th September 1964 and was replaced next day by the *Sun*, a new venture with modern, eye-catching design and a bold masthead of Eric's design. He also helped shape the scintillating launch campaign. The TUC's editorial stranglehold loosened and the content quality improved, but the limitations of Odhams' rotary presses prevented a physical format change.

It wasn't enough. Sales fell to a comatose 800,000 by 1969; the paper was losing money hand over fist, as newsprint prices rose inexorably. Rupert Murdoch bought it for a song after an approach by Robert Maxwell failed. Murdoch moved production to the *News of the World* presses which until then were idle six days a week. He changed the format to tabloid and, with no union commitments to honour, made a fresh start. The wintry *Sun* emerged from the clouds to scorch British journalism.

Eric never saw it. Tired, debilitated and disillusioned, he ignored encroaching illness until he could no longer function, dying in January 1967. A brief obituary in *The People* read:

"FLEET STREET LOSES AN ARTIST

A MAN whose work is known to every reader of "The People" died suddenly on Friday night.

He was Eric Nudd, one of Fleet Street's most original newspaper lay-out experts.

A pioneer of the technique of bold presentation, he applied his skilful projection to some of the most sensational exposure campagns [sic] *in newspaper history.*

His touch had a great influence on the development of this newspaper's distinctive appearance.

Evidence of his flair is visible outside newsagents' shops and on hoardings all over Britain today.

For he was the originator of the unique-style black and yellow "People" posters.

Mr Nudd, who was 54 and lived at Ruislip, Middlesex, entered hospital for observation last week. He leaves a widow and three sons."[lxxxix]

APPENDIX A:
ANTI-AIRCRAFT
ARTILLERY

T his is a quick tour of the technical and military background to the book. Feel free to skip it if you're familiar with terms like 'GL 3 Mk II' and 'Predictor No 10'. If not, fear not. I'll try to focus on the essentials.

It concentrates on British 3.7-inch anti-aircraft guns in the Second World War – with occasional digressions where they seem relevant. I recommend Brigadier Routledge's excellent work on the subject[xc] to anyone wanting to investigate further.

Figure 29 illustrates the three essential stages of an engagement:

1. Spot the target aircraft; check that it is hostile; measure its position, height, course and speed. Optical instruments were used if the aircraft was visible or gun-laying (GL) radar if not. The early radars were however scarce and couldn't measure height, which was estimated by sound location. If neither was usable the only options were predicted fire using sound location (useless once the guns opened up) or an un-aimed barrage in the approximate path of a raid. They could be effective in putting bombers off their aim but seldom hit much.

2. Calculate where the aircraft will be at a specific time and the gun

bearing, elevation and fuze setting needed to place an exploding shell at the same point. Early clockwork computers (predictors) were available for this purpose.

3. Set the fuzes, load the guns, point them in the right direction and – at the right moment – fire.

Or, in Eric's words:

> *"There's nothing very difficult about gun laying on predictor at night, but you have to be as quick as hell, and being dark makes it a bit tricky. We stay down in the dug-out until we get the call 'Stand by for 'Young' barrage'[54] and the guns have to fire 50 seconds from that time, or GPO* [Gun Position Officer] *cancels the shoot. You*

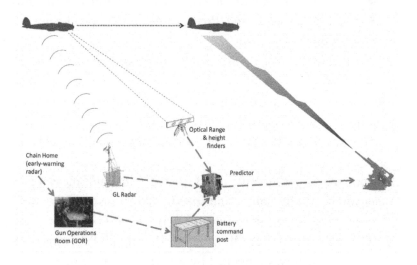

Figure 29: Anti-Aircraft Engagement Schematic

---

[54] A 'Young Barrage' seems to have been intense fire into the predicted path of a raid rather than an individual aircraft.

may be interested to know how this is arranged. First to report hostiles on the way are motor boats in the Channel, whose listening apparatus sets are so sensitive that they can report the planes massing for take off on the French airfields. [55] *This is flashed to our GOR (Gun Operations Room) at –! [Chatham] They plot the course of the plane and give us the number of a square on a graticule map[56] which the plane is approaching, also height of plane, and exact time when it will be at that certain point! Our Gun Position Officer measures the angle from Battery position to point of fire on square, shouts, say 'Bearing 110°.' Yours truly traverses like mad and fixes bearing by torchlight, and this simultaneously operates electrical pointers on the guns which the gunlayers follow, and the guns swing round with the predictor. At the same time an elevation is called 'Q.E (Quadrant Elevation) 65°.' Layer for Q.E. elevates, and the guns follow. Then Fuze, for height, (1,000 ft per fuze length) say 12, which is shouted to the guns, and which fuze setter fixes on his projectile. Predictor numbers report as soon as they are finished –*

'Bearing one-one-one set'

'Q.E. six-five set'

'Fuze one-two set'

'Fire'

Wham! Up they go!

*   'Battery stand easy' and down we go again to resume our arguments about one's favourite film actress! There's also a big dixie of cocoa on the stove, and some meat pies, if we're lucky."*

We shouldn't underrate the difficulty of this. Measuring a target's bearing, elevation and range simultaneously at least twice; building

---

[55] The early-warning radar chain was still VERY secret!

[56] A map marked with tactical grid squares.

a track and a fire control solution to allow for shell flight time and trajectory; and precisely timing the shoot were tricky tasks individually. They all had to work together for success, while the guns' behaviour constantly changed as the barrels warmed up and wore down.

The guns did not have to hit their target to be effective. Intense anti-aircraft fire forced attackers to fly higher than they would like, take evasive action and bomb less accurately. Formations could be broken up by gunfire, making RAF fighters' job easier, and raiders were often persuaded to abandon their attack or divert to a less important target. 'Pointer' rounds were also used to draw friendly pilots' attention to enemy aircraft. Finally, in a campaign to undermine the nation's appetite for war, there was the civilian morale boost of hearing the army shoot back.

Equipment

Guns

Anti-aircraft guns were classed as light (for defence up to about 5,000 feet) or heavy for targets above that height. Light artillery ranged from machine-guns to 40mm cannon. At first most heavy batteries were equipped with First World War vintage 3-inch guns, which were gradually replaced by modern weapons as deliveries came on stream.

There were also so-called 'Z' batteries which fired multiple, unguided rockets to roughly the same height as the heavy guns.

The late 'thirties saw belated recognition of the need for a better heavy anti-aircraft gun. This led to the development of the 3.7-inch weapon which, in various forms, was the mainstay of the British Heavy Anti-Aircraft (HAA) armoury throughout the war and for some time afterward. It was designed as a mobile weapon but the desperate need for as many barrels as possible led to the alternative fixed mounting, which was much quicker and cheaper to build, dominating early production. By the end of the war nearly 9,000 had been delivered in all.

It could engage airborne targets with predicted fire between 5,000 feet and 24,000 feet altitude. A skilled crew could fire up to 15 rounds per minute until the barrel overheated – at Boulogne in September 1944 the guns of 2nd Canadian HAA got so hot that the barrels drooped visibly.[xci] The main types of ammunition available were high explosive (blast effect) and fragmentation, used for low altitude and short range engagements. Both used timer fuzes which were initially powder-based, later replaced with a more consistent and reliable mechanical design.

The guns could be aimed visually but the bearing, elevation and fuze setting were usually transmitted from the Predictor by an electro-mechanical system called Magslip. At first the settings were displayed by indicators at the gun, which was cranked round by hand. Later this process was automated to improve speed and accuracy. The mobile gun was usually towed by an AEC Matador tractor.

Deliveries started, slowly, in 1938 so the rapidly-expanding anti-aircraft units were not fully equipped until well after the start of the war – a familiar story across all the armed forces.

The 3.7 is often compared with the feared German Flak 36, 88mm gun. The '88' was much lighter: 5 tons on its carriage as opposed to 9.5 for the mobile 3.7. It could be brought into action or packed up faster. The 88's higher muzzle velocity also gave it a better ceiling. The 3.7 on the other hand threw a 28lb shell as opposed to the 88's 19.8lb and had better horizontal range at about 11½ miles compared to 9¼.

The shortfall in numbers was partly addressed by adapting naval 4.5-inch guns for land use. The weight and bulk of this weapon dictated static mounting only. Over half were subsequently converted to 3.7-inch Mk 6 by lining the barrel diameter down to 3.7 inches while retaining the larger chamber, which greatly increased its muzzle velocity.

The complementary Light Anti-Aircraft (LAA) batteries were often equipped with the extraordinarily versatile Bofors 40mm gun for visual engagement of low-flying targets. Both were needed to defend a location, and they worked closely together in other tasks too.

Optical Instruments

There were well-established techniques to determine an aircraft's course, speed and height optically – provided it remained in sight long enough. This required a reasonably clear sky and either daylight or searchlights able to hold the target. The instrument used two telescopes on each end of a long bar (about 18 feet for the usual Barr and Stroud equipment). Range was determined by adjusting their angle so that both images combined in the eyepiece. Simultaneously other operators would mark time, bearing and elevation to calculate of the target's position at that moment. Two or more observations were needed to establish a track and predict where the target would be at a future time.

The calculations assumed the target flew a constant height, speed and course. Level bombers had to keep steady during a bomb run so that their gyroscopic sights had time to stabilise. In daylight they adopted close formation which helped defence against fighters but made evasive manoeuvring impractical. At night navigation was difficult enough without weaving all over the sky, so it was usually a fair assumption.

Dive bombers were a different game: the army's standard AA manual (published in 1924) stated "*… the case of an aeroplane dropping rapidly, which would practically eliminate the possibility of any accurate* *prediction, is also passed over.*"[xcii] Heavy batteries, driven by necessity, still evolved effective tactics. They fired a barrage on the attacker's bearing to detonate at a range and height that he would have to dive through to hit his target.

Predictors

The predictor was a specialised computer to calculate the 'aim-off' and fuze setting needed to explode the shell near a target aircraft. It was fed from visual or radar measurements of the target's course, speed and height, and sent laying and fuze settings to the guns.

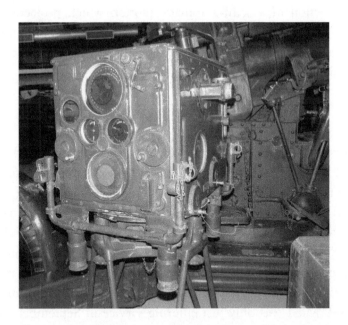

Figure 30: AA No 1 Mk III predictor in the South African National Museum of Military History, Johannesburg (Nick Roux, Wikimedia Commons)

Two types of HAA predictor were used throughout the war. No 1 was developed by Vickers, and worked by six operators with an NCO in charge. No. 2 was the US-developed M3A3, bought from Sperry to make up the numbers needed. It was slightly more advanced and used a team of four operators and a NCO.[xciii] Updated versions issued from 1944 were known as Predictor No's 4 and 5 respectively. All four were clockwork-powered mechanical devices.

Increased aircraft performance made ever-higher demands on the equipment, leading to the development of the 'Bedford Cossor' Predictor No 9 in 1943, and the later procurement of the much better, all-electric, Bell AAA Computer (Predictor No 10) used with the SCR 584 radar.

Fire-control at static sites improved in 1941 with the introduction of a semi-automatic plotter, which projected the target's radar track on a glass screen every ten seconds.[xciv] It improved accuracy by averaging more target plots than the predictor could. Mobile batteries had to make do without.

Radar

At first the only radar available to anti-aircraft batteries was the AA No 1 Mk 1, or GL I (Mk 1) set. This used two cabins, one for the large transmitter array and one for the receiver. The receiver cabin could be rotated bodily with its fixed antenna to find the target direction from the 'loudest' return signal. It had a range of about 30,000 yards (17 miles) and could give a continuous range output, with bearing updated every thirty seconds or so. It could not at first measure target elevation so height had to be estimated by other means.

GL Mk 1 was only just entering service in September 1939. Errors of up to two degrees and no height information meant it could not give a complete fire-control solution. Equipment rushed into production and manuals too secret for issue to the gun sites ensured its theoretical performance was seldom achieved in the field. 206 Battery's Cobham site firing by GL on 7th September 1940 noted: *"... that on almost every occasion the GL bearing & that indicated by the S/lights differed, sometimes as much as 15°"*[xcv]

Successful 'unseen' engagements were understandably rare, but not unknown.

An upgrade to E/F (elevation finding) standard partly overcame these limitations at the beginning of 1941. This added a second antenna to the receiver cabin, allowing a skilled operator to infer the target's elevation from the phase difference between the direct return signal and the ground reflection. An 85-yard horizontal wire mesh platform ('mat') around the receiver cabin gave a known, artificial ground plane for more accurate and consistent results – and created a national shortage of chicken-wire. Plotting a sequence of 'spot' bearing, range and height readings thus obtained gave a rudimentary blind-fire capability.

The AA No 1 Mk 2 (GL Mk 2) was an evolutionary development which replaced the Mk 1 and E/F in 1942. Output power and receiver performance were increased giving a detection range of up to 50,000 yards (28.4 miles) with improved accuracy but mats were still needed for height-finding. Two receiver arrays with separate display screens permitted continuous tracking. By the end of 1942 it was possible to feed radar data directly to the Vickers and Sperry predictors. The GL Mk 2 radar was credited with reducing the rounds-per-kill ratio from the Mk 1's 18,500 to 4,100. [xcvi] Targets could however be tracked only from around 14,000 yards (8 miles).

Toward the end of 1942 completely new radars designated AA No 3 Mk I (a Canadian unit also known as GL Mk 3C) and Mk II (a UK design known as GL Mk 3B) began to arrive. They boasted microwave (3 GHz) wavelengths and Plan Position Indicator (PPI) displays. Mk 3C used two cabins to cover tactical control and target selection. 3B had a single cabin and was suitable for gun fire control

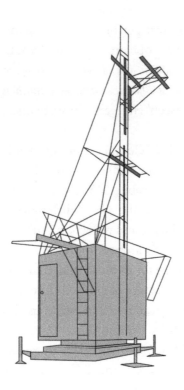

Figure 31: GL Mk 2 Receiver Cabin with antenna erected
Operators measured target bearing by rotating the entire cabin to find
the strongest signal.

only. The latter became the widespread standard, but needed a local warning (LW) set for target selection. Maximum detection range was initially 27,000 yards – later boosted to 35,000 by more power – but accurate tracking for prediction was limited to 14,000 yards by the Vickers No 1 Predictor. They did not rely on ground reflection to calculate elevation angles, so didn't need the expensive and cumbersome netting mats.[xcvii]

The local warning need was initially met by equipment developed in the Middle East for use by the Eighth Army: AA No 4

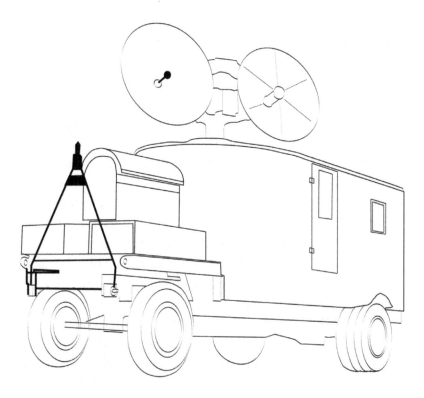

Figure 32: GL 3 Mk II Radar
Sketch showing single-cabin arrangement including generator,
transmit and receive antennae

Marks II and III. Two modified Air Ministry designs (No 4 Mk V/AMES Type 14 and No 5 Mk II/AMES Type 11) were later adapted for this purpose. Older GL Mk 2 sets were used where dedicated units were unavailable.

The final wartime advance was the US-built SCR 584 (known in UK service as AA No 3 Mk V). It arrived from late 1943 and provided outstanding performance when used with the Bell Telephone AAA Computer (aka Predictor No 10). It was used in the 'Diver' (anti-V1) and North-West Europe campaigns. Search range extended to 70,000 yards (aided by vertical scan) with target tracking from 35,000 yards.

A new use of artillery radar came out of the Italian campaign in 1944. AA operators watching for enemy air activity noticed that they could see the flight of shells. Further development allowed them to detect mortar positions accurately enough for counter-battery fire at Rimini (September 1944) and Forli (November 1944). Eventually this led to the formation of a Field Artillery Radar Regiment.[xcviii] Interestingly there was talk after the Battle of Normandy of removing AA radar sections from their batteries (which were by then used largely in the ground role) into a dedicated unit of their own. It came to nothing, but this may have been the reason.

Another use of AA radar was to detect enemy minelaying in the approaches to Arromanches and Port en Bessin after the Normandy landings. The point of mine release showed up clearly on the GL Mk 3B radar's display, and the resulting plots enabled the Navy to sweep them quickly and keep the supply route open.

Finally, a GL Mk 3B radar was used to guide landing craft in total darkness for the crossing of the Scheldt in 'Operation Vitality' on 24th October 1944.[xcix] In a back-handed compliment the assault troops found an enemy battery at Westkapelle equipped with four captured British 3.7s[57] and two 3-inch guns.[c]

Production

We have already noted the chronic equipment shortage at the start of the war for all types of military equipment – not least anti-aircraft. The planning target for HAA guns in 1935 was 544, rising to 608 in

---

[57] I believe the Germans rated the 3.7 highly enough to manufacture their own ammunition for it.

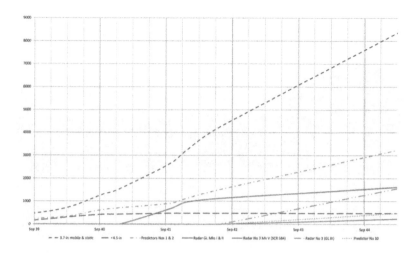

Figure 33: The Numbers Game – cumulative production totals
for key HAA equipment
Source – Routledge

1936 and 1,264 by 1938.[ci] Figure 33 illustrates the speed with which this was overtaken by events.

These are production totals and do not allow for equipment lost in action or retired.

Organisation

A heavy anti-aircraft regiment usually comprised three batteries of eight guns, each divided into two troops of four. Each troop would have optical instruments, a predictor and – as it became available – gun laying radar.

A battery kept its designation if moved between regiments – thus 206/58 (206th battery of the 58th regiment) became 206/60 when transferred to the 60th.

Figure 34: 206 Battery RA (probably at Evenly Hall Northamptonshire, April/May 1944). From the author's collection.

58th and 60th HAA Regiments, in which we take particular interest, were among the six raised as Territorial Army units between 1932 and 1935. Their numbers were filled out by conscription when it was introduced in 1940.

A battery needed support staff and equipment: headquarters, drivers, repair and maintenance, signals, admin as well as the gun and fire-control crews… quite a crowd in all. Figure 34 gives an idea of a mobile battery's scale.

Usage and Tactics

Anti-Aircraft

An air raid detected by the Chain Home early-warning system or coastal GL sets was tracked by radar over the sea and the Observer

Corps once it crossed the coast. The best information about its position, course and intention was plotted in RAF operations rooms (anti-aircraft guns were under Fighter Command tactical control). An AA liaison officer alerted the sector's Gun Operations Room (GOR) which called HAA batteries potentially in the raid's path. At this point bells started ringing.

Figure 35 shows the timeline for an engagement with an aircraft flying at 10,000 feet and just over 200 miles per hour. Its course takes it past a gun site at 15,000 feet (2.8 miles) closest approach. The aircraft track (the straight line on the chart) is marked at ten-second intervals.

The site has a GL Mk 1 E/F radar with an acquisition range of 30,000 yards (the outer arc on the chart) and a tracking range of 14,000 yards (the second arc). The third arc depicts the guns' maximum range, and the inner arc the range where radar loses sight of the target.

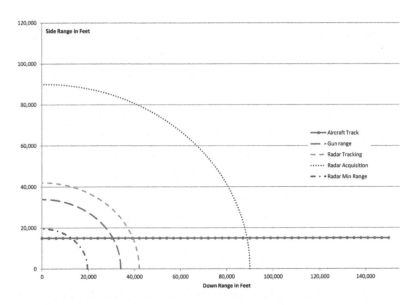

Figure 35: Anti-Aircraft Engagement Timeline

It takes about three minutes between the target's first detection and it coming into tracking range, during which the radar operators alert the Gun Position Officer who decides to engage it. Predictor and gun crews stand to as things start to happen fast.

By the time three radar plots have been taken at ten-second intervals the target is entering gun range where it remains for about one minute and forty seconds. The four guns of the troop will fire four rounds each at three-second intervals. A shell flight time of at least eight seconds means the fire order has to be given within eighty seconds, during which the predictor team must work out a fire-control solution, the gun crews crank the bearing and elevation onto their weapons, set fuze time and load. Finally, they have to fire at the correct moment: a 3.7-inch shell had a lethal radius of about 45 feet, or a third of a second flight time for our fictional target. It would probably have escaped.

Some of this is based on guesswork but the overall picture is pretty close. With manual handover from radar to predictor and predictor to guns, people working fast in the dark make mistakes. The predictor has to allow for imperfectly-known factors such as wind at different heights. The behaviour of the guns changes as the barrels heat up and wear. The Type 199 fuze then issued was not particularly consistent. All in all, the remarkable thing is not that the gunners didn't hit much at this stage of the war; it's that they hit anything at all.

Progressive improvement of every component and the links between them resulted, by the end of the war, in almost complete automation of static guns. The mobile units also benefitted from much of this work, which made life an entirely different story for the poor fliers.

Field Artillery

The 3.7 had a secondary role in field artillery, which came to the fore as the air threat faded in the war's last two years. The gun's accuracy, range, high rate-of-fire and all-round traverse were popular with field commanders, as was the ready availability of AA ammunition when other types ran short. On the other hand, firing at low angles was hard on a mounting poorly designed for it and the gun's flat trajectory made precise ranging difficult. Prolonged firing at maximum rate also caused barrel overheating and rapid wear.[cii]

The War Diary of 60th HAA Regiment illustrates the intensity of these tasks in North-West Europe, recording 2,450 rounds fired at ground targets between landing in Normandy and 26th August, rising to 25,000 by the end of October – an average of something like eight rounds per gun per day.[ciii] Imagine being the object of a full battery's attention – two rounds a second exploding over your head, and knowing that whatever happens next is going to be worse.

Some historians suggest that the strong AA component of the liberation army was at best redundant, at worst an active drain on resources. We should remember though that the guns were not only valued in the ground role, but that the *Luftwaffe* remained capable of strong local attacks until very late in the war. AA batteries were also active in defending Brussels and Antwerp against V1 attack, and in early attrition of those aimed at Britain.

Anti-Tank

Batteries on active service carried armour-piercing (AP) ammunition[civ] for the 3.7's tertiary anti-tank role. The gun's poor mobility compared to the German equivalent made it difficult to use in a fluid tank battle, but it was effective defending prepared areas against armoured attack. Examples include the defence of Boulogne in 1940 and of El Adem and Tobruk in 1942.[cv] These actions have not had the recognition they deserve, perhaps because

*Figure 36: 3.7-inch gun rigged for anti-tank use at Tobruk, 1941
(IWM E 4946)*

they happened in British defeats. Other instances such as the advance on Nijmegen in September 1944, when 165th HAA and 123rd LAA Regiments helped repel a determined counter-attack, are relative footnotes to the drama going on around them.[cvi]

Some 200,000 armour-piercing (AP) shells were manufactured for the 3.7, compared with nearly 11 million high-explosive. Crews also improvised anti-tank rounds when needed by firing anti-aircraft shells without fuzes.

APPENDIX B:
STORIES AND
POEMS

T his appendix brings together some of Eric's writing that doesn't fit into the narrative, makes no claim to literary immortality, but illuminates life and thought at the time.

Theory! Gertcher!

There was (mostly) good-natured tension between the technicians of the fire-control section and the gun crews. One group was stereotyped as effete, the other not very bright. The rivalry inspired Eric to write a short story while he was coping with the rigours and boredom of a Clyde posting.

> *"Theory" said the limber-gunner darkly "You keep your theory and much good it'll do you. Give me ten good men and a gun and I'll show you some straight shooting without any of these new-fangled contraptions. Take this Radiolocation for instance. That's what all the fuss is about over there, and to listen to 'em talking you'd think all our troubles were over. Like as not they've just started.*
>
> *"And them operators. Reg'lar wizards they think they are.*

357

Stuffed up with theory to the neck and jawing about condensors and electrical lengths and rejector what's-its all ruddy day. And their foot drill! Gawd!"

He stared gloomily at a small be-spectacled figure that detached itself from the group at work on the radiolocator and trotted past the gun-pit, carefully avoiding the sergeant in charge, but successfully entangling the latter's feet in a mass of trailing wire.

"Him!" resumed the limber-gunner when the storm had subsided. "Thought we'd seen the last of him and his theories since he tried 'em out the day the general come down with a party of Bigwigs and cleared off a damn sight quicker.

"Oh, he was a great theory lad was Horace. Came to us from that July intake and what he wasn't going to do to these here guns! According to him the Ack-Ack was in the bow and arrow stage and maybe the fourteen jerries we'd shot down was just an Act of God. He wasn't above getting up on his pins at the lectures and telling the Captain all about what he called our obsolete gun drill, and even a long spell in the Cookhouse couldn't take the bounce out of him.

"Well, one fine day he was drafted into our gun team and the boys kicked up such a stink you'd a thought he was something rather special in the leper line. Our Sergeant didn't say much, just gritted his teeth and eyed him for a few minutes, then gives him some cleaning rags and points to the ammo recess. 'You're ammunition number from now on' he says. 'Now get in there and start cleaning up them rounds, and one little crack about theory out of you, my lad, just one little teeny squeak and I'll proceed to knock seven colours of stuffing out of you. Get cracking!' We didn't get much trouble from Horace after that and the time he spent in that recess you'd a thought cleaning ammo was the thing he'd wanted to do all his life. You couldn't find a speck of dirt on 'em and even the Sergeant didn't find a reason to dislike him any worse. We all reckoned he was loopy when he began to spend his evenings over there, and old Fred who's a bit

on the nervous side spoke up and said he preferred a straight forward bomb to the thought of our Horace let loose among all that explosive.

"Then one day a General arrives to inspect the site and watch some practice firing, so we fall in and march down to the gunpits all spit and polish like, followed by His Nibs and a dozen other important blokes with red ribbons round their hats, Gunnery Instructors, I think they are, and only Horace and the General are out of step.

"They all make for our gun and we're up on action stations as quick as you like. The General points up at the plane that's towing the target. "Plane" says he as though we didn't know. "Engage" "Gun control". Doesn't half fancy himself at gun drill. "Traverse left – elevate – on target" shouts our Sarg, and out comes the first round with Horace on the end.

We're halfway up with it when everybody stops frozen like and stares at it as if they'd gone bats. The top's all covered with wires and knobs and evils and something that looks like an electric light bulb on the end. The General's the first to get his breath back. "What… what's this?" he gasps, like you'd say "Pinch me, Charlie, I'm dreaming". Somebody answers and it's our Horace.

"Radio-active fuze, sir. It's my own invention, sir and…" "Get that blasted infernal thing down, man!" roars His Nibs. "Get it down before something happens, I say. Get that…" It comes down all right because poor Fred who has hold of it is so scared by the General and the shell he just lets go. It comes down 'whop' at the feet of His Nibs, something goes 'pop' and she starts to splutter.

"You've never seen the like of the stampede. It's every man for himself and it's a treat to see the Sergeant beat the General over the sandbags and a brass hat go slap into the draining trench and forget to come up for air. I fancy the dug out myself but as three of us all think the same we end up on the floor and we get up I'm wearing a hat with a red ribbon round it!

"We get up because nothing seems to be happening bar a lot of *shouting. The General's shouting at the Colonel and the Colonel's raving at the Captain and the Captain's screaming at the Sergeant and the Sergeant's blinding at Horace, who seems awful worried because the shell hasn't gone off. It's no matter for wonder, as Horace is too full of theory to do anything right and we find he has fixed his blessed radio-active contraption on top of a dummy practice round.*

"Well, order is restored as they say. The other gun Sergeants who've been fair killing themselves laughing tell their teams to wipe the bloody grins off their faces, and Horace is marched off between two men and charged with crimes as fast the officers can read through King's Regulations. But instead of shooting him they send him on a radio course, as the Colonel says a bloke like Horace is sure to touch a high tension cable or something and get his lot that way. But here he is again large as life, all ready to work up another nice surprise for us, like as not.

"Theory! Gertcher!"

Little Nell

The introduction of mixed batteries – men and women working together and living in close proximity – prompted prudish and salacious conjecture. Eric was sceptical of women gunners but loved the comic possibilities.

Attention! Gunners, let me tell
the story of poor little Nell
Who from the straight and narrow strayed
And by a gunner was betrayed.
Here is the tale: you disbelieve it?
Well, please yourself, to take or leave it.

Our tale begins one winter's night
When the poor little maiden, in her plight,
Was booted forth into the snow… and
told to take her traps and go… so
Friendless, and in much distress
She forthwith joined the A.T.S.

It wasn't long before she heard
That soon she was to be transferred
Into the Royal Artillery…
"Here is my opportunity"
She said, and breathed a prayer
That she might find her lover there.

To prove misfortune hadn't licked her
She volunteered for the predictor:
And tho' her time was very near
She took part in 'Detachments Rear'
– But begged for No. 4 position
As best concealing her condition.

Then suddenly there was a Blitz
Scaring poor Nellie into Fitz –
Not so afraid of bombs or blast
As of that time approaching fast.
Aware of this, but loath to go
She bravely shouted "FUZE ONE OH!"
Essayed to fire that vital round
And then fell fainting to the ground.

The G.P.O. – a worthy man
Ordered "STAND FAST"

To Nell he ran… and
gathering her in kindly arms (not
unresponsive to her charms…)
Took her downstairs with beating heart
And laid her on the plotting chart.

He suddenly perceived her state
And sought assistance, most irate:
"It mustn't happen here, by Gad –
If I knew, I'd shoot the cad…"

Then did her comrades rally round –
From Nellie's team a nurse was found
And No. 5 soon proved to be
An expert in midwifery…
Thus, one by one, with great lament
They, two by two, assistance lent.
At last, to their surprise and joy
She had **(You've guessed it, Sir!)**
A boy.

So a Don R. was briefed to go
And fetch the battery M.O.
He came, but at the sight of Nell
He staggered, and grew deathly pale
And Nellie, opening her eyes
Her old betrayer soon espies
With word of love upon his lips…
But can this be? He wears three pips…

The grisly skein is soon untangled
Of how the Doc an intro wangled

Cloaking himself in gunner's guise
To take our Nellie by surprise.

He offers now to end all bother
And make an honest woman of her.
Predicts a wedding; bids her choose:
A Number four, could she re-fuze?

So all is settled: with a kiss
They consummate their wedded bliss…
Decide it's eminently sound
To call their offspring
PRACTICE ROUND…

Muster Parade

Out of camp the 'drunken and licentious soldiery' had a reputation
to live down to.

Attention! The O.C.'s
About to begin
It seems that the Town
Is a hotbed of Sin
The hospitals crowded
And temptation rife
So be warned: for a slip
May endanger a life.
Dismiss! The Parade
Has dissolved in a flash
The troops are away
In a desperate dash

To sort out their best
From appropriate shelves
And sally forth, eager
To see for themselves!

The Canteen Ball

The drumsticks fall and the saxophones bray
You collar a WAAF and you're on your way
A hazardous voyage on a stormy floor
Through an atmosphere thick as a fog off the Nore
A troublesome trumpet proclaims YOU'RE MINE
And the riot responds to each well-worn line
Till the ceiling shakes and the cobwebs fall
On the heads of the crowd at the Canteen Ball.

Small talk essayed mid the hullabaloo
Is addressed to the maid in the Air Force blue
She murmurs a non-committal reply
With an ashen cheek and a frightened eye
Guarding with vigilance undeterred
Her own sweet feet from the thundering herd
Determined that what-so-e'er befall
She'll emerge unscathed from the Canteen Ball.

Boots! Boots! Boots! – with an iron-shod core
Cutting a rug on the concrete floor
Dragging the fuddled musicians along
At double the lick of the Kipling song
Liquor flows fast and faster the beat
Of the overworked drum and the slap-happy feet

And fuddled spectators grin by the wall
Watching the dance at the Canteen Ball.

The partner replies with a questioning stare
To solicitous hints re a little fresh air
Out of the melee and into the night
Blast it! the atmosphere still isn't right
Dubious shadows and scamper of rats
Mingled with screams of adventurous ATS
Arouse her misgivings she cares not at all
For a promenade far from the Canteen Ball.

The riot's abated the last waltz played
A WAAF has departed her doubts unallayed
The transport is moving with feminine load
(Ecstatic farewells in the gloom of the road!)
We're speeding each truck with inebriate cheers
Then back to the bar for the rest of the beers
Enlivening comrades with anecdotes tall
Of the dances and dames at the Canteen Ball.

On Parade for Roll Call!

For brown-clad civilians-in-uniform it was always the pointless, mind-numbing futility of army routine – and no control over their own lives – that was most difficult to take.

ON PARADE FOR ROLL CALL!
– Chilling, mournful yell:
Percolating pleasant dreams
  Futile to expel

Cheerless is reality
  Darkness, wind and rain
Sergeant, if you gotta soul
  Call and come again!

Spirits sink to depths abysmal, bodies slightly turn
Matches, groped for, prove elusive: found, won't strike or burn
Futile yawning for belongings yields no major clue –
Save one shred of underclothing, wet with heavy dew.

  ON PARADE FOR ROLL CALL!
  Shaken from a trance
  dazed, bewildered forms collide
  Sorting out the pants
  Fighting o'er boots, rubber, knee,
  Chilled in every bone
  (Snatch the nearest jacket, lad
  and scram before it's known!)

Tattered nerves and fraying tempers everywhere abound
Loud the claims for all apparel in odd corners found
Menacing the conversation, fierce the free-for-all
Faster fly the precious seconds. Nearer yet the call –

ON PARADE FOR ROLL CALL!
  Falling, unaware,
Headlong into muddy holes
  Much too tired to swear.
Neighbour, on barbed wire impaled
  Bellows like a steer
Limping last man (two left boots)
  Bringing up the rear!

Non-commissioned whippers-in, shepherding the throng
Watching for the tardy few, dallying overlong:
Pounced upon is each offender, artifice is vain,
Segregated, castigated, abject they remain.

    ON PARADE FOR ROLL CALL!
    Limping slowly back:
    Gloomy thoughts of breakfasting
    On the same old tack.
    Stacking kit as radio
    Blares incessantly
    (Ugh!) "Only Forever" –
    (Oh, Miss Lynn, you're telling me!)

Dismal, futile sort of life. Bloody silly game!
Can no respite be devised – no reliefs from same?
Pray recount them, probe them, sound them; buoy that flagging hope
Transfer? useless. Discharge? hopeless. Arsenic or rope?

ON PARADE FOR ROLL CALL!
    – Half an hour ago.
Washing, jostling with the mob
    Dissipates the woe.
Suicidal tendencies
    Slowly melt away

ON PARADE FOR ROLL CALL!
    Starts the usual Army day.

Voice from the Ranks

"Well done! Well done! Good, steady going, men!"
The ranks are prone, the subaltern is not.
Five minutes for a breather. "Now we'll do the same again –
Ensure the spacing doesn't go to pot –
And HOLD THAT LINE. Remember this; these points may prove to be
Decisive, if our role is ever that of infantry –
So you'll gain tremendous benefit by doing this with me"

★ ★ ★ ★ ★ ★ ★ ★ ★ ★ ★

"Benefit, Sir? BENEFIT!"
"SICK benefit, maybe!"

Our Pal

You can cope with the unreal officers, sadistic sergeants, inconvenient enemy – but NOT deceit in your own hut.

He's really quite a decent sort of chappie,
    But his habits leave a lot to be desired.
We can put up with his crooning
    And his everlasting spooning
With the scores of pretty wenches he's admired.
    We forgive him when he swipes the manning rations
Taking twice his share and leaving us the bits –
    But what we cannot swallow
Is his thin pretence of sorrow
    When we catch the blighter 'going down' our kits.

He carts enough stuff for a general,
    Though what it all consists of is unknown –
For he'd sooner take what's handy
    From a kit that's nice and dandy
Than be bothered to investigate his own.
    When we beg him to sort out his vile collection
We're half afraid he'll take our good advice,
    And set up as a type o'
Royal Artillery Pied Piper
    With a record-breaking plague of rats and mice!

If you've lost a towel – he's left it in the wash house,
    And he thought your soap "too small" to bring away,
Your blacking – what a pity! –
It is all dried up and "bitty"
    Though he's sure he put the lid on yesterday.
If your braces are not holding up his trousers
    That's where your belt will obviously rest;
And God help you at inspection if inadequate protection
    Has enabled him to "win" your Sunday best.

So we have to mount a guard on our possessions,
    And vainly seek to stay the clutching hand
Of this trouble-hunting bird
    With a single obscene word
And a gesture even HE can understand!
    Oh, yes, he's quite a decent sort of chappie,
But some day we must tell him to his face,
    He's a useless little quitter
And a dirty thieving critter
    And here's hoping it will mend his little ways.

The Pay Parade

A tired, hungry life on two shillings a day was bound to kick up the odd vivid dream.

Friends, comrade gunners, can you spare a dime
*   To help a buddy o'er a troubled time?*
– A trifle each, for cigarettes and such
Until next pay-day – pray forgive this "touch",
*   I will explain; it was but yesterday*
When forth I sallied to collect my pay –
*   But cash, alas! ran short, and empty-handed*
Lacking a cent (and my best girl left stranded)
*   Broken and weary, much disposed to weep*
I staggered back to bed, and fell asleep.

*   A deferential shoulder tap*
*   Awakened me. I smelt a trap:*
*   ("Ha! Sloping, eh? Outside, you sap!")*
*   But fears were soon allayed,*
*   An office clerk with humble air*
*   Rebuked my long, suspicious stare:*
*   "I'm here, Sir, to conduct you there"*
*   I stuttered "What the – why the – WHERE?"*
*   He said "To PAY PARADE!"*

*   "No trouble, is it, Sir?" he cried*
*   "A car with escort waits outside –*
*   It's not above five minutes ride –*
*   You'll not be long delayed"*
*   Still slightly peeved, I answered "Oh,*

If that's the case, well, yes, I'll go –
But listen here, you so-and-so,
If I suspect you're going slow
To hell with PAY PARADE!"

We glided swiftly for a mile
Through ranks of guards in ledger file
Presenting pens in splendid style
Impressively arrayed;
The escort (such a dashing crew!)
Rode fiery steeds of sable hue
And brandished with a "View Halloo"
Their A.B.64s (Part II)
En route for PAY PARADE.

Alighting, somewhat mollified
I met a general, who sighed
"My boy, you have been sorely tried –
Inhumanly betrayed!
A scandal. Still, it might be wuss –
By Gad! We'll compensate you thus,
No waiting here – this one's on US
No signing; no saluting fuss –
The ideal PAY PARADE!"

Responding promptly to a call
I trod a vast and stately hall
A neon flashed from every wall -
"DEMAND. IT WILL BE PAID!"
Advancing in a blaze of lights
I savoured all these strange delights
Surrounded by my satellites

And luscious dancing girls in tights –
Oh, boy! Some PAY PARADE!

Came to a table, brimming o'er
With banknotes, stacks and stacks galore
And small change scattered on the floor –
AH! Would that I had stayed!
I'd barely touched the heavenly stuff
Resolved to gather just enough –
Then off to date my bit of fluff
And spend a riotous night, when – puff!
Alas! my PAY PARADE –

Dissolved in a second, I staggered up sobbing, my clothing
chaotic, my temples a-throbbing, too late for breakfast,
bawled out at inspection, obsessed by that dream – and the
bitter reflection that next week as usual I'll wait a
decade to answer my call on that damned

PAYPARADE!

Acknowledgements

F irstly thanks must go to my parents. Apart from the trivial matter of my existence, my father led the life this book is about and wrote most of it through his letters. My mother discovered them after his death and resisted her first impulse to destroy them, as private correspondence with someone else. She then spent a lot of time and effort transcribing them, without which I would have taken one look at his handwriting and given up.

My brothers, who knew Dad as adults, have corrected my memories and added their own. Geoff also contributed photos from his collection and developed the timeline model in Appendix A.

I have taken the liberty of correcting the (very) occasional error in spelling or grammar to avoid breaking the flow. Given the conditions under which he was writing there are amazingly few.

The authors and photographers I have contacted for permission to use their work have been generous and supportive. I would like to mention in particular Sir Anthony Pile, Max Hastings, Professor Terry Copp, Ray Watson and Martin Briscoe. Inevitably there were a few exceptions to prove the rule.

My wife Sue supported me burying my head in the 1940s when there were myriad other things I should have been doing. She is also a patient and meticulous reviewer without whom this book would read much worse and would certainly have far more commas.

John Hazel, one of my oldest friends, encouraged me throughout and constructively reviewed both the original plan and the completed book.

My niece Katie made time in her crowded professional and family life to do a final copy-edit, for which I am deeply grateful.

It goes without saying that the howlers are all mine.

Bibliography

13.4.41 (2011, 04 13). Retrieved 05 03, 2014, from Orwell Diaries 1938-42: http://orwelldiaries.wordpress.com/page/80/?orderby= date&order=ASC

206 HAA Bty (n.d.). War Diary, September 1939-June 1941. WO 166/2490. London, UK: The National Archives.

55 HAA Regt (n.d.). War Diary, August 1939-December 1941. WO 166/2345. London, UK: The National Archives.

58 HAA Regt (n.d.). War Diary, September 1939-December 1941. WO 166/2348. London, UK: The National Archives.

60 HAA Regt (n.d.). War Diary, August 1939-June 1940. WO 167/618. London, UK: The National Archives.

60 HAA Regt (n.d.). War Diary, January 1942-December 1942. WO 166/7444. London, UK: The National Archives.

60 HAA Regt (n.d.). War Diary, January 1943-December 1943. WO 166/11576. London, UK: The National Archives.

60 HAA Regt (n.d.). War Diary, January 1944-December 1944. WO 171/1145. London, UK: The National Archives.

60 HAA Regt (n.d.). War Diary, January 1945-December 1945. WO 171/4906. London, UK: The National Archives.

60 HAA Regt (n.d.). War Diary, July 1940-December 1941. WO 166/2350. London, UK: The National Archives.

AA Battery Kilcreggan (2014, 04 28). Retrieved 05 03, 2014, from Secret Scotland wiki: http://www.secretscotland.org.uk/index.php/Secrets/AABattery Kilcreggan

Andrew, C. (2009). The Defence of the Realm: The Authorized History of MI5. London, UK: Allen Lane.

Army Council. (1924). Text Book of Anti-Aircraft Gunnery (Vol. 2). London: HMSO.

Army Operational Research Group (1946). Development of Unseen HAA Fire Control 1940-1945 with special reference to work of AORG. London: AORG (National Archives record WO 291/303).

Beevor, A. (2009). D-Day – The Battle for Normandy. London, UK: Penguin Books Ltd.

Blizard, D. (2004). The Normandy Landings – D-Day, The Invasion of Europe 6 June 1944. London, UK: Octopus Publishing Group Ltd.

Collier, B. (2004). The Defence of the United Kingdom. Uckfield, East Sussex, UK: Naval & Military Press.

Connor, W. (1941). The English at War. London, UK: Martin Secker & Warburg.

Copp, Professor T. (2007). Cinderella Army: The Canadians in Northwest Europe, 1944–1945. Toronto, ON, Canada: University of Toronto Press.

Copp, Professor T. (1994). Counter-Mortar Operational Research in the 21 Army Group. Canadian Military History , 3 (2).

Cudlipp, H. (1962). At Your Peril. London, UK: Weidenfeld & Nicholson.

Cudlipp, H. (1953). Publish and be Damned! – The Astonishing Story of the Daily Mirror. London, UK: Andrew Dakers Ltd.

Cudlipp, H. (1976). Walking on the Water. London, UK: The Bodley Head Ltd.

Deighton, L. (1993). Blood, Tears & Folly – In the Darkest Hour of the Second World War. London, UK: Random House.

Delaforce, P. (2003). The Polar Bears – Monty's Left Flank. Stroud, Gloucestershire, UK: Sutton Publishing Ltd.

Dobinson, C. (2001). AA Command – Britain's Anti-Aircraft Defences of the Second World War. London, UK: Methuen Publishing Ltd.

Dudley Edwards, R. (2004). Newspapermen – Hugh Cudlipp, Cecil Harmsworth King and the Glory Days of Fleet Street. London, UK: Random House.

Eisenhower, D. D. (n.d.). Operations to Reach the Rhine. (P. Clancey, Editor) Retrieved 05 03, 2014, from ibiblio HyperWar: http://www.ibiblio.org/hyperwar/USA/SCAEF-Report/AEF-Report-12.html

Ellis, Major L. F. (2004). Victory in the West Volume II: The Defeat of Germany. (S. J. Butler, Ed.) Uckfield, East Sussex, UK: Naval & Military Press.

Grafton, B. (2001, 09 20). Bomber Command. Retrieved 05 03, 2014, from Military History Online: http://www.militaryhistoryonline.com/wwii/bombercommand/1941.aspx

Hastings, M. (2012). All Hell Let Loose: The World at War 1939-1945. London, UK: Harper Press.

Hastings, M. (2010). Finest Years: Churchill as Warlord 1940-45. London, UK: William Collins.

Hastings, M. (1993). Overlord – D-Day and the Battle for Normandy 1944. London, UK: Pan Macmillan.

Hickman, M. (2004, 04 22). Normandy. Retrieved 05 03, 2014, from The Pegasus Archive: http://www.pegasusarchive.org/normandy/frames.htm

Horn, Colonel B., & Wyczynski, M. (2003). Paras Versus the Reich: Canada's Paratroopers at War, 1942-45. Toronto, ON, Canada: Dundurn Group Ltd.

Horn, Colonel B. (2010). Men of Steel: Canadian Paratroopers in Normandy, 1944. Toronto, ON, Canada: Dundurn Group Ltd.

Ministry of Information. (1945). Roof Over Britain – The Official

Story of Britain's Anti-Aircraft Defences 1939-1942. London, UK: HMSO.

Moore, C. P. (2006). Fighting for America: Black Soldiers – the Unsung Heroes of World War II. New York, NY, USA: Presidio Press.

National Defence and the Canadian Forces Directorate of History and Heritage. (1949). Report No 26 – The 1st Canadian Parachute Battalion in France 6 June – 6 September 1944. Ottawa, Canada: National Defence and the Canadian Forces Directorate of History and Heritage.

Nesbit, R. C. (2004). The Battle for Europe – Assault from the West 1943-45. Stroud, Gloucestershire, UK: Sutton Publishing Ltd.

Odhams Press Ltd. (1944). Ourselves in Wartime. London, UK: Odhams Press Ltd.

Pile, General Sir F. (1949). Ack-Ack: Britain's Defence Against Air Attack During the Second World War. London, UK: George C Harrap.

Procter, H. (1958). The Street of Disillusion – Confessions of a Journalist. London, UK: Alan Wingate (Publishers) Ltd.

Prysor, G. (2011). Citizen Sailors – The Royal Navy in the Second World War. London, UK: Penguin Books Ltd.

Ramsey, W. G. (1995). D-Day Then and Now, Volume 2 (Vol. 2). (W. G. Ramsey, Ed.) London, UK: Battle of Britain Prints International Ltd.

Routledge, Brigadier N. W. (1994). Anti-Aircraft Artillery 1914-55. London, UK: Brassey's.

Rowley, R. (1994). The Attack on Boulogne. Canadian Military History, 3 (2), p. 83.

Royal Commission on the Ancient and Historical Monuments of Scotland. (2008, 06). Kilcreggan HAA Gun Battery. Retrieved 05 03, 2014, from Canmore: http://canmore.rcahms.gov.uk/en/site/107525/contribution/

kilcreggan+south+ailey+road/?&z=9

Steinbeck, J. (1958). Once there Was A War. London, UK: Penguin Classics.

Wakefield, K. (1988). The Blitz Then and Now, Volume 2 – September 1940 - May 1941 (Vol. 2). (W. G. Ramsey, Ed.) London, UK: Battle of Britain Prints International Ltd.

Wakefield, K. (1990). The Blitz Then and Now, Volume 3 – May 1941 - May 1945 (Vol. 3). (W. G. Ramsey, Ed.) London, UK: Battle of Britain Prints International Ltd.

Watson, R. C. Jnr (2009). Radar Origins Worldwide: History of Its Evolution in 13 Nations Through World War II. Bloomington, IN, USA: Trafford Publishing.

Wikipedia. (2013, 06 21). Casablanca directive. Retrieved 05 03, 2014, from Wikipedia: http://en.wikipedia.org/wiki/Casablanca_directive

Wikipedia. (2014, 04 30). Guadalcanal Campaign. Retrieved 05 03, 2014, from Wikipedia: http://en.wikipedia.org/wiki/Guadalcanal_Campaign#Ke_evacuation

Wikipedia. (2014, 04 21). Sten. Retrieved 05 03, 2014, from Wikipedia: http://en.wikipedia.org/wiki/Sten

Wikipedia. (2014, 04 26). The Blitz. Retrieved 05 03, 2014, from Wikipedia: http://en.wikipedia.org/wiki/The_Blitz

Wintringham, T. (1944). Your MP. London, UK: Victor Gollancz.

Picture Credits

Figure	Acknowledgement
Figure 1: Eric's brother and sisters at Kingsdown, probably before his arrival	Mr G Nudd.
Figure 2: Eric as a designer	From the author's collection.
Figure 3: Jennie and her father	Mr G Nudd.
Figure 4: Eric's Squad Ticket	From the author's collection.
Figure 5: Southover Hall from the northeast	English Heritage NMR BL12204.
Figure 6: Eric on ice	From the author's collection.
Figure 7: Kilcreggan Gun Site in 2011	Martin Briscoe.
Figure 8: 'The price of petrol has been increased by one penny. Official	Trinity Mirror Group.
Figure 9: The coast at Brighstone	From the author's collection.
Figure 10: Movement Order from Clacton to Ramsgate	From the author's collection.
Figure 11: Sergeants of 'F' Troop	From the author's collection.
Figure 12: Two postcards of Bayeux	From the author's collection.
Figure 13: 3.7-inch gun being towed by an AEC matador lorry through the ruins of Caen	Imperial War Museum; B 8768.

Figure	Acknowledgement
Figure 14: A Daily Sketch clipping pasted into the battery newspaper the following month	From the author's collection.
Figure 15: Cross-Channel gun emplacement at Cap Gris Nez, 1 October 1944.	Imperial War Museum; B 10465.
Figure 16: Canadian fun with a 9-ton gun in mud. (Original caption: 'Gunners of the 2nd Heavy Anti-Aircraft Regiment, Royal Canadian Artillery, pushing a 3.7-inch (9.84 cm) anti-aircraft gun through mud.')	Lt Ken Bell / Canada. Dept. of National Defence / Library and Archives Canada / PA-151554 / MIKAN 3211345.
Figure 17: Antwerp Leysstraat from a pre-war postcard	From the author's collection.
Figure 18: Bombing and 'Market Garden' left Nijmegen in a poor state	US Army Signal Corps via Wikimedia Commons.
Figure 19: The 1944 Christmas Party	From the author's collection. The identification is not certain.
Figure 20: A Sherman Crab flail tank in front of burning buildings in Arnhem, 14 April 1945	Imperial War Museum; BU 3515.
Figure 21: 3.7-inch guns of 60th HAA Regiment fire a victory salvo, 6 May 1945	Imperial War Museum; BU 5319.
Figure 22: 'Ode' to the editors of the 'Shower	From the author's collection.

Figure	Acknowledgement
Figure 23: A cartoonist's view of Hugh Cudlipp's career	From the author's collection.
Figure 24: Office horseplay	From the author's collection.
Figure 25: Never turn your back upon a Campbell!	From the author's collection.
Figure 26: Barbara Castle's 1964 election flyer	From the author's collection.
Figure 28: Nudd awaits the opening of hostilities	From the author's collection.
Figure 27: Design for a 1962 promotional leaflet	From the author's collection.
Figure 29: Anti-Aircraft Engagement Schematic	The author.
Figure 35: Anti-Aircraft Engagement Timeline	Mr G Nudd.
Figure 30: AA No 1 Mk III predictor in the South African National Museum of Military History, Johannesburg	Copyright NJR_ZA / Nick Roux, available under CC-BY-SA licence.
Figure 31: GL Mk 2 Receiver Cabin with antenna erected	The author.
Figure 32: GL 3 Mk II Radar	The author.
Figure 33: The Numbers Game – cumulative production totals for key HAA equipment	The author, using data from Brigadier N Routledge (*op cit*).

Figure	Acknowledgement
Figure 34: 206 Battery RA (probably at Evenly Hall Northamptonshire, April/May 1944)	From the author's collection.
Figure 36: 3.7-inch gun rigged for anti-tank use at Tobruk, 1941	Imperial War Museum; E 4946.

Glossary and Abbreviations

062647	Map Reference
AA	Anti-Aircraft
A/Borne	Airborne
Adv	Advance
ATS	Auxiliary Territorial Service
Att	Attached
Bde	Brigade
Bty	Battery
CF	Chaplain to the Forces
Comd	Commander
Def	Defence
Div	Division
Eqpt	Equipment
Gd	Ground
GDA	Gun Defended Area
GL	Gun Laying Radar
GOR	Gun Operations Room
GPO	Gun Position Officer *or* General Post Office
GTV	Gun Towing Vehicle
HAA	Heavy Anti-Aircraft
IAZ	Inner Artillery Zone
Inf	Infantry

LAA	Light Anti-Aircraft
Lt	Light
LW	Local Warning
PPI	Plan Position Indicator
QF	Quick-Firing
Rds	Rounds
Regt	Regiment / Regimental
Regtl	Regimental
Rep	Representative
RHQ	Regimental Headquarters
Sigs	Signals
SHAEF	Supreme Headquarters Allied Expeditionary Force
Tp	Troop
Tgt	Target
Trg	Training
Weapons Free	Weapons may be fired at any target not positively recognised as friendly
Weapons Hold	Weapons may only be fired in self-defence or in response to a formal order
Weapons Tight	Weapons may be fired only at targets recognised as hostile

References

[i] Hugh Cudlipp; *At Your Peril* (1962), Chapter 6.

[ii] William Connor ('Cassandra'); *The English At War* (1941), Chapter III.

[iii] 206 Heavy Anti-Aircraft Battery War Diary for September 1939 to June 1941; National Archives record WO 166/2490.

[iv] Ken Wakefield; *The Blitz Then and Now* Volume 2 (1988), Page 152

[v] Ken Wakefield; *The Blitz Then and Now* Volume 2 (1988), Pages 216/217. This was aircraft no. 4159 of 5/KG76 which crashed at New Barn Farm, Southfleet, Kent at 7.30 p.m. Three crew were killed and one missing.

[vi] Ken Wakefield; *The Blitz Then and Now* Volume 2 (1988), Page 283.

[vii] Ken Wakefield; *The Blitz Then and Now* Volume 2 (1988), Page 330. The identification is uncertain as the Regimental War Diary doesn't mention the engagement.

[viii] Colin Dobinson – *AA Command: Britain's Anti-Aircraft Defences of the Second World War* (2001), Chapter 6.

[ix] Basil Collier; *The Defence of the United Kingdom* (2004), Chapter XVII and Appendix XXX.

[x] Military History Online.com; Bomber Command 1941.

[xi] The Orwell Diaries 1938-42 website, entry for 13th April 1941.

[xii] William Connor ('Cassandra'); *The English At War* (1941), Chapter III.

[xiii] Brigadier N W Routledge, OBE, TD; *Anti-Aircraft Artillery 1914-55* (1994), Chapter 26.

xiv Broadcast on 22nd June 1941, quoted in the following day's *Daily Telegraph*.

xv Basil Collier; *The Defence of the United Kingdom* (2004), Chapter XVIII.

xvi Wikipedia; The Blitz.

xvii Ken Wakefield; *The Blitz Then And Now* Volume 3 (1990), Introduction.

xviii Basil Collier; *The Defence of the United Kingdom* (2004), Appendix XVII.

xix Brigadier N W Routledge; *Anti-Aircraft Artillery 1914-55* (1994), Chapter 17.

xx See http://www.secretscotland.org.uk/index.php/Secrets/AA BatteryKilcreggan and http://canmore.rcahms.gov.uk/en/site/ 107525/contribution/kilcreggan+south+ailey+road/?&z=9

xxi BBC Home Service broadcast on 8th February 1942.

xxii Reported in the *Sunday Chronicle*, 30th March 1942.

xxiii 60th HAA War Diary for 1942; National Archives record WO 166/7444.

xxiv Jessica Oliver; BBC WW2 People's War.

xxv General Sir Frederick Pile GCB DSO MC; *Ack-Ack: Britain's Defence Against Air Attack during the Second World War* (1949), Chapter XIX.

xxvi Max Hastings; *Finest Years: Churchill as Warlord 1940-45* (2010), Chapters 11-12.

xxvii *Daily Mirror*, 5th November 1942.

xxviii *Daily Express*, 19th January 1943.

xxix Ken Wakefield; *The Blitz Then and Now,* Volume 3 (1990), Page 204.

xxx Wikipedia; The Casablanca Directive.

xxxi Ken Wakefield; *The Blitz Then and Now* Volume 3 (1990), p216.

xxxii General Sir Frederick Pile GCB DSO MC; *Ack-Ack: Britain's Defence Against Air Attack during the Second World War* (1949),

Chapter IX.

xxxiii Wikipedia; Guadalcanal Campaign.

xxxiv Wikipedia; Sten.

xxxv 60th HAA War Diary for 1943; National Archives record WO 166/11576.

xxxvi *News Chronicle*, 5th June 1944.

xxxvii 60th HAA, Operation Order No 81 dated 26th June 1944 (National Archives record WO 171/1145).

xxxviii Brigadier N W Routledge; *Anti-Aircraft Artillery 1914-55* (1994), Chapter 22.

xxxix National Archives record WO 171/1145

xl Antony Beevor; *D-Day; The Battle for Normandy* (2009), Chapter 15.

xli National Defence and the Canadian Forces Directorate of History and Heritage; Report No 26 – The 1st Canadian Parachute Battalion in France 6 June – 6 September 1944.

xlii National Archives record WO 171/1017, quoted in the on-line Pegasus Archive (http://www.pegasusarchive.org/).

xliii Roger Rowley (1994); "The Attack on Boulogne", *Canadian Military History*: Vol. 3: Iss. 2, Article 11. Available at: http://scholars.wlu.ca/cmh/vol3/iss2/11.

xliv Terry Copp; *Cinderella army: the Canadians in northwest Europe, 1944–1945* (2007), p.78.

xlv *Daily Herald*, 11th November 1944.

xlvi Patrick Delaforce: *The Polar Bears, Monty's Left Flank* (2003), Chapter 34.

xlvii National Archives record WO 171/1145.

xlviii Major L F Ellis; *Victory in the West* (2004), Vol. 2, Chapter IV.

xlix Terry Copp (1994) "Counter-Mortar Operational Research in the 21 Army Group," *Canadian Military History*: Vol. 3: Iss. 2, Article 5. Available at: http://scholars.wlu.ca/cmh/vol3/iss2/5.

l Patrick Delaforce: *The Polar Bears, Monty's Left Flank* (2003);

Chapter 34.

li   Special Brigade Order of the Day, 8th November 1944, quoted in 60th HAA War Diary (National Archives record WO 171/1145).

lii   *Sunday Express*, 25th February 1945.

liii   Patrick Delaforce: *The Polar Bears, Monty's Left Flank* (2003); Chapter 36.

liv   Major L F Ellis; *Victory in the West* (2004), Vol. 2, Chapter XI.

lv   Terry Copp (1994) "Counter-Mortar Operational Research in the 21 Army Group," *Canadian Military History*: Vol. 3: Iss. 2, Article 5. Available at: http://scholars.wlu.ca/cmh/vol3/iss2/5.

lvi   *Daily Express*, 13th February 1945.

lvii   Report by the Supreme Commander to the Combined Chiefs of Staff on the Operations in Europe of the Allied Expeditionary Force 6 June 1944 to 8 May 1945 (http://www.ibiblio .org/hyperwar/USA/SCAEF-Report/AEF-Report-12.html).

lviii   US Naval Academy Office of War Information Survey No 114, 1/7/42; cited in Max Hastings; *Finest Years: Churchill as Warlord* (2010), Chapter 11.

lix   US Naval Academy Office of War Information Survey No 114, 1/7/42; cited in Max Hastings; *Finest Years: Churchill as Warlord* (2010), Chapter 11.

lx   *Daily Mirror*, 26th August 1942.

lxi   *Evening Standard*, 17th June 1940.

lxii   *Sunday Express*, 5th September 1945.

lxiii   *Daily Mirror*, 22nd September 1944.

lxiv   John Steinbeck; *Once There Was a War* (1958), 'Coast Battery.'

lxv   General Sir Frederick Pile GCB DSO MC; *Ack-Ack: Britain's Defence Against Air Attack during the Second World War* (1949), Chapter XV.

lxvi   General Sir Frederick Pile GCB DSO MC; *Ack-Ack: Britain's Defence Against Air Attack during the Second World War* (1949),

Chapter XV.

[lxvii] General Sir Frederick Pile GCB DSO MC; *Ack-Ack: Britain's Defence Against Air Attack during the Second World War* (1949), Chapter XVIII.

[lxviii] Imperial War Museum; Information Sheet No 42.

[lxix] Ken Wakefield; *The Blitz Then and Now* Volume 3 (1990), P.257.

[lxx] *Daily Mail*, 1st October 1942.

[lxxi] *Sunday Pictorial*; 6th September 1942.

[lxxii] *Daily Herald*; 22nd September 1942.

[lxxiii] *Daily Mirror*, 9th June 1944; Christopher Moore; *Fighting for America: Black Soldiers-the Unsung Heroes of World War II* (2006).

[lxxiv] Extract from a private letter by George Casey, then Sports Editor of the *Sunday Pictorial*.

[lxxv] *Daily Express*, 2nd November 1939; *Daily Herald*, 26th September 1940.

[lxxvi] *Daily Mail*, 31st March 1941.

[lxxvii] *News Chronicle*, 9th September 1943.

[lxxviii] *Daily Mirror*, 9th November 1942.

[lxxix] *Sunday Express*, 2nd July 1944.

[lxxx] General Sir Frederick Pile GCB DSO MC; *Ack-Ack: Britain's Defence Against Air Attack during the Second World War* (1949), Chapter XVII.

[lxxxi] General Sir Frederick Pile GCB DSO MC; *Ack-Ack: Britain's Defence Against Air Attack during the Second World War* (1949), Chapter III.

[lxxxii] General Sir Frederick Pile GCB DSO MC; *Ack-Ack: Britain's Defence Against Air Attack during the Second World War* (1949), Chapter XX.

[lxxxiii] Harry Procter; *Street of Disillusion* (1958), Chapter XIV.

[lxxxiv] Hugh Cudlipp; *Walking on the Water* (1976), Chapter 13.

[lxxxv] Letter of offer dated 6th November 1951.

[lxxxvi] Private letter dated 4th August 1960.

[lxxxvii] Private letter dated 23rd August 1960.

[lxxxviii] Hugh Cudlipp; *Walking on the Water* (1976), Chapter 17.

[lxxxix] *The People*; 29th January 1967.

[xc] Brigadier N W Routledge, OBE, TD; *Anti-Aircraft Artillery 1914-55* (1994)

[xci] Brigadier N W Routledge, OBE, TD; *Anti-Aircraft Artillery 1914-55* (1994), Chapter 23.

[xcii] *Text Book of Anti-Aircraft Gunnery*, Volume 2 (HMSO, 1924), Chapter VII.

[xciii] Brigadier N W Routledge, OBE, TD; *Anti-Aircraft Artillery 1914-55* (1994); Chapter 6.

[xciv] Supplement to the London Gazette, 18th December 1947. Colin Dobinson; *AA Command – Britain's Anti-Aircraft Defences of the Second World War* (2001), Chapter 8.

[xcv] 206 Heavy Anti-Aircraft Battery War Diary for September 1939 to June 1941; National Archives record WO 166/2490.

[xcvi] Raymond C Watson, Jr; *Radar Origins Worldwide* (2009), P.93.

[xcvii] Brigadier N W Routledge, OBE, TD; *Anti-Aircraft Artillery 1914-55* (1994), Chapter 9.

[xcviii] Brigadier N W Routledge, OBE, TD; *Anti-Aircraft Artillery 1914-55* (1994), Chapter 21.

[xcix] Brigadier N W Routledge, OBE, TD; *Anti-Aircraft Artillery 1914-55* (1994), Chapter 25.

[c] Major L F Ellis; *Victory in the West* (2004), Vol 2, Chapter V.

[ci] Brigadier N W Routledge, OBE, TD; Anti-Aircraft Artillery 1914-55 (1994), Chapter 7.

[cii] Brigadier N W Routledge, OBE, TD; Anti-Aircraft Artillery 1914-55 (1994), Chapter 21.

[ciii] 60th HAA War Diary for 1944; National Archives record WO 171/1145.

[civ] Brigadier N W Routledge, OBE, TD; Anti-Aircraft Artillery 1914-55 (1994), Chapters 6 & 8.

cv   Brigadier N W Routledge, OBE, TD; Anti-Aircraft Artillery
     1914-55 (1994), Chapters 11 & 12.

cvi Brigadier N W Routledge, OBE, TD; Anti-Aircraft Artillery
     1914-55 (1994), Chapter 23.

Index